ALSO BY CHLOE HOOPER

A Child's Book of True Crime

TALL MAN

THE DEATH OF DOOMADGEE

Chloe Hooper

Scribner

NEW YORK   LONDON   TORONTO   SYDNEY

SCRIBNER
A Division of Simon & Schuster, Inc.
1230 Avenue of the Americas
New York, NY 10020

Copyright © 2009 by Chloe Hooper

First Scribner hardcover edition April 2009

SCRIBNER and design are registered trademarks of
The Gale Group, Inc., used under license
by Simon & Schuster, Inc., the publisher of this work.

For information about special discounts for bulk purchases,
please contact Simon & Schuster Special Sales:
1-800-456-6798 or business@simonandschuster.com

The Simon & Schuster Speakers Bureau can bring authors to your
live event. For more information or to book an event, contact the
Simon & Schuster Speakers Bureau at 866-248-3049 or visit our website
at www.simonspeakers.com.

Designed by Kyoko Watanabe
Text set in Minion

Manufactured in the United States of America

1   3   5   7   9   10   8   6   4   2

Library of Congress Control Number: 2008038308

ISBN-13: 978-1-4165-6161-3
ISBN-10: 1-4165-6161-7

Photograph and map credits appear on p. 258.

For Justin and Nicholas

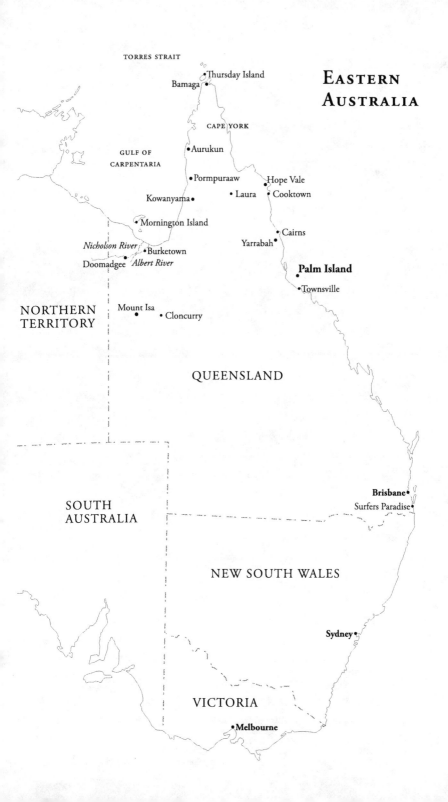

Contents

ONE

The Island   7

The Death   19

The Investigation   31

The Family   45

The Riot   56

Belief   69

The Inquest   80

TWO

Doomadgee   101

Burketown   119

THREE

The Inquest Resumes   137

The Funeral   159

The Submissions   166

The Findings   172

The Rally   182

FOUR

The Trial   193

The Accused   212

Amazing Grace   223

The Verdict   230

Postscript   251

Acknowledgments   253

TALL
MAN

ON AUSTRALIA'S REMOTE Cape York Peninsula there are spirits with long, thin arms and long, thin legs that move unseen in the night to do evil. By day they slide back into the country's sandstone cliffs, living in the cracks. On rock faces, in gullies and gorges and caves, their stretched-out bodies are painted in red ocher with all-seeing white eyes.

To find them I flew and drove to the tiny town of Laura, in Far North Queensland, and followed a guide along narrow walking tracks thousands of years old, up a steep escarpment. At the top, the guide yelled out a greeting to the spirits. Otherwise, he said, they would come and cut out our kidney fat.

It had been years since anyone had visited this place. Recent rains had left the saplings vivid green, and the ferns that grew from rocks made hanging gardens. This was a wet-season camp, a network of boulders and caves whose walls and ceilings were covered in layers of paintings maybe fifteen thousand years old: kangaroos, crocodiles, emus, dingoes, yams and their twisting roots, weapons, beehives with swarms of bees, stars; all the things of the cosmos drawn so they might multiply and release the bounty of the land.

Along one cliff wall, the orange and brown hues of the sandstone morphed into more recent figures: paintings of two white men lying down. They wore red half-moon caps and blue shirts, and were naked below their waists, their skin a pale, creamy ocher. Both men had rifles. They were police. This site was used for sorcery, *purri purri*.

On a cave wall a kilometer or so away, the guide had shown me a scene painted in the late nineteenth century of a European wearing jodhpurs and boots. He was midair, vainly holding to the reins as he was thrown from his horse. A rifle flew from his hands. A naked woman lay on the ground. Perhaps the man had stolen her; it was common on the frontier. Whoever painted this wanted to kill the European, to "doom" him, as the self-taught ethnographer W. E. Roth termed it a century ago. A man could be doomed to be struck by lightning or crushed by a falling tree, though it would not be the lightning or the tree that killed him, but the curse. The Aborigines called it "singing" him.

Sorcery paintings became more prolific while northern Australia was being colonized. In 1872—nearly a hundred years after Captain Cook claimed the continent for Great Britain—gold was discovered in a valley near Laura. When local Aborigines speared the Europeans' stock or pilfered their supplies, white settlers and then troopers—white and black—set out from the town in "dispersal" parties. The Aborigines tried to use *purri purri* against the whites' rifles, magic objects that could produce thunder and lightning. They tried to sing the guns and to sing the gun's "fruit" or "kernels"—the bullets—so they wouldn't fire straight. But the place-names marking Cape York's red-dirt roads tell the story: Spear Creek, Rifle Creek, Double Barrel Creek, Revolver Creek. A photograph of the Laura Native Mounted Police from around 1880 shows five Aboriginal troopers in their uniforms with peaked caps and rifles, flanking their tall white commander. Some traditional Aborigines lived like fugitives in these hills until the 1920s, but influenza and the troopers kept coming their way.

I stared at the blue-shirted men on the cave wall and thought that the motivation to paint them must have been strong. Blue pigment is very rare: someone had gone to great trouble to find and mix these paints. The smaller of the figures had two blue dots for eyes, the larger one brown-dot eyes and a cross that counted for a nose and mouth.

The second man was two meters tall and horizontal. Under his shirt he was reptilian. His pale skin had been crosshatched like a crocodile's—every part of it, including his penis. Below him a great serpent, painted in red ocher, reached four meters along the cliff face. The snake's tongue was striking the sole of the man's bare foot. This snake was the instrument of doom. Inside its body were stenciled handprints, like signatories to an execution. "I curse your foot, I curse your leg, I curse your heart, your shoulder, your neck," the guide said quietly. This was not a generic trooper. The people who painted him knew him. They knew his height. They knew the color of his eyes.

On the slow walk back down, nothing stirred in the bush. I asked the guide if he knew Chris Hurley, a white policeman who had once worked in the near deserted town of Laura down below. Hurley was popular in the Aboriginal communities and frontier towns where he chose to serve. He'd been decorated for his bravery. And he was tall, I said, two meters tall like the figure on the cave wall.

For two years I had been following his story: one morning, two hundred miles away on Palm Island, he'd arrested an Aboriginal man for swearing at him. Forty minutes later, the man, Cameron Doomadgee, was dead on a cell floor with injuries usually seen in fatal car accidents. Hurley claimed his prisoner had tripped on a step.

The guide did not know him. Policemen don't last long in these places. So many passed through, he said, that it was hard to remember one from another. But he knew the case. Everyone in Queensland knew the case. In a few months' time, Senior Sergeant Christopher James Hurley was standing trial for manslaughter.

ONE

The Island

PALM ISLAND'S GRIMY air terminal was decorated with a collection of the local fourth-graders' projects on safe and unsafe behavior. One, a rough drawing of a bottle with a cross through it, read: "Stop Drinking!" Another, "I feel safe when I'm not being hunted." The island lies between the Great Barrier Reef and the coast of tropical Queensland in the far northeast of Australia. Queensland, a boom state, is rich with minerals, cattle, tourists, and retirees—part Texas, part Florida, and twice as big as the two of them rolled together. The reef, with its luxury island resorts, is (as the state's advertising slogan goes) "beautiful one day, perfect the next." But no tourists come here to Palm Island. The Aboriginal mayor collected me and the two lawyers I'd traveled with and drove us into town along the narrow road fringing the water. Rocks jutted from the shore. On a boulder someone had spray-painted in purple TALL MAN.

In the township there was a jetty, a beer canteen, a hospital, a long-broken wooden clock tower, and one store. Outside the store a child sat in a rubbish bin while another cooled him with a fire hose. In the circle of shade under a tree, more children played a gambling game: some form of two-up, with bottle lids or seed pods landing in the dirt.

Two men who looked to be in their early thirties were stumbling around, leaning on each other.

"They're brothers," the mayor said. "They're blind."

"Obviously." I assumed she meant blind drunk. One of the brothers then shook out a white cane and I saw that the men were connected with a piece of string, the man with the cane leading his brother by the wrist. "How did they go blind?"

"Nobody knows."

Two white women—teachers, or nurses, or police—were walking briskly through the heat in shorts and T-shirts. They looked as awkward and out of place as I felt. "Who are they?" I asked the mayor.

"Strangers," she answered.

One of the women smiled at me, curious perhaps, and briefly I was unsure whether to reciprocate. I felt incandescently white.

Traveling to Palm Island had been like a sequence in a dream: the pale green sea so luminous and the plane flying so close I could almost see the life in it—dugongs, giant turtles, whales. All around were moored small pristine islands. Then, on the horizon, like a dark green wave, came a larger island. As the plane turned to land, the wilderness unfolded. Mountains of forest met the palm-lined shore, which met mangrove swamps, the coral reef. Then the dream shifted.

Tropic of Despair, Bitter Paradise, Island of Sorrow were the headlines I'd been reading in Queensland's newspapers. Three months earlier, on November 19, 2004, Cameron Doomadgee had been arrested by Senior Sergeant Chris Hurley for swearing. Forty minutes later, Doomadgee was dead with a black eye, broken ribs, and a ruptured liver. Hurley said he had tripped on a step while entering the police station, and the state-appointed pathologist reported no signs of brutality. The community did not agree: a week later, a mob burned down the island's police station and the senior sergeant's house. Chris Hurley went into hiding on the mainland.

A FEW WEEKS before coming to Palm Island, I'd happened to meet Andrew Boe, a Burmese-born Brisbane criminal lawyer who was visiting friends in Melbourne, where I live. An elegant, monk-bald figure with glasses, and a tattoo on his biceps in Burmese that meant "freedom from fear," he was best known for defending Australia's notorious serial backpacker killer, Ivan Milat. Boe had read of Cameron Doomadgee's case in late November and had flown to the

island in December, volunteering to represent the community pro
bono at the state coroner's inquest into Doomadgee's death: an open
hearing that would seek to establish how he had died. Boe had
attended his funeral. Many hundreds of mourners, on a scorching
day during the buildup to the rains, silently followed the coffin
through the streets for kilometers, all the way to the graveyard.

Boe wanted someone to write about the case. The inquest would
take a week or two, he said. I agreed to come along. I had spent most
of my twenties living overseas, and I knew very little about Indigenous Australia. Like most middle-class suburbanites, I grew up
without ever seeing an Aborigine, except on the news. The Reconciliation Movement—our country's fitful attempt to bridge relations between the first Australians and all who followed—is a cause
pursued by thousands who do not actually know any of the 2 percent of the population who are Aboriginal. "I suspect you are yet to
understand how complex and 'hopeless' the state of the indigenous
situation is," Boe had written to me after our meeting. And it was
true that until I had met him, I had never heard of Palm Island. Not
that I told him so—he did a hard line in moral earnestness. Among
his reams of suggested reading—scholarly articles on traditional
Aboriginal swearing rituals, case law, government reports, the five
volumes produced by the 1991 Royal Commission into Aboriginal
Deaths in Custody—he'd included a list of what would be inappropriate to wear. "Be mindful of exposing underwear unduly. Don't try
to be feral."

"Do you ever rest?" I wrote back to him.

"Rest . . . ?" came the hand slap. "We have to use our freedoms
and privileges to see what respite we can give to those less equipped
to deal with their challenges."

It was now early February. In two days' time, the state coroner—
the government-appointed investigator of deaths—would arrive on
Palm Island for a pre-inquest hearing to resolve where the inquest
would take place in three weeks' time. Boe and his junior partner,
Paula Morreau, a bright-eyed, dedicated young lawyer, had arrived

to prepare their case. Boe had brought with him files of witness statements and the surveillance tape from Doomadgee's cell on the morning he died.

PALM ISLAND IS a place where history is so close to the surface, so omnipresent, it seems to run parallel to daily life. According to the original inhabitants, the Manburra people, Palm and its adjacent islands—Orpheus, Fantome, Eclipse—were formed in the Dreaming, the time of all creation, when an ancestral spirit, the Big Snake or Rainbow Serpent, broke up and left behind fragments of its body. When on June 7, 1770, Captain James Cook anchored the *Endeavour* among these tropical islands—shards of the Snake's backbone— he saw "several large Smokes upon the Main, some people, Canoes, and we thought Cocoa Nut Trees upon one of the Islands." He sent some men ashore but "they returned on board having met with nothing worth observing."

A century later, the sea lanes along the east coast of Australia were well traveled and the islanders were accustomed to pearlers and fishermen, their seas being rich with bêche-de-mer, the sea cucumbers the Chinese believed were aphrodisiacs. North Queensland by the end of the nineteenth century was a multiracial community of Chinese, Japanese, Filipinos, and Pacific Islanders, in addition to Aborigines and Europeans. Southern states called it Queensmongreland. The historian of the Australian frontier Henry Reynolds argues that the Federation of Australia in 1901 was the equivalent of the American Civil War, but in reverse: the South conquered this steamy, racially diverse, "occult" North with its vision of White Australia. Asian immigration was restricted and thousands of Pacific Islanders were deported. "Unity of race is an absolute essential to the unity of Australia," said the founding father Alfred Deakin.

Deakin and his ilk were less perturbed by the fact a diverse group of more than 350 Aboriginal tribes had been living on the continent for at least fifty thousand years, from the time land bridges existed between Cape York and New Guinea. By Federation, it was believed, they were doomed, and even in the 1940s Europeans wrote of their duty to "smooth the pillow of a dying race"; it was the general view that within decades the Aborigines would either die out or be bred out.

In 1897, Queensland had introduced the Aboriginal Protection Act making all "full-blood" Aborigines and female and underage "half-castes" wards of the state. "They are and will always remain children, and therefore must be protected, even sometimes against their will," wrote the ethnographer W. E. Roth, now officially deemed "northern protector of Aboriginals." Every district in Queensland was assigned a protector, most often a local policeman, not always an upstanding one: "Sgt on verge of DTs, eyes propped out, face lean but purple dewed with constant sweat," wrote one observer. The protectors had responsibility for forcing people from their traditional lands onto reserves, which were predominantly run by Christian missionaries. Before long, the need for another, separate reserve was identified: a place for those who protested their treatment.

In 1916 Palm Island's potential struck the Queensland government. An official found it "the ideal place for a delightful holiday," and the remoteness also made it "suitable for use as a penitentiary" to confine "the individuals we desire to punish." From 1918 until the late 1960s, hundreds of Queensland Aborigines were sent to the Palm Island Mission, which served as a regular reserve as well as an open-air jail. Although the state Parliament had been advised that "the grouping of many tribes in one area would mean continual warfare amongst themselves and practically survival of the fittest," members of more than forty different tribes were nonetheless sent to Palm Island, in a grouping together of people with incompatible territorial, language, and kinship ties. Adults often arrived in handcuffs or leg irons, deemed variously "troublesome characters," "larrikins," "wanderers," or "communists." Some were sent there for practicing traditional ceremonies or asking about wages. Children were sent alone or in groups and were placed in the island's dormitories.

In the mission's isolation it became increasingly authoritarian—

a kind of tropical gulag. The island's white superintendent, who "got the law in his own mouth," issued permits to fish and permits to swim. To discourage traditional ceremonies, there was European dancing, and those who did not participate were questioned by police. A brass band learned to play jazz and marching tunes, and failure to attend band practice could result in a jail sentence. To leave the island, to marry, or to draw wages from a bank account, the Aboriginal inhabitants had to seek permission from the protector. Permission, as this letter to a new bride attests, was not to be assumed:

Dear Lucy,

Your letter gave me quite a shock, fancy you wanting to draw four pounds to buy a brooch, ring, bangle, work basket, tea set, etc., etc. I am quite sure Mrs. Henry would expend the money carefully for you, but I must tell you that no Aborigine can draw ⅘ of their wages unless they are sick and in hospital and require the money to buy comforts . . . However, as it is Christmas I will let you have 1/5/- out of your banking account to buy lollies with.

In the end, countless people never saw their savings. Aboriginal wages were appropriated by government departments or taken by protectors who forged the *X* of most workers' signatures.

By 1967, the year Aborigines and Torres Strait Islanders were granted equal rights, Palm Island was still a completely segregated community. In 1970 a commentator described the white administration as "monarchical" and the island itself as "the most extraordinary of all Aboriginal settlements . . . completely unlike life in ordinary Queensland." An Aboriginal Council was given some autonomy in the mid-1970s, but just as a new beer canteen was opened with alcohol abuse an instant scourge. Palm Islanders have come to call themselves the Bwgcolman, after the traditional name for the island. Today, with a population around 2,500, it is home to one of the largest Aboriginal communities in Australia.

To get to Palm you take a two-hour ferry trip or a fifteen-minute flight from Townsville (population 150,000), the largest town in North Queensland. Seven hundred miles north of Brisbane, the state capital, Townsville is an army center with four military bases. It's a hot and dry and tough town. Like many places in the North it still retains a feeling of being the über-Australia that should have been. Big-city lawyers and southern liberals are given short shrift. At its airport the lawyers and I were picked up by a taxi driver in shorts and a starched short-sleeved shirt. His face was a rash of cancers. As he drove us to the terminal, where we could fly out to a thousand-dollar-a-night resort or to Palm, he began complaining about people arriving from down south. He could always pick them.

"How?" I asked.

"Because they're fuckwits," he answered.

ERYKAH KYLE HAD been Palm Island's mayor for a year. She was in her early sixties, with light brown skin, glasses, and graying curls under a hat crocheted in the red, yellow, and black of the Aboriginal flag. Erykah's maternal grandfather was white, and mixed relationships were illegal. That's why her grandmother and her mother, a half-caste, were ordered by police to Palm Island. Her mother was placed in the dormitory; her grandmother was sent out to work on one of North Queensland's vast cattle farms, where her family presume she died. Erykah's father's family, who came from the Burdekin River, inland from Townsville, was also sent to Palm Island, in 1918, probably so their homeland could be cleared for farming.

Erykah took us for a quick tour of the island. In the tropics, buildings seem to ripen—then sag and wilt and rot. People spilled out of houses into yards, onto the street. We stopped at a beach hemmed by the island's densely forested hills—ancient volcanoes. Two chestnut horses were foraging nearby, wild ones left over from the mission stockyards. They roamed the hills and township, grazing on nature strips and gardens.

Boe, Paula, and I were to stay in an accommodation known as

"the motel." Surrounded by a high Cyclone-wire fence, it was a series of spotless rooms with no apparent overseer. My room had barred windows, a steel-frame bed, a ceiling fan, and a nail on the wall with a coat hanger.

Boe wanted to explain the legal process to Cameron Doomadgee's family. At his suggestion I went with Erykah to pick up the Doomadgee sisters for a meeting.

Erykah had known Cameron since he was a young boy. As a man, she said, he was happy-go-lucky; he loved to hunt and fish, and worked two days a week on the work-for-the-dole scheme, selling mud crabs on the side. Cameron had been a good friend of her own son, who two years earlier had been found dead in his cell in a mainland prison. An inquest took an hour to decide that he had committed suicide. There were no signs of foul play, but not knowing what had happened in the last hours of his life had left Erykah with an open wound. She showed me a photograph of her son diving into a water hole: he was young and strong, the water dappled in light.

Driving, we passed a group of young men walking uphill with their shoulders hunched. One carried a spear. "Who knows their abilities?" Erykah said.

She parked in the Doomadgees' driveway. Theirs was one of the island's newer houses, a white kit home. Large rocks had been dragged onto the block to landscape the garden. Frangipani branches stuck out of the sun-blasted earth, as did other cuttings: lychee, pepper, guava. A woman came briefly to the door, then for no apparent reason Erykah reversed out of the driveway. Something had been wordlessly arranged. The family were eating and wanted us to come back in twenty minutes.

Erykah told me that in the mission days her people found ways to communicate under the missionaries' radar, with their eyes and hands. W. E. Roth had noticed something similar in the late 1890s: all across northern Queensland there were hand signs, subtle and complex, for different plants, animals, birds, snakes, fish, weapons, emotions, and ideas. There were signs for "sunset," "forgetfulness,"

"Silence: be quiet!" for "bad person," and "run!"—which, he wrote, was "Both fists closed and circular movement with each: the feet hurrying onwards."

To kill time, we kept driving. Erykah talked about growing up on the island. One of twelve children, she was always top of her class, but got caned a lot: she had a defiant streak. She was not allowed to walk down Mango Avenue, where whites lived, and she was supposed to salute any white person she passed. Whites got the choice cuts of meat, blacks got the bones, and only in adulthood did Erykah taste milk that hadn't been watered down. In the 1950s a man could be arrested for waving to his wife or for laughing at the wrong moment. Anyone who complained was sent for solitary confinement to nearby Eclipse Island, and put on a diet of bread, water, and any fish they could catch with their bare hands. She remembered a man called Mr. Starlight, who spoke out against the missionaries. He was always being sent to Eclipse Island. Her father smuggled over *Reader's Digests* for him. Mr. Starlight ended up in an insane asylum.

Outside the island's store sat an elder from her tribal group, whom Erykah took me to meet. As we walked toward him I felt like I was wearing the heat on my body, or like it was wearing me. "Uncle," she called to the old man, "will you sing your Whale Song?" Partly blind from glaucoma, he sang in his first language about standing on cliff tops watching a whale below. Erykah clapped as he sang. She said she wished she could give him something. I gave her $10; she slipped it to him.

Back at the Doomadgees', two naked toddlers were playing under a tap. Elizabeth Doomadgee stood at the door. In her early forties, a striking, straight-backed woman with tight dark curls, she had an almost stately quality, a force to her that could make her seem haughty, or as if she were controlling—just—a steady rage. Elizabeth called to her younger sister Jane. She too was tall and slender and in shorts and T-shirt. They got into the mayor's car and we drove to the Palm Island Council building. In the council board-room, with its sepia prints of high-achieving Aborigines hung on the faded walls, Boe and Paula sat with the sisters and talked about the coroner's inquest beginning in three weeks. Elizabeth was poker-faced, skeptical, as if deciding whether to trust the lawyers. Jane was softer but silent.

Boe soon put the sisters at ease. He was attentive, convincing, and he also seemed to have a deep, instinctive sympathy. Boe's family had fled Burma when he was four. On the tarmac of the Brisbane airport his father gave his five sons new, Irish Catholic names to help them fit in. After high school, Boe studied law while working to pay the fees and support himself. A star lawyer with his own practice by twenty-four, he was now thirty-nine and had six children, two of them adopted, with an Aboriginal magistrate. Palm Island's tropical heat reminded him of Burma, the Doomadgees of his own family.

Boe asked the sisters whether there was a traditional name by which he should refer to their late brother.

"*Moordinyi,*" said Elizabeth.

It meant something like "the departed one." In the Gulf of Carpentaria, people traditionally used Moordinyi instead of the deceased's name for a period after death, to prevent the living calling back the dead. But Erykah transcribed *Mulrunji* and showed it to Elizabeth, who nodded coolly. (She had trouble spelling.) Perhaps people still used the correct term back in Doomadgee, the Aboriginal ex-mission town near the family's ancestral lands in the Gulf region, from which they had taken their name. On this deracinated island, however, the family and witnesses continued to call the dead man Cameron. In the months following his death, only the lawyers and journalists used Mulrunji.

Elizabeth, at that moment, was less worried about tradition than she was about the inquest, in particular about witnesses being asked for the timing of events; no one on the island wore watches. She and Jane feared a trap. Boe told them not to worry. By representing the community, he would work to highlight not only the culpability of Hurley but the systemic flaws in Queensland policing. He had organized two highly regarded barristers to fight solely for the family.

Boe explained what would be happening. In two days, on February 8, the state coroner and the legal teams representing the police and the Doomadgees would fly to Palm Island for the pre-inquest arguments. Inquests were supposed to be held as close to the place of death as possible. Boe believed this one should be on Palm Island; the police lawyers would argue that the island was unsafe and the inquest should be held in Townsville. Wherever it was held, the coroner's broad task was to decide what had caused Cameron's death and to recommend measures that might prevent similar deaths from occurring. The coroner was not to make a finding of criminal guilt, but if he suspected any crime he was obliged to refer the case to the director of public prosecutions, who would determine whether Hurley should be charged.

Elizabeth told Boe she was concerned that her epileptic sister might throw a fit during the inquest and frighten the coroner away. Jane was worried that the tumor with which she'd been diagnosed would stop her learning her police statement by heart. They asked if Boe could help them borrow two hearing aids from the hospital for another sister and a niece. Both were partly deaf, probably due to untreated childhood ear infections, and would have difficulties hearing the evidence. Elizabeth herself was diabetic—like deafness, that was endemic in Aboriginal communities. She did not take medication, she told me, because God was protecting her. Fifteen minutes from the mainland, they all lived in a different country.

Starved of information, without any sign of legal progress, Elizabeth was prepared to believe that this serious figure in an Armani beanie and a swagger that was part arrogance, part idealism could be her savior come. A fervent Christian, she told me Boe's arrival was proof that "God believes enough is enough."

Elizabeth and Jane were anxious to see the cell-surveillance tape, and Boe told them he would play his copy—but first they wanted to assemble the rest of the family and get some tissues.

The store was closed, so Erykah and I drove around the corner to the hospital and she spoke to two young white nurses. They didn't recognize Erykah. When she asked for the tissues, the nurses opened a few cupboards and said they couldn't find any.

Back in the council boardroom, Jane said tissues would be no use anyway: she'd need a towel for her tears. She had naïve, unblinking eyes but held her face as if always braced for bad news. A dozen people had gathered. Cameron had been one of ten siblings, of whom, Jane explained, "Only three are dead." Sitting in the boardroom were five of his sisters: the eldest, Carol, in her early fifties, along with Victoria, Elizabeth, Jane, and Valmae, the youngest at thirty-four. (A brother and sister had both died; another brother, Lloyd, lived back in Doomadgee; another sister, Claudelle, lived on the streets of Townsville.) Also present were Cameron's brother-in-law, his aunt, his niece Doreen with her young baby, and Tracy Twaddle. Tracy, Cameron's partner of ten years, was a pretty woman with big finger-waved curls, bow lips, and a stunned, private air. Her cheeks were streaked with tears. The family looked like they'd come in from a storm. Their sleeplessness, their grief, their anger all submerged in polite and embarrassed silence.

The lights were turned off. The family sat in the dark, hunched close around a laptop. On the screen, the police cell was suffused with yellow-green light. In solemn quiet, the Doomadgees watched, hoping to find out how Cameron had died.

The Death

FRIDAY, NOVEMBER 19, 2004, was just another perfect, grinding day. By 9 A.M. it was around ninety degrees, and the humidity made it feel hotter. Senior Sergeant Chris Hurley had gone to Palm Island's hospital after the three Nugent sisters had been bashed. The sister with a smashed jaw would have to be medevaced to Townsville. The sister with a black eye had asked for a lift home.

Hurley said no at first, he was too busy. But Gladys Nugent, a big, gentle-looking woman, was diabetic and needed an escort to collect "sugar" (insulin) from Roy Bramwell's fridge. Roy was her partner, and it was he who'd just beaten Gladys and her sisters. So shortly after ten, Hurley and Lloyd Bengaroo, the island's Aboriginal police liaison officer, took her to Bramwell's place in Dee Street. Hurley told her to go in and come straight back out.

The senior sergeant waited in his van: the archetypal sheriff, clean-cut with deep-set dark eyes in a strong, handsome face, bristlingly physical and tall. Everyone had to look up to him as if to a man upon a horse. He had been promoted to senior sergeant two years before, at the age of thirty-four, and was now officer in charge of the island, with a staff of six white policemen and an Aboriginal liaison officer. He was "Boss Man," and he'd risen through the ranks young and fast.

In front of him was the sea; the mountains reared up close behind. On Dee Street one house was salmon pink, the next dark blue, then light blue and lime green and yellow—a tropical mix, bright colors to disguise that every second house had broken windows, graffiti, small children playing around beer cans. This was now Hurley's natural environment. He had become a creature of the Deep North, a specialist in places on the edges of so-called civilization, Aboriginal communities and frontier towns in Cape York and the Gulf of Carpentaria, places where the streets, the days shimmered as if you were in a kind of fever—all of it, with its edge of menace, like some brilliant hallucination.

The senior sergeant had done his training in Cairns and was transferred as a twenty-one-year-old constable to Thursday Island, the administrative center of the hundred or so windswept islands in the Torres Strait. Local custom is a mix of Aboriginal and Papuan cultures, and the people speak a creole known as Torres Strait Broken (*Oli Gos* = Holy Ghost; *broke skin* = sex; *algita* = crocodile; *lugaut* = beware; *plisman* = policeman). This was the high tropics, where the tarmac lifted in the heat and buildings looked decrepit the moment they were built. Only a few years earlier they'd taken down the pictures of Queen Elizabeth and the maps of the British Empire from classroom walls. English missionaries had come to Thursday Island in 1871 to teach the natives "shame," the wearing of clothes, and to stamp out, more or less, the Darkness Time practices of head-hunting, idolatry, and sorcery. The missionaries' arrival was still celebrated every year by locals and visiting Christians in the Coming of the Light ceremony. A dinghy rowed through the maze of coral reefs and mangrove swamps, carrying the gospel ashore; then there was a church service and drumming, feasting, and dancing.

Hurley liked dancing. He liked to party. He had a personality to match his outsize build. He'd swing girls over his shoulder, spinning them in the air. He'd stand in the center of a crowd, telling jokes: a cocky, exuberant larrikin. Thursday Island had made him a different man. He told an Aboriginal friend that he'd once found himself in a police boat searching for some islanders lost at sea, angry at having his plans for the night spoiled. It was then he realized he was a racist, and decided to change.

His conversion led him deeper into Aboriginal Australia. After two years on Thursday Island, he spent the next five working in Cape York: Aurukun, Kowanyama, Bamaga, Pormpuraaw, all Aboriginal or Torres Strait Islander communities set up by missionaries to protect the natives from the violence of the frontier and to bring "light to the darkness" of their lives. The churches were mostly gone now. The places had become impoverished ghettos of alcoholism, petrol sniffing, brutality, arrests, and early deaths. Hurley had found a niche in these communities, and in the towns nearby: Cooktown, Laura, Burketown. They were in part the last outposts of racists, crocodile hunters, war veterans, hermits, and every kind of heathen, along with young teachers and nurses and cops who wanted to party, then get out. But Hurley had applied for these places. And the locals seemed to like him. He was kind, and wonderful with their children, always joking around or playing sports with them. He was popular with old people too, protecting the grandmothers from young men threatening them for their bank cards.

He'd done a stint back in civilization, in the tourist resort of Surfers Paradise, but he seemed to gravitate to the tough places. And Palm Island was tough. During his first year, stories had been published about the cruelty of the children who rode the island's wild horses like bicycles rather than creatures of flesh and blood. They rode them in wet board shorts and the horses had sores the size of dinner plates. Animal welfare inspectors found that the kids drove the wild ponies out into the water until they were exhausted, until they drowned. A horse was found in a fishing net out at sea. Another was found brain dead with a bucket around its head. Children had put petrol in the bucket. A mare had been stabbed when in foal. Another had had battery acid poured over its open wounds.

Hurley had done two years on Palm Island and had signed up to do another year. He and the other officers kept sane by hiking or cycling the bush tracks, snorkeling the reefs, going fishing in the police boat, Jet Skiing—to the locals' chagrin—on the dam, and spending sultry evenings drinking and playing pool. But now he sat waiting for Gladys Nugent, who had been bashed and was still half drunk and probably wouldn't thank him for his trouble, but turn her eyes down like they all did.

Through the closed window of the van, he and Police Liaison Officer Lloyd Bengaroo could hear a young man yelling abuse from Roy Bramwell's front yard. It was Gladys Nugent's nephew Patrick, a thin boy whose mother was one of the women Bramwell had beaten. Drunk and high from sniffing petrol, Patrick was calling the police "fucking queenie cunts."

"Are you hearing what he's saying?" Bengaroo asked.

Hurley got out of the van.

Patrick's grandmother asked the senior sergeant to arrest him. Hurley didn't need any convincing; Bengaroo held open the back doors of the police van while Hurley put his prisoner into the cage.

At that moment Cameron Doomadgee walked past barefoot. He had with him his dog, Bulbush ("great hunter"), and a pack of orangey neighborhood mutts. "Bengaroo," he said to the police aide, "you black like me. Why can't you help the blacks?"

In his fifties, Lloyd Bengaroo was overweight and overburdened, with a craggy face and buried brown eyes. He'd grown up on Palm Island. For twenty years he'd been a community police officer, with the power to arrest, but his role had changed. He was now supposed to be working to bridge the gap between police and blackfellas, and he could no longer even touch offenders. This was meant to be for his own good, to spare him the loathing of his fellow islanders, but the community reckoned Bengaroo was a police "watchdog" or "errand boy"—and told him so constantly.

"Keep walking or you be arrested, too," Bengaroo told Cameron.

Cameron Doomadgee, thirty-six, was lean and fit and proud of it. (He'd joke to his fishing companions that they had more fat than the turtles they hunted.) This morning he was on a full-scale bender of beer, cask wine, and "goom"—methylated spirits mixed with water. For all he'd drunk, he was "walking pretty good, staggering but not falling over," according to Gerald Kidner, his drinking buddy, who was walking ahead of him.

When Cameron had gone on another thirty meters or so—Hurley was later to claim—he turned and swore at the senior sergeant. Lloyd Bengaroo said he didn't hear it. Neither did Gladys Nugent, now back in the van with her insulin. Kidner reckoned Cameron was singing "Who Let the Dogs Out," a one-hit wonder by the Baha Men that went:

Who let the dogs out (woof, woof, woof, woof).
Who let the dogs out (woof, woof, woof, woof).

But Chris Hurley, who had endured every insult in existence, heard something more offensive, and this time he decided not to let it go. Perhaps he was still riled by Patrick's "fucking queenie cunts." Perhaps he was thinking of the abuse flung at Lloyd Bengaroo, who'd recently asked for a transfer after being hospitalized for stress. Perhaps he was thinking of the three women who'd just been beaten by a drunk like this one. Or perhaps in the heat his uniform was sticking to his skin, and he could feel the sweat in the roots of his hair, and this whole island was vibrating, the whole place out of control, and it was up to him to still it.

"Who is he?" Hurley asked.

"Cameron Doomadgee," Bengaroo answered.

The two men got back in the van and Hurley reversed toward Cameron. "What's your problem with police?" The senior sergeant didn't wait for an answer. He was out of the van instantly and arresting Cameron for creating a public nuisance. "I'm locking you up, Mr. Doomadgee."

Lloyd Bengaroo opened the cage doors again. Nobie Clay, watching from a nearby balcony, said Cameron didn't struggle but yelled, "You're locking me up for nothing." She reckoned she then saw Hurley pick up Cameron's legs and spear him into the van. She heard the bass note of his head hitting the inside of the cage. It was 10:20 A.M.

With Cameron and Patrick locked in the back, Hurley and Bengaroo dropped Gladys at her sister's house and by 10:26 had returned to the station. Outside, in Police Lane, Penny Sibley, a frail, gray-haired Aboriginal woman, was waiting to get money from Bengaroo. She was taking his goddaughter to Townsville to a land rights meeting. Hurley pulled into the garage, and when he opened the cage doors, she saw Cameron "going off, drunk, singing out, and everything."

Then Cameron struck the senior sergeant on the jaw.

Hurley was stunned. No one on the island had ever hit him before. Penny Sibley said his face went "wild." She and another witness, Tiny Bonner, said they saw Hurley punch Cameron in the ribs. In the garage, the two men struggled; Hurley tried to force his prisoner inside the station. As she watched them fighting, Penny Sibley began to cry. She said they entered the station, then the door slammed shut.

But Chris Hurley, Lloyd Bengaroo, and a young constable standing watching from within the garage all said that when Hurley and Doomadgee got to the station's doorway, the two men tripped over a step and fell inside.

Standing by the door, Bengaroo did not move to see if his boss was hurt. The next day he told investigators: "I was thinking, um, if I see something I might get into trouble myself, or something." Constable Kristopher Steadman, who had arrived on Palm Island fresh from the police academy the day before, also stood outside. He heard Hurley yelling angrily, but like Bengaroo said he waited until he thought it safe to enter.

Inside, Roy Bramwell was sitting by a filing cabinet, waiting to be questioned. The day before, he and the three Nugent sisters had started drinking at 11:30 A.M., and by midnight Roy had drunk forty cans of beer. He got up early next morning and had six more. Standing on the sisters' veranda, Roy—"plenty drunk"—became angry because Gladys wouldn't go home with him to take her insulin. They started to fight. In his statement, Roy later said:

During this argument I punched her sister, this is Anna
Nugent, and hit her in the face. I punched her with one punch
and this knocked her out. This was in the front yard. I
punched Anna because she was being smart with her mouth.

I then punched the other sister, this is Andrea Nugent, and
punched her once to the face and this knocked her out. I
punched Andrea for the same reason. I dropped her on her
knees and then the smart mouth did not get back up.

I then got into Gladys. I punched her once to the face and
knocked her out. This was in the front yard as well. Gladys
dropped to the ground and was on her knees. I started kicking into her and kicked her about three times. I kicked her in
the face. I did this cause I was angry with her cause she didn't
want to come home with me.

After beating the three women, Roy went home alone and had a
shower to cool off. Then he headed to the post office to pick up his
welfare check. While he was waiting there, the Nugent sisters' uncle
Tiny Bonner found him, and another "tongue bang" (argument)
began. That was where Sergeant Michael Leafe had found Roy, and
that was how he came to be at the station.

But in his struggle to control Cameron, Hurley did not notice
him.

The next day, and the next week, in separate police statements,
Roy claimed:

Chris dragged him in and he laid him down here and started
kicking him. All I could see [was] the elbow gone down, up
and down, like that . . . "Do you want more Mister, Mister
Doomadgee? Do you want more of these, eh, do you want
more? You had enough?"

Roy's view was partially obscured by the filing cabinet, but he said
he could see Doomadgee's legs sticking out; he could see Hurley's

fist coming down, then up, then down. "I see knuckle closed." Each time the fist descended he heard Doomadgee groan. "Cameron, he started kicking around and [called] 'leave me go' like that now. 'Leave me go—I'll get up and walk.'"

Roy said Hurley did not stop: "Well, he tall, he tall, he tall, you know . . . just see the elbow going up and him down like that, you know, must have punched him pretty hard, didn't he? Well, he was a sober man and he was a drunken man."

Sergeant Michael Leafe, who'd just arrested Roy, was inside the station but he told investigators he didn't see or hear anything. He claimed he left Hurley alone with Doomadgee for ten seconds while opening the door to one of the station's two cells. When he returned the prisoner was limp. Leafe and Hurley each took Cameron Doomadgee by a wrist and dragged him on his back into the concrete cell. When they were done, Roy Bramwell said he saw Hurley rubbing his chin. The officer had a button undone.

"Did he give you a good one?" Roy asked.

"A helluva good one," Hurley replied.

Then, Roy claimed, Hurley asked him if he had seen anything. Roy said no, and the senior sergeant told him to leave. Roy went back to the post office to get his welfare check, along the way warning some friends, "Chris Hurley getting into Cameron." They told him, "Go tell someone, tell the Justice Group." But Roy didn't tell the Justice Group, a community program run by elders to settle conflicts. None of them did anything. They went on drinking.

Meanwhile Hurley and Leafe went to get Patrick Nugent out of the van. He was so drunk they had to carry him through the hot, cramped box of the police station and dump him beside Cameron in the cell. Then Hurley put a videotape in the cell surveillance monitor and tried to get on with his day.

ELEVEN WEEKS LATER, Cameron's family sat in the council boardroom, enveloped in the bile-colored glow of this video, watching their brother die.

From high in the cell corner where the camera was installed, the two men sprawled on the concrete floor look like they've fallen from a great height. Cameron writhes. He calls out, "Help me!" The sound is distorted. It's a desperate, agonized, animal cry. "Help me! Help!" he calls again. Patrick, half paralyzed with drink, feebly pats Cameron's head and Cameron rolls closer to him, for warmth or for comfort. They lie there inert for a minute or so. A digital clock runs on the top left of the screen.

Hurley enters—rangy in his blue uniform, with sideburns, a hint of a pompadour, and a glare. From this angle he looks enormous. He stands staring down as if at two dolls. When he leaves, Cameron lurches away from Patrick. Then he's still. They're both still. The seconds on the digital clock flick over. Life is escaping. Ten minutes, twenty; neither man moves.

The Doomadgee family sat in silence, watching every frame.

After half an hour, Sergeant Leafe comes into the cell. He kicks Cameron. When there's no response he kicks him again. At the inquest, this is called "an arousal technique." Leafe leans over the prisoner. He touches his skin. Then he goes to get Hurley. The senior sergeant returns with a torch and flashes the light in Cameron's eyes. He hunches over Cameron, puts his hand under Cameron's nose, feeling for breath. He searches for a pulse, and for a moment seems to think he's found one. But he hasn't. It's his own adrenaline surging. He rushes out; at 11:22 he calls an ambulance. When at last the ambulance officers arrive, they pull a defibrillator out of a medical bag and place it on Cameron's chest. Chris Hurley stands against the cell wall, watching. It's too late. The ambulance officer shakes his head. Hurley slumps down the wall with his head in his hands.

ELIZABETH DOOMADGEE walked out of the council building and sat on a bench under a mango tree. Nearby stood the wooden clock tower, each of its four faces broken. From here she could just see her daughter playing on the jetty. Kids rode up on wild horses and ran and backflipped into the water. Elizabeth stayed still. "The light shining on Hurley now," she said finally, "but when the sun go down he a bad person."

Everyone on Palm Island had a story about what happened on that day. And everyone had a story about Senior Sergeant Hurley. He denied that he had ever been violent toward Cameron Doomadgee. His supporters claimed he was "gutted" by the allegations made against him. They pointed to the extensive volunteer work he'd done with Aboriginal children and to his Aboriginal friends. He even had a skin name; he'd been adopted into an Indigenous family in Cape York, and in his midtwenties he had an Aboriginal girlfriend. Old colleagues said Hurley would restrain other officers if they lost their temper.

In the wake of Cameron's death, the senior sergeant was emerging as a model cop. Before going to Palm Island, I read this glowing article about Hurley in Brisbane's *Sunday Mail* of December 5, 2004:

A Cop Who Cared

At 200cm tall, Palm Island policeman Chris Hurley was always going to make an impression on the remote Aboriginal communities he made it his life's work to serve. Before the death of Cameron Doomadgee on November 19 and continuing unrest on the island, that impression appears mostly good.

One of his postings as a constable aged just 21 was to Thursday Island, where the community quickly warmed to the gentle giant.

Worried about the high crime rate among children there, in 1989, he took it upon himself to establish a sporting club for young people, writing dozens of letters to organisations seeking donations to equip the club.

When a Brisbane shopping centre offered equipment if he would travel down to collect it, he arranged for three young islanders to join him and get their first taste of the big smoke.

A photograph taken on Thursday Island shows smiling children clambering over the young officer as he told *The Sunday Mail* his dream was for the "kids up here to be better known for their sporting ability than getting into trouble."

A second photograph unveiled on Thursday Island this week is another reminder of his stay. It is part of a new photographic exhibition on Aboriginal reconciliation and is accompanied by his words: "Reconciliation is a two-way street; it's going to take a lot of effort by all Australians. At the end of the day there are more similarities than differences between Aboriginal and non-Aboriginal Australians."

In the exhibition photograph, a darkening sky is filled with rolling clouds. Hurley stands on a bridge and behind him a river runs wide but twists out of sight. He looks serious and strong. Wearing a broad-brimmed police hat, he leans over a map spread out on the hood of a police van. His eyes are narrowed as if seeing something just emerging on the horizon, as if it is coming toward him.

THE FIRST NIGHT I spent on Palm Island there was no moon. Cicadas tuned in and out of the heat. As it grew darker, I sat on the motel veranda drinking with the lawyers. Boe had the manner of someone lumbered with exchange students in a war zone. "What have you learnt?" he kept asking, wanting epiphanies. Virgin forest surrounded us. We heard unknown creatures begin their nocturnal rounds. In theory we were safe: the motel stood between the police station and the police barracks. But the barracks were surrounded by a high barbed-wire fence that was heavily padlocked. As I watched officers lock themselves in and out, it was unclear who needed protecting.

Erykah Kyle dropped by to speak to Boe. Like the Doomadgees, she had invested her hopes in him. The pair had an easy rapport, sharing ideals of activism that seemed to belong to an earlier age. As a young woman, Erykah had been inspired by the American black power movement, and in the early 1970s she'd spent time at the rebel Aboriginal Tent Embassy in Canberra, campaigning for land rights. Now she had written and printed a pamphlet that was to be distributed all over the island.

COMMUNITY NOTICE

THE STATE CORONER IS COMING TO PALM ISLAND
FOR THE START OF THE INQUEST INTO THE DEATH OF
OUR BELOVED BROTHER, PARTNER, FATHER, SON,
COUSIN, NEPHEW, UNCLE AND MATE WHO DIED IN
POLICE CUSTODY ON 19 NOVEMBER

PEOPLE WHO WANT TO ATTEND SHOULD
BE ALLOWED TO LEAVE WORK FOR THIS

COMMUNITY SUPPORT IS NEEDED TO MAKE SURE
THAT JUSTICE MIGHT COME THROUGH THIS TRAGEDY

From the veranda, I could see through the Cyclone-wire fence to a group of cops in a mess room playing pool with some nurses. Two officers drove in, parked their van, and heaved an old mattress over the windshield. Every night Palm Islanders threw rocks at the barracks: all its windows were covered by wooden screens.

I wondered what I was doing here, but my lawyer companions were on a mission and had no such doubts. We were two doors down from where Chris Hurley had lived. His white house was now a burned, vacant lot: a clue to what had happened in the riot a week after Cameron Doomadgee's death. As the cops played pool on the other side of the fence, Boe raised his glass and proposed a toast to the revolution.

The Investigation

SOON AFTER DAWN the cicadas resumed their electrical humming, as if releasing some live current into the air. I woke in a low single bed in a room whose walls had strange stains. This island was on some other frequency. Its element was different, like when you enter a hospital and the air changes. I thought of Chris Hurley on the surveillance video, slumping down the wall with his head in his hands. What did that slump mean? That this was a cop's worst nightmare? That he was distraught because a young man had lost his life while in his care? Or was it guilt? Had remorse hit his bloodstream and made his legs crumble underneath him?

The morning Cameron Doomadgee died, when the ambulance had gone and the surveillance video stopped running, there were five men in the police station: four officers—Chris Hurley, Michael Leafe, Lloyd Bengaroo, Kristopher Steadman—and Patrick Nugent, unconscious in a cell. There was also Cameron's body.

"We were sick," Hurley said later. "Lloyd was upset, he was crying." Lloyd was part-Kalkadoon, from around Mount Isa in northwestern Queensland, and he had a connection to Cameron's mother. He reckoned they should tell the family Cameron was dead, but Hurley told him to stay put and keep quiet. Hurley asked one of his officers to print out the pages in the Queensland Police Service's *Operational Procedures Manual* (*OPM*) dealing with black deaths in custody.

The 1991 Royal Commission into Aboriginal Deaths in Custody had investigated ninety-nine deaths over a ten-year period, calculating: "If non-Aboriginal people had died in custody at the same rate . . . there would have been nearly 9,000 deaths." But after painstaking research, the inquiry found no evidence that any of the deaths were the result of foul play. Rather, Aboriginal people were chronically overrepresented in jail (making up 2.4 percent of the national population but 22 percent of the prison population), were in appalling health, and were given inadequate care while incarcerated. The commission found that police investigations into these deaths in custody "had usually been perfunctory," and now, thirteen years later, there were strict guidelines dictating what police had to do if they found themselves in this situation.

Hurley and Leafe moved Patrick Nugent to the station's other cell and sealed off Cameron's cell as a crime scene. Hurley then rang the Townsville District Police Communications Center: "We've had a death in custody . . . bloody came in, he was bluing and carrying on . . . calling out fuckin' . . . fuckin' white cunts and carrying on basically, walking down the street and calling Lloyd a black cunt."

The officer in charge of the communications center, Senior Sergeant Stephen Jenkins, telephoned his superior, Inspector Greg Strohfeldt, on a closed line to notify him of the death. Jenkins then contacted the region's acting superintendent, a higher rank again. Those in the chain of command were now aware there had been what they called a SIGEV—a significant event.

Within minutes of finding Cameron dead, Hurley also called his close friend Darren Robinson. This was not an *OPM* directive, although "Robbo" was the detective on the island. He and "Hurls" had worked, lived, and bonded there for the past two years. Robinson had been a good mate when, earlier that year, Hurley's girlfriend had left him and gone back to the mainland. The previous day, Robinson had escorted a prisoner to Townsville, and that's where he took the call.

After the men spoke, Robinson called his superior, Detective Senior Sergeant Joe Kitching of the Townsville Crime and Investigation Bureau. Kitching was also a friend of Hurley's. During Hurley's posting in Burketown, on the Gulf of Carpentaria, Kitching had worked "nearby" in Cloncurry, a pastoral center eight hours' drive away. They knew each other "reasonably well," Kitching would tell the inquest. "If I saw him in the street, I'd certainly say g'day to him and stop and have a talk."

Robinson then placed a call to Kitching's superior, Detective Inspector Warren Webber, the northern regional crime coordinator. Webber had done a two-day disaster management course with Hurley and held him in high esteem. He believed community and police relations on Palm Island had been improving under Hurley's leadership.

The *Operational Procedures Manual* stated that in "custody-police related incidents" the regional crime coordinator (in this case Webber) "should appoint an investigator from a police establishment other than from where the incident occurred, or where the officers or members directly involved in the incident are stationed." Webber decided that Townsville, though only fifteen minutes away, was separate enough from Palm Island to fulfill this requirement, and appointed Kitching and Robinson to the investigation. It was true that Robinson had worked on the island for the past two years, but he would be a junior investigator. Webber himself had never set foot there.

The phone calls made, there was a knock on the station door. Hurley opened it to see Tracy Twaddle with Cameron's sister Carol and a small child. In her police statement Tracy said she had heard Cameron yelling from the back of the police van as it drove past their house, and she'd brought him some lunch. But now, "Chris Hurley's face was funny; he didn't know how to look at me. I thought there was something wrong." She asked when Cameron would be let out.

He said, "Were you with him?"

"Yes, I live with him, I'm his de facto."

"Were you with him [this] morning?"

"No, he went when I was asleep."

"Did you have anything to drink the night before?"

"We had about one and a half cartons of beers."

"Come back at three o'clock and I will talk to you."

Hurley claimed to have no recollection of ever seeing the dead man before. On computer records he found that Cameron Doomadgee had been arrested a few times for being drunk and disorderly in Townsville. As well, he found that they were the same age—thirty-six. The child at the door might have belonged, he thought, to the man lying on the cell floor.

Hurley later said he felt his stomach giving way. This was not meant to be happening to him. Until 11:22 A.M. he'd been a man with a tight, hard plan, who'd worked his guts out in a string of places other cops thought were shit holes, and as a result the insignia on his uniform had been constantly upgraded. Another embroidered chevron, then another, until as senior sergeant he had an embroidered crown circled by laurels. He was ambitious, he wanted to go all the way in the police force, and in each posting he'd earned not just a chevron but the respect of a lot of people—including a lot of black people. It was not part of Chris Hurley's plan to be standing in the doorway lying—or whatever it was—to the woman of a dead blackfella.

Hurley still did not know the cause of Cameron Doomadgee's death. But he and the other Palm Island officers had more than three hours in which to compare notes on the SIGEV before the investigators arrived. Hurley, Leafe, and Bengaroo sat "throwing around ideas" about how it might have happened. Possibly they were too distressed to realize this contravened the *OPM*'s clear directive that "members directly involved in the incident should not discuss the incident amongst themselves prior to being interviewed."

Hurley's investigators were on the 2:30 flight from Townsville. Fifteen minutes later, the senior sergeant was waiting at the airstrip to pick them up. The *OPM* says a death in custody must be investigated as a potential homicide, but Inspector Webber, the senior investigator, told the inquest he considered the case of Cameron Doomadgee not to be an actual homicide investigation but rather a "potential homicide" and more a "homicide-type investigation, if you like." He had no actual suspects, but "persons of interest were obviously anyone that was in the station at the time."

Inspector Webber was in his fifties, short, balding, gray, bespectacled, with a squint that merged easily with a frown. He did not record any conversation he had with Hurley that day. "I didn't go into great depth," he said. "We didn't engage in any great conversation. It was simply a matter of 'All right, what's happened?' and a two-minute conversation to secure the scene, put the forensic team into the cell." A crime scene photographer took pictures of the police station and of Cameron lying dead in the cell. The body would be moved to the hospital that evening before being flown to the mainland for autopsy.

It was Inspector Webber who went to Dormitory Lane, to Cameron's mother's bright blue house, to tell Doris Doomadgee that her son was dead. The *OPM* requires officers to inform the deceased's next of kin immediately, but recommends that a senior member of the Aboriginal community be asked to do this. Though Webber was aware that Hurley had not met this requirement, he told the inquest that he thought "it was appropriate for a senior officer to reassure the mother of the deceased that a thorough and proper investigation would be conducted of that death." He also felt it was inappropriate for the family to be advised by "one of the persons of interest." This did not stop him, however, taking along Sergeant Michael Leafe, who had earlier that morning attempted to rouse Cameron with a kick.

Carol, Cameron's sister, recalled the officers' visit: "The detective had a red book with him, and he read it out to us telling us we lost Cameron." Doris Doomadgee was in a wheelchair. She was emaciated, dying of cancer. She asked Webber to notify her family in the Gulf region town of Doomadgee. Two weeks later, she too was dead.

Webber then went to inform Tracy. She was waiting at home, "wondering what happened, [why] I've got to wait till three o'clock, for Cameron. For to talk to them . . . They told me that Cameron was found on the police cell an hour after he got locked up; they found him dead."

Elizabeth Doomadgee did not even know her brother had been arrested. She was gardening when an Aboriginal hospital worker came and told her the news. She felt choked and could not speak. She'd been waiting for Cameron with a pack of smokes he'd asked for.

Later that evening, Elizabeth and Jane went to identify their brother's body. He was wearing his favorite shirt. It was torn and he had a black eye. "He was not at peace," Elizabeth said later. "Cameron had his eyes half open and I looked into his eyes and I could see struggle."

Lloyd Bengaroo, at the end of his working day, went back to the house he shared with his sister. Agnes Wotton, who lived across the road, was visiting. She thought it strange Bengaroo didn't say hello. He went straight to his room and closed the door and stayed there.

WHILE CAMERON'S FAMILY was hearing of his death, Chris Hurley was being interviewed by his two friends Officers Robinson and Kitching.

Darren Robinson was a fitness fanatic. The locals often saw the thin-lipped policeman with the impish face and upturned chin running or riding his mountain bike around the island. Although he had "conducted minimal investigations . . . essentially none" before arriving on Palm Island, he was putting together evidence against the island's suspected child abusers. He had bought magic tricks with his own money as aids to interviewing children who'd been molested. Kitching, who outranked Robinson, was a balding redhead with orange eyebrows and mustache, and the kind of bright, supernatural tan that comes over years to the very pale. He wore an onyx ring with a gold crucifix on it.

The taped interview began at 4:04 P.M. and concluded at 4:36 P.M. In it the detectives focused almost exclusively on Cameron punching Hurley. A dead body lay nearby, a dead body with a pronounced black eye, but the officers did not ask Hurley if, when Cameron hit him, the senior sergeant hit back. In old-school policing, punching a cop was considered enough provocation to teach the offender a hard lesson.

"I observed that he had a small amount of blood that was, ah, coming from a very small, ah, injury above his right eye," Hurley said.

"How did he receive that injury?" Kitching asked.

"I don't know."

Neither officer asked him to speculate. Instead, Robinson wondered whether Hurley had sustained any injuries himself.

"Just a tiny scratch on my arm there," Hurley replied, "probably from the ah . . . the little wrestle that we had. That's the only thing I can see."

Then Robinson, perhaps giving his friend an out, asked, "And you didn't fall on top of him?"

Hurley could not have been more emphatic. "No, I landed beside him."

That night, Robinson and Kitching and Webber met Hurley at his house, and Robinson cooked dinner. Sergeant Leafe joined them afterward and they all sat out on the balcony, talking, drinking beer. At the inquest, Hurley said he had no recollection of what was discussed. He was too distressed. Anyway, Robinson and Webber, he said, were barely speaking to him. "I wasn't treated like a friend . . . I was treated like a leper."

Robinson was asked at the inquest, "Did you make an effort to console him, or to offer him support if not console, saying things like *don't worry about it*?"

Robinson responded, "Ah, no."

"Or, *don't blame yourself*?"

"No."

"He's a good friend of yours, isn't he?"

"He is a friend of mine, but I'm not there to give him a pat on the back about what happened."

"But if a friend of yours is highly distressed, you usually do what you can to alleviate that distress, don't you?"

"Ah, not in this situation, no."

This was not the first time Webber had instructed Robinson to investigate Hurley. (In fact, Webber had once instructed Robinson to look into a complaint against his own conduct, to investigate himself.) Robinson had cleared Hurley of wrongdoing at least once—and he knew his friend could be quick to use his fists. Robinson had seen Hurley hit another Palm Island resident, a drunk schizophrenic who'd come into the station one evening and mouthed off at Hurley and five other officers who were sitting around talking. Hurley said he threw the punch when he thought the man was going to head-butt him. The punch put the drunk on the floor.

At 8 A.M. on Saturday, the day after Cameron's death, Darren Robinson went to Dee Street and found Roy Bramwell. None of the officers, including Hurley, knew whether Bramwell had actually witnessed anything. Robinson and Kitching interviewed him at the police station. Bramwell said he'd seen an assault. His view had been partially obscured by a filing cabinet, but Hurley was a big man with long arms: "I could see the elbow gone down, up and down, like that . . . 'Do you want more Mister, Mister Doomadgee? Do you want more of these, eh?'" Roy said he'd watched Doomadgee's feet writhing as Hurley's elbow went up and down. Asked why he didn't move, he told the officers, "If I got up and seen where the punches were hitting he would have hit me, he would have threw me in the bloomin' cell."

NEARLY TWO YEARS later, on October 6, 2006, when Roy Bramwell was in prison for his assault on Gladys Nugent and her sisters, he called in a Legal Aid representative. His nephew Patrick Nugent had just been arrested again and he was frightened for him. Roy made a sworn statement:

> On the 20th November 2004 . . . I was visited by four demons [police officers] who obtained a statement from me regarding what I had seen . . . One of the four detectives present was

Darren Robinson and after my statement was signed he threatened me with if anything happens to his friend Chris Hurley, he would come looking for me. I did not tell anyone of this threat until now as I am now scared for my safety and also for my family.

In 1987, after the media had aired claims of high-level corruption within the Queensland Police Force, a judicial inquiry was set up, headed by Tony Fitzgerald QC. Fitzgerald exposed a police service linked to illegal prostitution, gambling, and kickbacks, an organization "debilitated by misconduct, inefficiency, incompetence and deficient leadership." Endemic corruption led all the way to the state's long-serving, ultra-right-wing premier, Sir Joh Bjelke-Petersen, and to his anointed police commissioner, Sir Terence Lewis. In September 1987 Sir Terence was forced to resign and later went to jail for ten years on corruption charges. Chris Hurley was sworn in as a police officer the following month. The month after that, in November 1987, after nineteen years at the helm, Sir Joh spent his last moments in office shredding incriminating documents.

The Fitzgerald inquiry identified within the force a pervasive unwritten "code," which required that police "not enforce the law against other police, nor cooperate in any attempt to do so, and perhaps even obstruct any such attempt." Police justified this code to themselves by claiming they "need to trust each other." Fitzgerald found that it "effectively places police officers beyond the law."

ON THAT SAME Saturday morning when Robinson and Kitching interviewed Roy Bramwell, Inspector Mark Williams arrived on Palm Island. Williams was from Ethical Standards, the police division required to sign off on deaths in custody. At 10:52 A.M. he and Inspector Webber conducted a video interview with Bramwell, wherein he repeated his claim of having seen Hurley's elbow going up and down three times.

A few feet away, Hurley sat in his office with the door closed.

When the interview was finished, Webber, Williams, and Hurley went to Dee Street to look at the scene of the arrest. The two investigators' conversations with Hurley immediately following their interview with Bramwell were not taped. At the inquest, Webber denied telling Hurley of Bramwell's allegation: "I certainly did not, and certainly in my presence no officer did." But Webber could not say where, in or around the police station, Hurley had been after 8:15 A.M., when Roy first made his claim, or which officers he had spoken to.

Back at the station once more, Hurley had his own video interview with Webber and Williams, recorded at 11:53 A.M. Hurley is shown standing loose-limbed and slouching. He is tense. He can't keep his hands still; he clenches his fists and flutters his fingers, flexing them. His long arms look like they have a lot of leverage. He knows how to box and demonstrates four different punches in the space of a few seconds, to show how Cameron hit him. This relaxes him. Hurley is articulate when he's being physical. He starts describing their "figh—" before correcting himself and calling it a "tussle." "I knew there's going to be a tussle on if he's going to hit a copper," he tells the inspectors in a voice that seems to expect agreement.

Inspector Webber plays the part of Cameron while Hurley reenacts his story: he'd been hit, he said; they had "tussled" on the way to the door and tripped and fallen through it side by side. But now he adds a new element.

The video shows him standing near the filing cabinets, as Roy Bramwell said he had been. But where Bramwell said he saw a punching motion, Hurley demonstrates a "picking up" motion. He leans down to the floor and bends his elbows up and down. When he straightens, his head nearly touches the ceiling. He explains to the inspectors that he was trying to lift Doomadgee by his shirt. Rather than saying, "Do you want more, Mr. Doomadgee? Do you want more?" as Bramwell claimed, he was calling on Doomadgee to get up: "Get up, Mr. Doomadgee! Get up!"

This interview is striking for its camaraderie. Webber refers to

Hurley as "mate" or "buddy"; Hurley calls him "boss." When he demonstrates trying to lift Cameron by the shirt, Hurley laughs with the investigating officers—they joke about not tearing Inspector Webber's shirt the way Hurley had torn Cameron's faded Hawaiian one. Neither inspector asks Hurley why Doomadgee was taken into custody in the first place. They don't ask why he had objected to his arrest. They don't ask whether Hurley hit Cameron back. They don't ask how the dead man got a black eye.

After conducting the reenactment, Inspectors Webber and Williams sat down to watch the cell-surveillance tape. "Senior Sergeant Hurley actually had to operate it for us," Webber told the inquest. They could not remember if Hurley watched it with them, just as Robinson and Kitching could not remember if he had watched it with them the day before.

Next morning, Sunday, November 21, two days after Cameron's death, Detective Senior Sergeant Kitching tracked down Penny Sibley, the Aboriginal woman who had been standing outside the police station when Hurley struggled with Cameron. She had left Palm Island and was staying in the sugarcane town of Ingham, an hour's drive from Townsville. She had not yet heard Cameron was dead: "I got the biggest fright." Penny, who'd known Cameron all his life, described him in traditional terms as her nephew. She told Kitching she had seen him strike Hurley's face, then Hurley "got wild" and punched Cameron back. She said that when she saw this she started to cry. Kitching asked her if she was on any medication. Penny admitted she was on "a helluva lot of drugs" for "heart, high blood pressure, sugar, yeah, diabetes." Penny's daughter wondered if her mother should be talking out against Hurley: "All this things that Mum doing," she asked Kitching, "this can put in danger?"

Darren Robinson, meanwhile, had heard a rumor that Cameron had been drinking bleach, and was researching alternative causes of death. On Monday morning, November 22, Kitching suggested he stop by the hospital to get the dead man's medical records. This was what Robinson found: Doomadgee had been admitted in 1991 with hepatitis; in 1993 with a head injury; in 1994 with an alcohol-related seizure and also renal trauma; in 1999 with multiple stab wounds to his chest and stomach. In 2000 he was admitted with stab wounds in his right thigh and a fractured arm; in 2003 it was lacerations to his hand and lip from fighting; and later that year he was admitted with broken ribs. This was life for a young man on Palm Island. From around the time of Robinson's visit to the hospital, the rumor emerged—popular with the police—that Doomadgee had been in a car accident just before Hurley arrested him.

Kitching, of the onyx Christian ring, signed the police report on Cameron Doomadgee and sent it to the pathologist. He did not include Roy Bramwell's allegation of assault: the cause of death was a fall.

But by Monday afternoon, Bramwell's story of seeing and hearing Hurley beating Doomadgee had made its way around the island. Mayor Erykah Kyle had been calling on any witnesses to come forward and speak on a PA system she'd had set up in the town square. Around a hundred Palm Islanders listened as Roy Bramwell—now a kind of hero—told his story: Cameron had been lying on his back; Hurley's knee was on him and he was punching down. Afterward a mob went to the police station demanding to know what was happening with the investigation. To their surprise, it was Chris Hurley who came out.

Rising to his full six foot seven, Hurley stood facing the crowd. He told them he'd done nothing wrong. Nothing—and since he'd been on the island it had become a better place. He seemed angry, affronted that they were questioning him. People started yelling out abuse, and other police officers came to see if Hurley was all right. According to one officer, someone threatened "to drag him out of the station and bash him to death the same way he had supposedly done to the offender Doomadgee."

A group of older women, including Erykah Kyle, ran and stood between the crowd and the police.

One woman, Rosina Norman, said she couldn't look at Hurley.

It made her cry. "Stop it!" her sister told her. "He might guess what you're thinking."

"He did something to him," Rosina replied.

Despite having assembled the crowd, Erykah told me she was "almost pleading" with them to leave. "We are not going to find the answers here," she said. "This will achieve nothing."

After the protesters dispersed, Hurley walked from the station across the dirt of Police Lane to his home, a high-set white weatherboard house surrounded by palms and trimmed with white lattice and wooden window guards. Dark vines were overtaking the Cyclone-wire fence. Unlocking the gate, he crossed his neatly trimmed lawn and went up the side stairs. He had set his place up with every comfort, padding himself from the grind of the job. Did he start to pack, knowing he would leave and not come back? Did he start with the basics, then add the things he did not want to lose?

Within a few hours Hurley was at the airstrip with two large bags of clothes and personal effects. He was joined by Lloyd Bengaroo, who had started receiving death threats. The two men boarded a plane and flew off the island.

Detective Senior Sergeant Kitching traveled to Cairns on Tuesday, November 23, and attended Doomadgee's autopsy, which took place later that afternoon. When he and the pathologist, Dr. Guy Lampe, discussed the evidence, Kitching again failed to mention the allegation that Cameron had been assaulted.

A doctor involved in the case told me in confidence that because of Cameron's black eye, both the initial police investigation and the autopsy proceeded on the assumption that the cause of death was a head injury. In fact, the autopsy revealed four broken ribs, a ruptured portal vein, and a liver almost cleaved in two. Blood had quickly filled Doomadgee's abdominal cavity, restricting the flow to his vital organs. His internal injuries were so severe that even with instant medical attention he would not have survived. On the autopsy certificate, Dr. Lampe reported that Cameron had died from an intra-abdominal hemorrhage caused by a ruptured liver and portal vein. Under "Antecedent Causes" he wrote "Fall."

The next morning, Dr. Lampe rang Detective Senior Sergeant Kitching and told him that his superiors did not want him to include "Fall" on the certificate for fear it "may be seen to be assisting police with a cover-up." He would have to reissue the certificate. Later that day, November 24, the Crime and Misconduct Commission (CMC), a Queensland government organization born out of the Fitzgerald inquiry and known as "the filth" by the police they investigate, took the case away from Hurley's associates.

On November 30, a second autopsy was performed by Dr. David Ranson, an English pathologist based in Melbourne. He had been called in by the Queensland state coroner, who wanted an outsider to give a second opinion. Ranson concurred with Lampe that Cameron Doomadgee had died due to blood loss from internal injuries. But Ranson also discovered further bruising on Cameron's right eye and eyelid, his forehead, the back of his head, the upper part of his back, along the right side of his jaw, and on his right and left hands.

Unfortunately, as a CMC insider put it to me, by then the police detectives had already "stuffed things up." In the five days they controlled the investigation, the truth had begun to evaporate. When the CMC interviewed Lloyd Bengaroo, he had clearly decided to keep his mouth shut.

Crime and Misconduct Commission: "Did Senior Sergeant Hurley assault Mr. Doomadgee whilst he was on the floor?"

Bengaroo: "I can't recall that one."

The Family

ELIZABETH DOOMADGEE invited the lawyers and me to dinner. She covered the table with a purple batik cloth and upon it laid a large economy packet of biscuits and two bowls full of fruit. Her house was fastidiously tidy, and spare of furniture other than mattresses and a set of bookshelves with Bible stories and family photos. In one frame a young Elizabeth was laughing, a hibiscus in her hair: a beauty. She had three daughters—the youngest, Sylvia, ten years old—but six other small children, some still in diapers, sidled up to us for the biscuits; they climbed onto our laps as if we were all old friends, struggling to be held and cuddled and given attention. Aborigines call their elders Aunty or Uncle as a sign of respect, but I was Miss, like the teachers at school. The children eating biscuits were Elizabeth's grandnieces—some of whom she fostered—and neighbors' kids who had spilled in from the street and the warm night: it was her policy that any child was always welcome. Seeing the Palm Island children had made Andrew Boe decide to take on Cameron's case. Now these kids took turns to play with him.

The coroner had come and taken a brief tour of the island on February 8. After a pre-inquest hearing in the local gymnasium, he had ruled that when the inquest began on February 28, the Palm Island witnesses would give their evidence on the island and the police witnesses would give theirs in Townsville.

With dinner ready, the rest of the family went to watch television and Elizabeth brought two large bowls of stir-fried wild goat and rice to the table. The goat, I later realized, had been hunted by

Cameron. Elizabeth thanked God for the food and prayed for those who did not have as much. She prayed for Sylvia's sore foot to heal, and for any children in the hospital: "May God with his great hands heal them." She thanked God for our being in her home: "Only you know what's in their hearts." She prayed for the lawyers' mouths, so that at the inquest they would be bold, and for my ears, so that I would not miss any important details.

Elizabeth laid three plates on the batik cloth, and the lawyers and I were served the dead man's bounty. Really, this dinner was in honor of Andrew Boe. For the Doomadgees, like many Indigenous families, to be drawn into the law was to be drawn into an impenetrable labyrinth, all walls and no exits. Boe could lead them through. He could find out for sure what had happened to Cameron. I was welcomed warmly, as if his disciple. And later I looked back on this meal as the moment that I too was hooked in and set upon a quest.

After we'd refused second helpings, the rest of the family ate in the kitchen. Among them was Eric, Cameron's only child, a quiet, polite sixteen-year-old wearing an American basketball shirt. Cameron used to take his son diving and fishing and hunting for possum, goat, and echidna, using dogs and a spear. Eric lived down the road with his aunt Valmae at his grandmother's old house. Twenty-two other relatives also lived there. Some of them had drinking problems. If Valmae had trouble she called in Jane and Elizabeth.

"We go and straighten them out properly," Jane told me.

"How?" I asked, laughing; they were both slight women.

"Either with our fist or hit 'em with a stick."

Valmae told me she was worried about her nephew. "He lost if you ask me. Sit down with you and like he's thinkin' thoughts long way away. It's showing out in him now." She had been trying to keep him interested in boxing lessons with an ex-boxer who lived on the island. "Keep his mind busy," otherwise "he's just falling away slowly."

Valmae showed me a photo of her and Cameron in their late teens, both of them striking, glowing with youth. Now in her early thirties, with five children, she had long, curly hair that she liked to tint red, an impulse she attributed to having a Scottish ancestor. A very sweet, sensitive woman, she was easily wounded and in deep mourning—not just for her brother. Shortly after his death, Doris Doomadgee had died. Mothers, Elizabeth had told me, would always try to protect their sons; hers was following Cameron to the afterlife to look after him.

Not all the siblings had the same father. The older children's father was Arthur Doomadgee, from the Ganggalida tribe near the Gulf of Carpentaria. He had been banished to Palm Island from the mission community of Doomadgee in the mid-1950s, after knocking out all the teeth of a missionary who'd flogged his uncle to near death. Arthur was put in leg irons and sent to the island along with his young wife, Doris, who was of the Waanyi tribe from around the Gulf region's Nicholson River. On Palm Island, Arthur became an alcoholic. Doris bore her last two children, Cameron and Valmae, outside the marriage. Their father was Francis Anderson, who had grown up in the Palm Island dormitory. The two children lived in Townsville with Anderson until he died. As six- and five-year-olds they came to live with their mother and the stepfather who gave them his name.

All the Doomadgee children grew up listening to Doris telling them Dreamtime stories. The Dreaming, or *Wanggala* to the Waanyi, is for Aboriginal people the equivalent of Genesis, a saga of creation rich in complex, philosophical layers about how rivers and water holes, the sun, the moon, and the stars were created. According to the great Australian anthropologist W. E. H. Stanner, "One cannot 'fix' The Dreaming *in* time: it was and is everywhen." It was and is "an age of heroes," when the Ancestral Spirits in animal and plant form journeyed, stopping to fight, make love, give birth—and leave the evidence of their adventures on the landscape. Doris's children would hear tales from the Dreaming and protest, "Oh! You're getting it from library books." But Doris had got it from stories she'd been told as a child.

At night the young Doomadgees would listen as their mother sat alone, talking in Waanyi to her dead father, Jack Diamond, who she believed returned as a crow if anything was wrong. She believed that he still sent her signs.

Before he died, Arthur Doomadgee returned to his homeland of Doomadgee to see his mother, Lizzy Daylight. Doris and the children accompanied him. Lizzy Daylight, whose bush name was Yella Gundgimara, is remembered by contemporary anthropologist David Trigger as "the grand old lady" of the Ganggalida people. Trigger wrote to me:

> Lizzy Daylight was known to be in touch with the spiritual forces connected with Rainbow (Snake) Dreaming, and hence to such phenomena as storms, cyclones, lightning and so on. She [could sing] songs said to have the power to either stir up or placate Rainbow and hence also the physical phenomena connected with that Dreaming. And when she died, people spoke of how they saw rainbows both to the north (her mother's coastal Ganggalida country) and the west (her father's up river Waanyi country).

In many parts of Australia, the Rainbow Serpent—although its traits and abilities vary—is considered the most powerful Ancestral Spirit, a symbol of fertility that rules water and the weather. The old people from Doomadgee believed Bujimala, the Rainbow Serpent, carved out the landscape, leaving tracks for water. Its voice was thunder, lightning its tongue; sacred trees were its ribs; a falling star, perhaps, the serpent's eye as its body writhed in the dark. "You can see shadow standing, rain time—pretty color," one old woman told a land-rights judge in the 1983 Nicholson River land claim. In other words, a rainbow was the serpent's body in the light. Valmae told me, "You know how [there are] all these books about Aboriginal things; they all true. We just couldn't get over it. They real all right."

Sylvia, eating her dinner, listening, now told me a secret: there was a plug on Palm Island, and if there was ever a war, the elders could remove it and the island would disappear.

"What would happen to all the people?" I asked her.

"They'd swim," she said, as if I must be crazy.

I asked Sylvia what she wanted to do when she grew up. She wanted to work in the kitchen of the island's new Police Club Youth Center. Her seventeen-year-old sister, named Doris after her grandmother, wanted to be a doctor, as she had ever since she'd had a heart bypass as a twelve-year-old. But the Palm Island high school went up to only tenth grade and she had not matriculated. Another of Cameron's nieces wanted to be a model; her mother told me she'd have to get her off the island before . . . and she held her knuckles to her cheek, meaning before her daughter's looks were ruined by beatings.

Jane, who was in her forties, said she wanted to be a fighter pilot because when she played video games in a Townsville arcade she was so fast that people crowded around to watch. If not a fighter pilot, then she wanted to be a cook, and if not that, a security guard. But just then she was not working.

The inquest was scheduled to begin in two weeks and Chris Hurley would be appearing. Hurley had been transferred to the plum posting of Surfers Paradise, on the Gold Coast, Australia's answer to Miami. He might have been enjoying police work amid the sun, surf, sex, revelers, and retirees, but Queensland's *Courier Mail* had reported that the senior sergeant was "suffering" as he waited to tell his side of the Palm Island story. "He is just gutted," a source said. "Mostly he feels let down by the community. This bloke spent most of his career in Aboriginal communities trying to help people and he just feels they turned on him."

Andrew Boe asked Elizabeth how she felt about going to the mainland to see the police testify.

"I'll forgive them what they done, because Jesus said, *Love thine enemy.*"

"If you say that, then it doesn't matter what happens," Boe suggested.

"It doesn't matter," Elizabeth answered, "because it's in God's hands."

"I'm not that patient," he replied.

"Aboriginal people got no choice but to be patient. If I didn't have God in my life . . ." She paused.

Elizabeth had something more than Christianity in her life: she had blackfella protocol. Although Chris Hurley had been relocated, Lloyd Bengaroo had been denied a transfer and was back working on the island, helping white cops make their arrests. Elizabeth had seen him in the street and he couldn't look at her. Were she a different kind of person, she told me, she would take his clothes off his washing line and send an item to her relatives across the border from Doomadgee in the Northern Territory. They would use them to do magic that would make Bengaroo grow sick and die. But instead Elizabeth tried to love him and to be patient. In prayer meetings she had been praying for justice. "We want justice for Cameron . . . that's to make his spirit free. We want the truth. We want to hear the truth."

Elizabeth was both Christian and blackfella, New Testament and Old. She could afford to love her enemy because she believed fiercely in divine retribution. "I work for God, so he gotta work for me." She had been doing a course in firefighting. One day, standing close to a fire, she thought: This is what hell must be like. This is what whoever killed Cameron will feel. Where they'll go. Just imagine how dry it will be. You'll want to drink and drink and drink.

After dinner, the lawyers and I walked down to the jetty. It was eleven o'clock; the Milky Way was close above, and people sat along the jetty's edge holding their fingers, with baited strings attached, over the water. They were mainly women and children, perhaps getting away from the drinkers. One child lay in the center of the jetty, asleep on a pillowcase; two others were dozing in their strollers. I wouldn't have thought there was much to catch at low tide, but the children used a torch to spotlight the dark water. If they found a fish they tailed it with the light while their friends dropped in lines nearby.

I sat on the jetty's edge, the sea breeze a balm after the heat of the day. Water lapped around the wooden pylons. There was no horizon: the sky was connected to the water. It too was liquid, its stars like phosphorescence. In an article on Aboriginal astrology, I'd read: "Like the stained glass windows of medieval cathedrals [the night sky] provided, in effect, an illustrated textbook of morality and culture during the thousands of years when the only means of relaying the accumulated wisdom of the tribe was oral tradition." People navigated and predicted seasonal shifts by the stars, but they were also the subject of religious stories. The Milky Way was commonly believed to be a river, with the brightest stars fish, other stars waterlily bulbs, and the dark patches lagoons. Some tribes thought that the dead lived in this sky world of great bounty.

Around Australia, as the frontier spread through the nineteenth and into the twentieth century, the Aborigines understood the white invaders to be the spirits of kinsmen returning from the dead. In northern Queensland, W. E. Roth wrote in 1903, many names for "white person" translate as "bogie man," "ghost," "corpse," or even "grave." And the names, of course, took on a terrible irony. The Aborigines showed these white ghosts where the water was. The white ghosts brought sheep and cattle and occupied the traditional hunting grounds and sacred sites. They took black women. And in North Queensland, as in many other places, every act of Aboriginal retaliation was answered with violence far exceeding it. "Shoot those you cannot get at and hang those that you do catch on the nearest tree as an example to the rest," exhorted the *Northern Territory Times* in 1875. The Aborigines of the Gulf region, where Cameron's family came from, called this frontier period Wild Time. The survivors were cleared onto missions; and this period was called Mission Time.

When I was at school in the 1980s, we never learned about Aboriginal history; we didn't know the name of the tribe who'd inhabited Melbourne pre-settlement, let alone anything of Aboriginal religions or cosmology. Somehow we picked up basic tenets. We knew that land was central to Aboriginal identity, that in fact blackfellas saw themselves as inseparable from the land. No land meant no Dreaming, and no Dreaming meant no identity, no meaning. Wild Time was, among other things, a violent religious upheaval. It meant the smashing of those stained-glass windows in the night sky.

Palm Island was settled with refugees from Wild Time; they lived cut off from the religion and culture of their traditional lands, and the despair that went with their removal was often fatal. Around the turn of the twentieth century, W. E. Roth heard old people on a mission singing a song: "This [country] made him die. The place he did not belong to. It was this [that made him] die."

On the jetty a thin, white-haired Aboriginal woman sat with three of her daughters, one of whom was a hopeless alcoholic, of the kind the islanders call "drones." The mother looked to be in her eighties, but was probably closer to sixty. Boe perched next to her and they started talking. She told him she thought things had been better in the missionary days. Palm Island was spotless then. Everyone had a job, even if they weren't paid. There was a market garden, stockyards, a turtle farm, boat builders. All the houses were immaculate, and gardening competitions ensured that everyone's yard was beautifully maintained. There were Christmas trees for the children. Dances. A football team. Drinking was banned. There was far less violence.

Like most older people I met, this woman, a half-caste, had been taken by police from her parents, from the "retarding influence of the old myalls," the traditional Aborigines, and sent to live in Palm Island's dormitory. This was an island of stolen children.

Across Australia, it is estimated, between one in three and one in ten Aboriginal children were forcibly removed from their families in the period 1910–1970 and transported to distant missions, orphanages, or foster families. Many children were separated from their siblings. They were often told that their parents had died, and they were given new names. One Palm Island woman, Bethel Smallwood, told me that her mother was haunted all her life by not being able to remember her own mother's appearance. She could picture her outline, but could never give her a face.

Children in the Palm Island dormitory were ordered out of bed at 5 A.M. and made to attend church three times on Sunday. The missionaries found it easier to teach children that Jesus would save them; adults were grounded in their traditional beliefs. Children caught speaking tribal languages had their mouths washed out with soap. Beatings were routine. Often there was not enough to eat.

"You were given a tin plate and cup, and if you forgot it, had to wait for others to finish and then look through the slops for what you could bear to eat," Bethel Smallwood said. Girls wore dresses made from burlap bags and if they misbehaved they had their heads shaved. Native police escorted the girls everywhere. One of the girls was Amy Atkins, who now lives in Brisbane. She told me that in the 1950s the dormitory windows were nailed shut so the girls couldn't run away. When she cried for home she was locked in jail for the night. The girls were taught basic literacy, numeracy, and housekeeping. When they came of age they were often sent to the mainland to work as domestic servants.

During the 1940s, Cameron's mother was raised in the girls' dormitory at Doomadgee; his stepfather, Arthur, in the boys'. The couple were sent to Palm Island in their early twenties, and like most people were allowed to raise their own children until they turned five, then the children were required to live in the island's dormitories. Cameron Doomadgee's three eldest sisters, Henrietta, Carol, and Victoria, were taken from Doris, and so that she could see them for more than a few hours a week, she took on a dormitory job. Henrietta Doomadgee was making a cubby outside the dormitory in some long grass when "a white man," not realizing she was there, poured out petrol and set it alight. She died in her mother's arms.

That night on the jetty the lawyers and I also met three boys. They looked no more than thirteen, but said they were sixteen. One, who had a cigarette butt tucked behind his ear, sidled up to Andrew Boe and asked him for a smoke. Boe shook his head. Of his six children, the eldest, an Aboriginal foster son, had been in trouble with police. He was only a few years older than the smooth-skinned, keen, curious boy who now sat alongside Boe, wanting to talk.

The boy boasted that he drank Jim Beam. He teased one of the others, a quiet, chubby kid, for drinking camel's piss, XXXX beer. He took the butt from behind his ear and tried to light it and when finally he succeeded the three shared the tiny stub between them. I asked the third boy where, if he could have a ticket to anyplace in the world, he would go. He said Brisbane, because he'd heard it had a park with a swimming pool that offered a free feed once a week.

"Are there drones in Brisbane?" he asked Boe.

"Yes," he answered.

"Do you ever give them money?"

"Sometimes."

"Miss, what song you like?" the quiet boy asked Paula.

She thought for a while.

They liked rap: Eminem, Usher, and Destiny's Child. Michael Jackson was "Sharpnose."

The leader stood to perform a dance routine. The boy who wanted to go to Brisbane showed us some punches he'd learned in boxing. The quiet one made a series of birdcalls with his hands. They were full of spirit, full of life.

Boe asked them why TALL MAN had been written on the boulder near the airstrip. They didn't know. But they knew who the Tall Man was. They'd been brought up with him, the island's combination of Big Foot and the bogeyman. The Tall Man was dangerous, while another spirit haunting the island, the Hairy Man, was short, ugly, and mischievous. In all sincerity, the leader pointed to a nearby light post to show the Tall Man's height. "His feet as big as a giant's. You can see his red eyes when the lights turned out on the football field."

When I asked other children about the Tall Man they reported: "He smells of stinkin' things." "He smells as bad as a bin." "A bin tipped over." A teenage girl, Rae Rae Clumpoint, told me: "At night when you're by the campfire, big wind blow and you smell dead goat, you smell it, it's strong, it's stinkin' and them wind blow, there's Tall Man, they stand up behind trees and they move with the wind, they blend with the wind, they very tricky." She told me she had been in Townsville once on top of a hill. "We smell dead goat, we knew that thing was hanging around us. If it takes you they will bash you, but they won't kill you. That's all they do to you."

The boys on the jetty said the Tall Man lived in the hills but came down and watched people while they were sleeping. For no reason he would slap you across the face.

"He tall, he tall, he tall, you know," Roy Bramwell had said of Hurley. Another witness, an old woman, had recalled: "The tall man get out and arrest him. I saw the tall man grab him by the arm . . ."

When we started to walk back to the motel the boys followed. At the end of the road, contractors were guarding the new police station. The boys had seen the old one burn down in the riot.

"What do you do for sport?" Boe asked them.

"Throw rocks at coppers."

Boe reached into his pocket and made a dare. He'd give $2 for each rock that hit the old, long-broken clock face.

Not one shot missed.

Headlights warned of a police van approaching and the boys bolted. They were gone before we even said good-bye.

The Riot

SEVEN COPS WERE usually stationed on Palm Island, but in the days following Cameron Doomadgee's death there had been twenty-two. A gray-haired Aboriginal grandmother turned to one newly arrived constable at the airstrip and asked, "Why don't you cunts fuck off?"

A fever was rising. At night barrages of rocks hammered the roofs of the police station and barracks, and when the officers went out into the dark they couldn't see the perpetrators. On the evening of Thursday, November 25, six days after the death, the island's young doctor, Clinton Leahy, met with the Doomadgee family and Erykah Kyle to explain the findings of the first autopsy. That night was unnervingly quiet. It was pay week, although even in off-pay week there were always parties going on somewhere. Revelers blasted loud music, kids were out playing, people fought. Now the streets, lit by a full moon, were silent and deserted.

Two constables were on patrol. Around eleven they parked their vehicle and sat on the veranda of an old man playing his piano accordion. People came out of their houses yelling, "Fuck off cunts! White shit! White trash!" The constables bolted. In the next shift, police picked up a woman with a black eye and two busted front teeth whose husband had bashed her and called her a "copper cunt" because she defended Chris Hurley. Otherwise, that night was the quietest anyone could remember: "just silence all night."

In the morning the state coroner gave Erykah permission to inform the community of the pathologist's findings. In jerky video footage taken by an onlooker, men, women, children, and dogs line the edges of the mall, a paved area outside the store and council buildings, to hear how Cameron died. It is a bright, hot day. The amateur exposure of the camera floods the scene with sun and shade. Erykah Kyle stands at a portable PA system holding a microphone. She wears a black shirt, skirt, and, despite the heat, black pantyhose. Notes clasped in her hand, she is both dignified and at sea. The Doomadgee sisters are behind her, alongside Tracy Twaddle, who holds a handkerchief to her face. Elizabeth stares at the ground.

Erykah asks everyone to stand for a moment's silence. Hundreds of people bow their heads. She tells them the pathologist believes Cameron's death was the result of an accidental fall and that he'd found no sign of police brutality.

"We understand you want answers," Erykah says finally, "because this is a mystery to us all." She pauses and then reads from her notes: "There was an accident somewhere around the cell at about 10:40. He was found at 11:23 that day. There was a fall and the doctor, Dr. Clinton, explained it was compressive force on his body; four ribs were broken and a rupture in his liver and from that a lot of bleeding . . ." She emphasizes "a lot." "There was a big blood loss, a huge blood loss. That's all the information I can give today," she says. "No more questions to the family. Please show them your respect and think about the life of this man. We thank God for the life of Cameron Doomadgee."

The crowd stands watching. They have heard this announcement as a verdict of "not guilty." They've heard that Cameron's death is going to be written off as yet another accident, another whitewash. A voice calls out for more information. But Erykah stands flailing. She doesn't have the words.

"It will go to the CMC and from there . . ." Turning to people behind her, she pleads, "I need some help." But there is no one who can give it. Her notes blow in the breeze. She might be thinking of her own son, who played with Cameron when they were children, and who had committed suicide in jail two years before. "You never get over losing a child," she said to me one day, "never ever."

The video records people yelling. The situation is too much for Erykah. She turns and walks back inside the council building. The Doomadgees follow her.

A thirty-seven-year-old plumber called Lex Wotton had been fixing a pipe nearby and joined the crowd. He'd planned to fly to Townsville that morning to go grocery shopping, but then the pipe had burst and the only other plumber on the island was drunk. Now he steps forward and takes the microphone, bare-chested in jeans and with red reflective sunglasses.

As a child, Lex had heard the mission bells telling people when to wake and when to sleep. Back then people still lined up for rations. In an old shed where he used to go and sit, he'd found an illustrated Bible. He couldn't read well but was fascinated by the pictures of Samson, who was clever and heroic and strong, and who would break his bonds no matter how often the Philistines tied him up, and taunt them with his unnatural strength. Lex would look at Samson wrestling a lion, or slaying an army with the jawbone of an ass; even with his eyes gouged out he could push down the temple of his oppressors. Lex's own father was a Kalkadoon, from a warrior tribe known for their ferocity and their ability to vanish from their enemies. In 1884 they made their last stand against the Europeans at Battle Mountain, with their spears held like lances, charging downhill straight into gunfire. The Kalkadoon word for bullet means "hole maker." It is said that for years afterward their bones lay scattered over the ground.

The adult Lex has the muscular, V-shaped torso of a man who works out. He has scars running from shoulder to armpit on both sides, legacies of football and fighting. One of eleven children, he left school at fifteen, a talented athlete and a heavy drinker. He'd been to jail, but sober for a decade, he now commuted to work in Townsville, where shop people put his change on the counter rather than in his hand.

"Come on, people!" Lex calls. "Will we accept this as an accident? *No!* I tell you people, things going to burn. We'll decide when. I'm not going to accept it and I know a lot of you other people won't. So let's do something!" On the video, half of Lex's eloquence is in his body. Instead of decrepitude there is strength and muscle and presence. He is a fantasy of a figure before white contact.

Another man walks up to the microphone. David Bulsey is tall and slender, with a wonky dignity and a stare lit with fury. He grew up in the dormitory, but taught himself to read and write in a mainland jail. His brother had died in jail after being convicted for murder. Bulsey points like a preacher to the sky and then to the crowd. "I done the wrong thing!" he yells. "I went to prison. So have a lot of boys. So why should *he* get away with murder?" People are clapping. "We don't want trouble on this island, we want bloody justice! If he get away with this, it's going to happen again and again and again!"

Then Bulsey changes tone, speaking quietly, knowingly, and hits his target. "If you people don't stand up, it's going to happen again, and it may be one of your children next time."

DETECTIVE SERGEANT Darren Robinson had a feeling something was going to happen. He sat at his desk in the station that Friday eating a steak sandwich, listening to the crackling PA system in the mall: "a familiar sound," he told investigators the next day. "Come Christmastime they'll all be down there doing Christmas carols and shit." He knew the results of Cameron's autopsy were being announced, and for his friend Hurley, the findings of a split liver were going to be controversial. Nothing in Hurley's account of events explained how Cameron had sustained such a massive injury.

It was one o'clock. As Robinson put down his sandwich he heard breaking glass and knew. "I thought to myself . . . *It's on. They're coming.*" He ran into the next room; glass was strewn over the desks and the floor. All around, windows exploded behind the bent, jagged Venetian blinds; police were moving desks and filing cabinets to barricade the doors. The building was a box with nine cops inside it.

There were people running on the roof. Stones hit the walls. "I was just waiting for this moment," Robinson later told investigators. "I knew we're in big trouble here."

He ran outside. The highest-ranking officer, Inspector Brian Richardson, was trying to reason with the mob. The inspector, his wife—Detective Kathleen Richardson—and Senior Sergeant Roger Whyte stood looking out upon, as Whyte put it, "copious amounts of Indigenous people." Two hundred Palm Islanders stood behind Lex Wotton, calling out about "that murdering cunt Hurley." Why was he not in custody? Why had he not been charged with murder? Seeing a blue uniform made them angrier. Every cop was Hurley. Women were screaming. Adolescents threw rocks. Little kids gave officers the finger. Boys no older than ten held milk containers full of petrol.

But Darren Robinson had never seen anyone as angry as Lex Wotton. Lex was all biceps, abdominals, white teeth with ragged edges, and rage. He carried two enormous Stillson wrenches—long cast-iron plumber's tools. Lex swung the wrenches round his head and smashed the station's walls. "Oh, Lord God, remember me and strengthen me!" Samson had cried as he pulled down the Philistines' temple. "You fucking killed him!" Lex screamed. "You murdering white cunts! You cunts killed him!"

For the first time in his two years on Palm Island, Robinson wanted his gun. He and the other officers "fucking literally ran inside" and opened the safe where the firearms were kept. Inspector Richardson suggested they lock themselves in the police station, but Robinson thought that was "bullshit . . . we're going to die, mate, they're going to burn us." Most of the crowd faced the front of the station. Robinson led his fellow officers out the side door and over Police Lane to Hurley's yard, then through a gate to the police barracks.

Ten other police officers were there waiting for them. Three more coming in from the airstrip had been radioed; they watched the crowd from a hilltop as if "watching a shoal of fish." Of the offi-

cers, twenty were white, one was Aboriginal, one of Torres Strait
Islander descent; only three were regular to the island. Now a high
wire fence separated the police in the barracks from the crowd gathering outside. No one seemed drunk, Robinson noted. "They were
cold sober."

"We are going to burn you!" they called. "White cunts!" "Kill the
cunts! The Captain Cook cunts!"

The police could hear windows smashing next door at Hurley's
house. People were throwing anything they could find: coconuts,
mangoes, paving stones; a six-foot star picket came over the fence
like a spear.

"I saw kids walking with shopping bags full of rocks," one officer said later, "all of them throwing whatever object they could peel
off the ground or pull off a tree." This was an outbreak of visceral
loathing. It was payback: the symbolic clash of two laws. The furies
had been unleashed, not just over Cameron Doomadgee's death but
over all the black deaths in custody, all the black deaths and all the
injustices since Wild Time. Thick dark smoke started spewing from
the police station.

Video footage shows Palm Islanders of all ages standing on the
other side of the lane, watching the station burning. The Doomadgees
stood there too. The cell in which their brother had died was razed.
Some cheered as it went down. All the power vested in those walls was
vanquished. Later, the crime scene photos would show decomposed
bulletproof jackets and Glock handguns, their polymer frames now
puddles of plastic.

A siren began to wail and the police trapped in the barracks realized kids had broken into the police van and were switching the
lights and siren on and off. A gas tank exploded. Bright orange
flames came from next door: Hurley's residence. The police could
smell gas.

"Oh, shit! This is the Alamo!" cried one cop on the phone to
command, begging for the army to fly in. "We've got to get the fuck
out . . . It's a simple fact they will take us." The officers started to wet

towels, filling any containers they could find with water, but then the water ran out. Lex Wotton had turned it off.

Many of the officers believed they were going to die. They passed around a mobile phone and rang their families to say good-bye. Men asked their wives to tell their children they loved them. Wives were crying but the husbands had to hang up and give the phone to the next man.

Then Senior Sergeant Roger Whyte went outside and walked over to the fence with his hands up. He had spent six years working in the ex–mission communities of Cape York and he had "an intuition" about how "far you can take 'em. I said to my inspector, I said, 'Listen, boss, we're gonna get overrun here, we need to attempt to communicate . . . otherwise . . . we're gonna have to shoot one.'" As Whyte approached the fence, more rocks came toward him.

But Lex Wotton, who had been trying to jimmy open the gate's padlock, now ordered the crowd to stop throwing rocks. They did so. "You've won! You've won!" Whyte called. He negotiated for an hour's grace, sixty minutes to get off the island. The Torres Strait Islander cop, Bert Tabaui, heard Wotton yell, "We'll give you an hour to get off our island, then we'll kill you!"

The crowd returned to the mall around the corner and waited. As the fire roared behind him, Senior Sergeant Whyte addressed the other police. "There may be a case where you'll have to discharge a few fuckin' rounds in the air to scare the shit out of these cunts!" According to Robinson, Inspector Richardson added the command to "fire . . . a warning shot in the air, and if that didn't work it was fine, you know, you have the support of the Service to start shooting people."

The police knew there were very few guns on the island, although some worried that if they opened fire they'd be beaten to death. Those with guns counted their bullets. Those without looked around: one man took a pick handle off the wall, another man a cricket bat, another a set of pool cues, which he snapped in half and gave to those with nothing. One man took a barbecue lid to use as a shield.

They cut a gap in the wire fence and moved quickly down Mango Avenue, the street where blacks had once been forbidden. The hospital was two hundred meters away. When they had all reached the ambulance bay, they formed a guard while Inspector Richardson went inside to check on the reinforcements with command. In the background, the view was paradise: blue sea and tropical islands. In the foreground, the crowd re-formed: two hundred people, armed with pieces of wood, screwdrivers, spears, iron bars, or even butter knives. The police could hear rocks hitting the hospital behind them. People were still yelling: "Kill them whities!" "Kill them, they're murderers." "This is our island." Ash and debris floated through the air. The smoke got thicker. All around were the sounds of crashing timber and buckling iron—the sounds of the station and Hurley's house falling down.

A group of Palm Island men stood under the hospital's great mango tree drinking beer they'd stolen from the police barracks. A ten-year-old drove a sedan around the streets. Each time he passed, the crowd cheered. A cop holding a spade for protection was told he would be killed and the spade used to dig his grave. The Indigenous officers were called "whiteman lickers" and ordered to "cross the line."

Lex faced the police. He was still angry, but the anger was now controlled. "Time's up!" he called. "All I wanted was for you to get off the island!"

Erykah Kyle, who had stood back watching as the crowd exploded, was shocked at how far things had gone. She and Lex began to argue. "You had your time to talk!" he yelled at her. "Now I'm taking over."

An older woman next to Erykah interjected, telling Lex: "We want the police here. Who is going to protect us from you men if they go?" Others started abusing her, and she and Erykah walked away.

As the rioters and the police stood staring at one another, each perhaps saw its reverse. The blackfellas saw men from stable families, men who'd had fathers, men who'd finished school, men with jobs, who owned houses, who had traveled, who'd had chances, men whose deaths would be properly investigated. They saw the police who had put them and their brothers and their fathers in jail.

The police saw "pack animals" turned wild, ungrateful children. And they believed themselves to be the real victims—poorly paid coppers called on to do society's dirty work.

The cops told Lex they couldn't leave. They had no transportation. A car drove past and Lex flagged it down, telling the driver he wanted to give the cops the car to get to the airstrip. The driver refused and kept driving. Lex then organized for two council cars to be offered up; they were parked outside the hospital with the keys in the ignition. The police believed this was a trap. They'd heard that an ambush had been set up on the road out of town.

Lex Wotton didn't know it, but police reinforcements had arrived at the airstrip and were making their way to the hospital. Darren Robinson walked into the crowd, trying to stall the riot leaders until help arrived. The air was leaden with smoke. People stood with shirts over their mouths. "I'm just talking shit to get us more time," Robinson explained to police investigators the next day.

Incredibly, he chose to deliver a lecture to the Palm Islanders. Local police, he told them, needed to be part of the community. He had great rapport with the children. He had spent his own money on magic tricks to develop that rapport. He told the crowd that as the Palm Island detective he was "doing more child sex offenders than ever before and . . . um, it's probably hit home at that stage that they have destroyed evidence against pedophiles in the community, people that raped kids, that they only have themselves to blame that they were letting sex offenders walk around in this community."

When asked by the investigator how the crowd responded, he said, "Oh, everything that came out of their mouth was white cunts, you know. Get off our island . . . going into this stolen generation thing . . . you know, and I'm just shaking my head, in fucking disbelief that they're bringing up that shit at this time."

The thunder of helicopters filled the smoke-clouded sky. Extra police had now arrived and still more were coming. Inspector Richardson came outside and told Lex, "We are not leaving this island. We are the police. You are the ones causing the problem . . . we are not going anywhere! No way in Australia!"

Lex Wotton turned around and faced the crowd. The revolution had failed. His idea that the police would leave the island had been biblical in ambition and naïveté, a declaration of war he had no chance of winning. His actions would draw national attention to Cameron Doomadgee's death, but at that moment he knew he would soon be the one inside a jail cell.

"The party's over," he called, "we'll all go home!" Then he turned to the police. "You can come around later and pick me up."

HURLEY'S WHITE HOUSE was burned to the floorboards. A crumpled mass of corrugated iron, once his roof, lay on the ground, peeled off to expose rooms of ash. "He had absolutely his whole life in that house, he had thousands and thousands of dollars of stuff," a young constable later remarked. Kids had broken the lock on Hurley's front gate. Finding petrol near his lawn mower, they threw it on his motorbike and bicycle and on the police van, setting them alight.

Darren Robinson found his door kicked in and his rooms ransacked. Clothes and CDs and books were scattered over the floor. Food was out of the fridge. A television lay on its screen. His futon frame was broken. He started making a list of things missing: knives from his knife block, five games for his Sony PlayStation II, a tin of coins ("value approximately $100"), beer, cordless phone, fishing reels, spear gun, mountain bike, ski rope, Calvin Klein jeans, Adidas running shoes, Nike thongs. Also gone were his magic tricks.

That night, Robinson became the most important cop on Palm Island. He was the only one able to recognize any of the rioters besides Lex Wotton. By order of the police commissioner, there were now eighty officers on the island, carrying trash bins full of batons and stun guns and semiautomatic rifles. Detective Inspector Warren

Webber, originally the senior investigator of Cameron Doomadgee's death, had just been removed from the case by the Crime and Misconduct Commission. Now he had a new gig: coordinating the riot response. Webber declared an emergency situation under the Public Safety Preservation Act 1986, which allowed police greater powers.

Going from house to house through the dawn of Saturday, November 27, Darren Robinson led a team of twenty-four officers in balaclavas and riot gear, including thirteen from the Special Emergency Response Team (SERT), who were newly trained in counterterrorism tactics; seven officers from the Public Safety Response Team; two dog handlers with Rottweilers; and two police negotiators. First he took them to Lex Wotton's low-set, mustard-colored house on Farm Road, where Lex was shot in the chest with a Taser. He dropped to his knees and was then, according to his wife and children, surrounded by cops who struck him on the legs with a baton, handcuffed him, and dragged him away.

Altogether the police raided eighteen houses, but in five found no one they were looking for. In one house a man who couldn't speak or hear, who usually only opened his door when his elderly mother shook a rattle outside it so he felt the vibrations, had his door kicked down and was made to lie on the floor with dogs and guns facing him. Children and pregnant women had the red lasers of rifles playing over their faces. Some youths arrested at remote Wallaby Point alleged the police told them that if they were shot, no one would know what happened to them.

The CMC later disputed the legitimacy of Webber's declaration of emergency. It was difficult to investigate the conduct of individual officers because they were all wearing balaclavas and called one another by code names, such as Horse, Hippy, Speed, Buzz, and Law.

Eighteen men and three women were charged with rioting. The men were flown to Townsville and incarcerated. After ten days they were granted bail on the condition that they not return to the island.

•   •   •

NINETEEN OF THE twenty-two police officers involved in the riot prepared victim impact statements, the first step toward receiving a compensation payout. The officers said they were suffering post-traumatic shock. They couldn't sleep, had nightmares, and cried uncontrollably. Nine went into therapy, two went on medication. Some now felt fear, others hatred.

One officer wrote that his children no longer played sports on the weekend because they didn't want to mix with black kids. One officer said he cared nothing for the people of Palm Island, and "this I feel has diminished my humanity a little." Another said that he had quit his role in three charities. And another claimed to have trouble socializing with anyone not a cop. There was an officer who felt he had lost his Catholic faith, and now "I do not trust Indigenous people for fear of violence . . . I fear for my family because if they can try to burn my body, they will burn and hurt my loved ones." Another stayed up all night guarding his infant son because he was scared blacks would find his house and attack him. He had sold up in case whoever stole his identification from the Palm Island police barracks came seeking retribution.

Another officer wrote, "I will spend my last dollar on alcohol," and another that he had considered shooting himself ever since the riot, when he'd "placed a bullet in my top pocket in case I had to shoot anyone and I ran out of bullets I could have one bullet left to shoot myself as I was convinced they would murder me and or burn me to death."

The sole policewoman at the scene wrote:

> I had concerns I would not only be bashed but also raped if they overpowered us. The thought of this happening in front of my husband and colleagues was always on my mind and to this day, still haunts me. I told myself that they would have to rape a dead body as they wouldn't take me alive, I was prepared to fight them to the end.
>
> I imagined that my front teeth would be knocked out. It

is a common occurrence for Aboriginal women to have lost their front teeth because of the violence they endure from their spouses. I honestly believed that at the very least, by the end of the day, I would be in the hospital with no front teeth. Either that or dead.

There was an officer who wanted "to make all the people involved in the riot feel the same helplessness that I had just endured. I wanted revenge." "Right or wrong," wrote another, "I have harbored unhealthy desires to seek revenge which often consume all my thoughts." This was now a kind of war.

Belief

IN LATE FEBRUARY 2005, the Sunday before the inquest began, Elizabeth took me to her church with her daughter Sylvia. It was a plain wooden building with white pews, arrangements of plastic flowers, and broken windows. Two white-haired men played steel guitars while we twenty or so people swayed and sang: *All I had to offer Him was brokenness and strife, but He made something beautiful out of my life!* Everyone clapped for what God had made out of their lives. Then we sang: *Stand up, stand up for Jesus!* Children squirmed like church children everywhere. A little girl in white frills and bows played up and down the aisle. Babies were passed around the congregation and held as if they could bestow some blessing.

The preacher was late, and while we waited we sang, and one parishioner stood up and spoke in praise of the clear blue sky and brilliant sun. A man arrived with his German shepherd. He sat and the dog made small circles until it found a shady spot under his pew.

It was now three months after the riot, and the eighteen men who'd been arrested in the dawn raids were still banned from returning to their homes and families on Palm Island. They were on bail in Townsville under a 7 P.M.–7 A.M. curfew, reporting daily to police. They were not allowed contact with other alleged rioters and could not participate in any "event in relation to the death of Cameron Doomadgee." The police lawyers had argued that if the men returned to Palm Island to attend Cameron's funeral on December 11, they would use it "as an excuse to further damage property and attack police." Typically the alleged rioters were staying on the couches of their relatives in Townsville. When, every couple of nights, the police came to check that the men were obeying the curfew, they came between 1 A.M. and 4 A.M. and woke the whole house.

Framed on the church wall was a small needlework warning:

> How shall we escape
> If we neglect so great salvation.
> Flee from the wrath to come.

There were four churches on Palm Island; Elizabeth's was Pentecostal, although we were singing a Lutheran hymn: *Stand up, stand up for Jesus! The strife will not be long. This day the din of battle; the next the victors' song.* In the 1930s and 1940s Catholic and Anglican missionaries on Palm Island had engaged in bitter competition. Six miles from Palm lies Fantome Island, which until 1973 operated as an Aboriginal leper colony, with a "lock hospital" for those with VD. The two denominations fought over souls, and dying lepers were sometimes baptized more than once.

Christianity had washed easily into Aboriginal religions. People who believed in sorcery had no trouble with miracles or the devil. The transformations that their Ancestral Spirits performed were akin to transubstantiation. And those who had lost everything welcomed the promise that they would see God and inherit the earth.

Elizabeth shared her hymn sheet with me, pointing to a line if my singing slackened. She was happy to be here, inconspicuous in the back row. It gave her relief. "Without this, out there," she said, gesturing to the community, to the world, "there's nothing."

W. E. H. Stanner described the Dreaming as offering a "poetic key to reality," a mythic lens through which to interpret daily life. For Elizabeth that poetic key had become the Bible. She quoted lines of scripture at random, metaphors that carried her through. They would help her in the following week when she would see in court the man she believed had killed her brother.

In the middle of a hymn, the black preacher made her entrance—

a big, stern woman with a long gray plait, and reading glasses on the end of her nose. Her dress hung from her bust like a tent. She sang the loudest, in a high-pitched, strident voice. "Tribulation times are coming!" she cried at the end of the hymn. "And they're going to be very hard, brothers and sisters!"

She'd been browsing the Web, she said, and now saw the end of the world was nigh. "The returning Lord will come at an unexpected time, but a time with specific observable signs. There are signs all around us. There are murders, there are rapes, there are all kinds of things going on." I assumed she was talking about Palm Island, but astonishingly she continued: "We are fortunate in this community because nothing has happened to us yet."

The preacher gestured behind her, perhaps to the steep hills covered in boulders, and told us that, come the apocalypse, stones would rain down. "When he speaks, just at his voice even the rocks cry out and praise him as they smash. Little pebbles crack like his word tell us." She asked us to ask ourselves: "Am I really clear of all my sins, am I really ready for when he comes, am I prepared?" Millions of people, including a lot of Christians who were not fully committed, were going to have a bad time at the apocalypse. "When he closes the door," she boomed, "it will be shut to us like the door to the ark after he took Noah and his family in! And the rest of the world was lost! What have we got to say to that?"

From where I sat, the door seemed to have shut a long while ago. I had heard horror stories so casually told of stabbings and beatings between siblings, between lovers. In the past six weeks, a man had critically knifed his brother over a beer. A woman had bitten off another woman's lip. A man had poured petrol over his partner and set her alight. The unemployment rate was 92 percent. Life expectancy was more than twenty years less than the national average. This place was a black hole into which people had fallen. Rocks may as well rain down.

We stood to sing: *Yes, Jesus loves me / Yes, Jesus loves me / Yes, Jesus loves me / The Bible tells me so . . .*

Through the window I watched children tossing an inflatable plastic ball, patterned as a globe, bouncing it like capricious gods. Sitting next to her mother, Sylvia was feeding a bottle to a toddler, but she wanted to go out and join the other children. She deposited in my arms this plump baby with dark skin and uncannily bright blue eyes. She was the preacher's granddaughter and she lay in my lap, sucking at the milk, the fingers of one hand wrapped in mine. Around us, exhausted-looking parishioners sat praying. There were twenty people in this church, trying to hold back the tide.

THE DAY BEFORE, I'd met a policeman, dressed in shorts and a T-shirt, fishing off the jetty. As soon as he caught anything, birds swooped down and took it. I asked him how he liked the island. He said he couldn't believe there were three thousand people here and not even a barber shop. That was strange, and it was strange as well to be locked each night inside the police barracks. All the regular officers had been taken off the island after the riot: he was here on a three-month rotation.

While we were talking, little children approached him. "Can I have a jig, sir?"

He showed them how to use the nylon line with small hooks and colored glass beads to attract fish.

The kids' young mother was sitting on the other side of the jetty with her back to the water, staring at the policeman. Oblivious, he looked out to sea. When the children turned to her, excited at having used the jig, she mouthed at them: "He a copper." She smiled as she did this.

The policeman sat jiggling his line. The sun was setting. The sky, swathed orange and lilac, was shockingly beautiful, but around us it grew dark. While the locals seemed friendly, he said, it frightened him that at any moment they could turn. He recommended I didn't walk around at night alone. "They are a very violent people," he said quietly.

Why would a police officer choose to work solely in these communities? In the old days, these were punitive postings, or places for coppers who needed to be hidden from sight. Chris Hurley had put his hand up for such assignments—because Hurley was ambitious. One acquaintance of his told me Hurley had a particular and clear vision of how he planned to progress, one he liked to talk about. Everything had been carefully calculated, tallied. Hurley knew that for a man tough enough to stick it, these communities were the fastest way up the ladder.

"I'm going the whole way," he'd boasted to an old friend. Hurley was from a police family: his older brother was an officer, and this friend told me that Hurley's uncle, also an officer, had earned the rank of inspector. Hurley wanted to get at least that far as well. As senior sergeant he needed just one more promotion. So he suffered the discomfort, and put the extra money paid to officers serving in remote communities into a property portfolio; already he had two waterfront apartments in the booming beach town of Burleigh Heads.

But ambition was only part of the explanation. Remote places can be addictive. A well-regarded inspector who served on Palm Island for six years told me how, early in his tenure, he'd been viciously beaten by the locals, but he decided not to be transferred and had subsequently won great respect. "I saw violence mainstream people can't understand," he said, violence from which there was no respite. Living on the island was "like living in a fishbowl. There's no escape. Every bugger knows your business and if they don't they make it up." Still, he reckoned those were the best years of his life. Days on Palm, he explained, seemed more vivid, more intense. Somehow life was closer to the surface. And he felt he was making a difference.

There might also be a darker appeal. For someone who feels like an outsider in the mainstream, or undervalued, or unsuccessful, or overlooked, these can be good places, places every Mr. Kurtz can go and stockpile ivory—or raw power. Police in these communities have enormous control over people's lives. "I was like the king of the island," the inspector recalled. I suggested that this was a temptation some officers succumbed to: the community became their fiefdom. "No," he said, perhaps misunderstanding what I was getting at. "It was just that it was my place."

What I didn't ask the inspector was this: Can you step into this dysfunction and desperation and not be corrupted in some way? In a community of extreme violence, are you, too, forced to be violent? If you are despised, as the police are, might you not feel the need to be despicable sometimes? Could anyone not be overcome by "the growing regrets, the longing to escape, the powerless disgust, the surrender, the hate?" Or had I read *Heart of Darkness* too many times?

I wondered if Chris Hurley had heard the story of Palm Island's first superintendent, Robert Curry. Mr. Curry, known as Boss or Uncle Boss, was a veteran of the Great War who oversaw the settlement of the island throughout the 1920s. The Aboriginal inmates cleared the land and erected buildings, without even a horse or dray, and when eventually a dray came—with no horse—Uncle Boss ordered the men to haul it themselves. It was he who introduced European dancing, and the jazz band and garden competitions. He fired his gun at Christmas. He fired his gun on the beach at seagulls, and while boating, at passing whales.

A Conradian figure himself, Uncle Boss resented the interference of other white officials on the island. As one of them noted, "Mr. Curry practically regarded this settlement as a child of his brain." When rumors spread on the mainland that he was flogging young Aboriginal women, Curry suspected his rivals. But the allegations were true. Without these whippings, he told his superiors, his "authority . . . would have been weakened." The violence was his way of maintaining control. He'd turned tyrannical in a place he described as akin to "living on the rim of a volcano."

Curry hated the Palm Island doctor, and his enmity intensified when his wife died in childbirth. Drinking heavily in his grief, and dosed on novocaine for neuralgia, Curry donned a long red bathing suit, a bullet belt, and with a gun in each hand, went on a rampage. First he dynamited his own house with his drugged children inside, then he went out to shoot the doctor and burn down the settlement buildings: to kill the child of his brain. As they burned, white officials gave a gun to a young Aboriginal man, Peter Prior, and deputized him to shoot Curry—and then they hid.

Prior was charged with murder and locked up for six months. The charges were then dropped, but for the rest of his life, Prior would dream of Robert Curry.

Tony Koch, a senior writer for the national newspaper the *Australian*, told me he interviewed Peter Prior when he was very old and both his legs had been amputated due to diabetes. Prior started crying because he was scared to die. God said, "Thou shalt not kill," and he had.

Like Kurtz, Uncle Boss died in a land he had mistaken for his own. *This country made him die,* sang the old people on the mission. *This place he did not belong to. It was this that made him die.*

AFTER OUR MORNING in church, Elizabeth took Boe, Paula, and me on a trip to find taro, a tuberous root vegetable that's a tropical staple. This diversion was not just hospitality. Elizabeth and the lawyers were going into battle together; she wanted to keep them close to her before the inquest began.

Halfway up a mountain, Boe could coax the borrowed four-wheel drive no farther. "Think of Jesus," Elizabeth urged him. But Boe was an atheist. He parked and lay under a tree while we three women set off through the old mission's abandoned plantation. I was carrying a shovel, and Paula a pair of Elizabeth's boots.

Enormous pine trees stretched above us. "This remind me of *Blair Witch,*" Elizabeth said. Along the dirt road, to the right, was a view of the surrounding islands. To the left I could see valleys where wild horses grazed on the banks of a creek.

"How much farther?" I kept asking. "To the bridge," she kept answering. Through the heat we passed huge gray boulders, wildflowers, a tree with foliage gathered on each branch like a bouquet. No bridge ever materialized.

I asked Elizabeth about the Tall Man.

"He like Big Foot." She believed he'd always been in these hills.

The Aboriginal activist Murrandoo Yanner told me that Tall Man stories exist all over Indigenous Australia. In the Northern Territory's Arnhem Land, there are mimihs—tall, thin rock spirits capable of evil. There's also the figure of Namorrorddo, described by rock-art expert George Chaloupka:

> A malignant spirit, a ghostly, spectral figure [he] is usually portrayed in rock paintings as a very tall, thin and extremely elongated being with long slim arms and legs, and with claws instead of fingers and toes. It is not unusual to find images representing this being that are more than 8 metres long. He moves about only at night, when he may be seen for a split second rushing across the sky. When the people see the trail of a falling star they know that it is Namorrorddo going to a locality where somebody is dying. He is said to fly in search of sick people, waiting to rip open their chest, take away their "breath" and carry away their heart. The brighter the star the more important the dying person. When a person dies during the day, their "shadow" is taken away by birds who are said to be Namorrorddo, or who act on his behalf.

I'd seen contemporary bark paintings from western Arnhem Land of the giant called Luma Luma. There was a Luma Luma Street on Palm Island. Elizabeth told me the Tall Man was a traveler, a creature that could change shape at will in order to move around freely. This was also one of the abilities of Luma Luma.

In the 1920s and 1930s many Aboriginal people were sent to Palm Island from around Laura, in southeastern Cape York. Near Laura there was said to be a giant who ate people, called Turramulli, as well as many tall spirits, good and bad, who, like the mimihs, were rock spirits. These spirits were called *quinkans,* and were said to have stone axes extending from their knees and elbows that they would use while flying down and striking enemies. Laura elder Tommy George explained:

> *Quinkans* are malevolent spirits. They hide in dark places and come out at night. That's when they are active. Our stories say they live in the sandstone, the cracks and narrow places. It's dark there and you can't get in. They come out at night and sneak around over the rough country. That way they can hide quickly if they have to. They just slide into a crack in the rock. Those long legs and arms let them hide easily behind and in the trees too. That night work they do can be evil. It still make people worry a lot. That *purri purri* belief is still very strong.

Fifty thousand years ago, the Aborigines did live among giants. The megafauna included three-meter-tall kangaroos, and giant wombats, koalas, snakes, crocodiles, and lizards. Their bones found across the land were readily explained as evidence of the giant Ancestral Spirits of the Dreaming.

Elizabeth led Paula and me down a steep embankment covered in long grass. At the bottom stood a mahogany-colored horse straight from a young girl's fantasy. As we picked our way through the rocks and deep grass it stared at us, quizzical. In a shallow creek bed, taro grew: tall green stalks with wide leaves on which mud and water ball like mercury. Elizabeth put on her boots and began to loosen the roots with the shovel.

Then she stood back, expecting me to pull the roots out—and I did. The job was ridiculously primal. I squatted and clutched the stalk, pulling as hard as I could, sliding farther into the mud. An enormous tuber sprouting muddied roots slowly emerged. As it came free, mud splattered all over me, giving off an intense vegetable smell not unlike manure. It was overwhelming, the whole thing. Before long Paula and I were both roiling in mud trying to birth these bulbous taros. Elizabeth's mother had taught her to do this, and perhaps her mother before her.

For Elizabeth, traditional food gathering was one custom the Palm Island missionaries could not destroy. The same was true for men on the island: her brother had been much admired for his hunting.

The Christians had tried to stamp out "tribal sorcery and super- stition ... savage life ... medicine men and rainmakers of barbarous nations." Like a lot of people on Palm, Elizabeth had her own way of reconciling traditional spirituality with Christianity. She worried that the Rainbow Serpent, her grandmother Lizzy Daylight's totem, was the snake in the Garden of Eden, but she still believed the Ances- tral Spirits were all around.

I passed the taros to Elizabeth, who sliced off the stalks with the blade of the shovel. The tangled roots looked like hair. It was as if I were filling our bag with human heads. Paula and I were now com- pletely covered in mud, while Elizabeth remained spotless. I realized how far we would have to carry the bag and stood staring at it gloomily.

"What's that?" Elizabeth asked suddenly. "It's the Warning Bird calling!"

I strained to hear birdcall.

"It's warning us it's now time to leave." She moved quickly and I picked up the heavy sack and followed. Elizabeth was strict but warm, wily but protective. It was impossible to tell if she was teas- ing us. "Thank you very much," I heard her say to any resident spir- its. "We're going now."

The people in Elizabeth's church had been searching for grace. Elizabeth was searching for grace and for answers. Father Tony, the island's Catholic priest, later told me that on the island he'd had the- ological discussions of more substance than in many other places. Among families so ravaged by alcoholism and violence, there is another dimension to forgiveness.

Father Tony had invited Elizabeth to go to Townsville with him to speak at a church service. She told the story of her brother's death, and a white policeman stood up and started to cry. He said he'd seen terrible things done to Aboriginal people; he said how sorry he was.

"He cried brokenhearted," Elizabeth told me. She had gone over and hugged him. "Brother, I forgive you."

The Inquest

THREE AND A HALF months after Cameron Doomadgee and Chris Hurley fell through the door of the Palm Island police station, the coroner's inquest into Cameron's death began. The riot had made the case front-page news in Queensland, and on the first morning, along with the star lawyers, small planes delivered star journalists to the island. After one plane's arrival, an Aboriginal man stood waiting for the passengers to disembark. "The white people fly in," he sniggered, "so we fly out."

"What do you think will happen?" I asked him.

"The same as usual: nothing."

Court convened in the gymnasium of the newly opened state-funded multimillion-dollar Police Club Youth Center. Under the basketball hoop, a desk was set up for the coroner. On the wall behind him hung a sheet reading:

THE PALM ISLAND COMMUNITY WELCOMES YOU
TO THE CORONER'S INQUEST HEARING OF
THE LATE MULRUNJI DOOMADGEE.
MAY THE BLESSED BEAUTY SHOW HIS MERCY AND BOUNTY
UPON HIS BATTERED, BLESSED SOUL FOREVER.

The colorful sign had been appliquéd by Lex Wotton's sweet-looking, bespectacled mother, Agnes, who had learned to sew and embroider in the mission's dormitory. Unfolding the umbrella she used to keep off the sun, Agnes told me she was having a second career as an activist. Along with her son and daughter, she had been charged with rioting. The women had not been sent off the island, but on the sign she had listed the names of the banned men, alongside this message:

BWGCOLMAN WARRIORS TOOK A STAND FOR JUSTICE.
WE WANT JUSTICE.

Despite the workload of the inquest, Andrew Boe had applied to have the men's bail conditions reversed. Now he sat along the bar table with seventeen other lawyers, all of them white. They knew one another, having worked together on different trials over the years. They knew who among them were the drinkers, which ones were gamblers, who was fast on his feet, who was slow. This was a club with old loyalties and old grievances. Running the inquest, as counsel assisting the coroner, was the trim, wry barrister Terry Martin SC, who was himself assisted by two other lawyers. Martin would examine all the witnesses. Other counsel would then have an opportunity to cross-examine. The coroner had to determine what had caused Cameron's death. If he suspected Hurley was guilty of a criminal offense, he was required to refer the matter to the director of public prosecutions, who had the power to lay charges.

Every party with an interest in the outcome had legal representation. Appearing for Senior Sergeant Hurley were the barrister Steve Zillman and solicitor Glen Cranny. Cranny, along with another barrister, was also appearing for the other police who'd been in or at the station at the time of Cameron's death: Lloyd Bengaroo, Michael Leafe, and Kristopher Steadman.

Barristers Peter Callaghan SC and Tony Moynihan, and solicitor Stephanie Hack, all funded by Legal Aid, had come from Brisbane to represent the Doomadgee family; Boe and Paula Morreau were to represent the Palm Island Aboriginal Council. Two lawyers from Townsville's Aboriginal and Torres Strait Islander Legal Aid were representing Tracy Twaddle. The Queensland police commissioner also had two lawyers. Another lawyer, Jonathon Hunyor, was appearing for the Human Rights and Equal Opportunities Commission.

Although this was an inquiry, not a trial, and the proceedings were not meant to be adversarial, the lines were firmly drawn: five lawyers for the cops, trying to persuade the coroner that Hurley had no case to answer; ten lawyers for the blackfellas, insisting that he did. Agnes Wotton was made to remove her sign.

Under the basketball hoop, in linen shirt, trousers, and new boots, sat the state coroner, Michael Barnes. His wide-brimmed hat rested on the floor. Barnes looked like someone who had tried to dress down but only succeeded in making himself look like a colonial planter. Now he rose and said good morning—and shot himself in the knee.

> Firstly, I think I need to place on the record my previous involvement in some matters involving one of the principal witnesses, namely Senior Sergeant Hurley. From 1992 to 2000, I was Chief Officer of the Complaints section of the Criminal Justice Commission.* In that position I was obliged to make a determination in relation to all complaints made to the Commission. A review of the files of complaints made against Officer Hurley shows that I dealt with a number of those matters in that capacity . . . I have no memories of any of the matters. I do not believe that my involvement will in any way reduce my ability to impartially consider the evidence in these proceedings.

This was Queensland: even the state coroner had only one degree of separation from the main suspect. The coincidence was like a red flag to the Doomadgees' lawyers. They had written to the

---

*The Criminal Justice Commission (CJC) was established in 1989 to investigate claims against the Queensland Police Service in the wake of the Fitzgerald inquiry into corruption. The CJC was replaced with the Crime and Misconduct Commission (CMC) in 2001.

state coroner's office a number of times over the past month seeking access to Hurley's complaint files. They were looking for "similar fact" evidence, trying to find out whether Hurley had been accused of assaulting prisoners before. Quick and aggressive, Peter Callaghan now declared he wanted immediate access to these files, to gauge the coroner's involvement—and to see what the complaints were.

The police commissioner's lawyers opposed him; so did Hurley's barrister, the lean, coiled Steve Zillman, who claimed that most of the complaints were "unsubstantiated" or led to "informal resolution . . . there's nothing in them."

Callaghan stood again. He was forty-two and in Brisbane's legal ranks considered a rising star. He had been drawn into this case by Boe, who knew Callaghan was haunted by work he'd done fifteen years earlier on the "Gulf circuit": Callaghan, a twenty-seven-year-old government prosecutor, would fly to the Gulf of Carpentaria's Aboriginal communities for the day, meet Aboriginal rape victims for the first time in the courtroom, and then have to fight for them with no counselors to assist, no resources, and no time for preparation.

Peter Callaghan said to Coroner Barnes: "I will object to you continuing to hear the inquest, and ask you to disqualify yourself, on the basis that you have disclosed previous dealings with this man [Hurley] and for not allowing us access to the materials that relate to those dealings, which can only entrench a perception of bias."

The coroner ruled that Callaghan could review the files, but they were back in Brisbane. And seeing everyone was gathered and waiting to start, he said, the inquest would continue.

Elizabeth sat with her sisters and Tracy Twaddle in a line at the front, watching the lawyers' facial expressions to gauge what was happening. The women wore Sunday best and held kitchen wipes in case they needed to dry their eyes. Earlier, Elizabeth had led her lawyers in prayers and ordered them to stand up straight with their heads held high. I'd also overheard her asking Erykah Kyle if onlookers could be banned from taking notes. "We got our writer here," she'd said, gesturing to me.

It had been raining lightly. "Blessing rain," Valmae said. She had not been able to find a hearing aid and was sitting by a speaker, straining to follow the evidence. Also sitting near the speakers were fifteen or so journalists, photographers, and cameramen from around Queensland, sweltering. Among them was the *Australian's* Tony Koch, who'd done the most to publicize the Doomadgee affair. In his midfifties, Koch was both hard-bitten and gentlemanly; he'd been writing about Indigenous issues for twenty-five years. The son of a country cop and the brother of cops, Koch was considered a traitor by the Police Union for criticizing the riot response. While all the other journalists were embedded under police control, he had stayed with a local family and gone out on the streets reporting.

About a hundred Palm Islanders sat at the back or stood close to the door, as if being able to get out fast were more important than being able to hear.

The inquest was like a great, old-fashioned crushing machine, slow to crank up but, once in motion, processing its victims with brutal efficiency. Tracy Twaddle, wearing black, was the first witness to be called by Terry Martin. In a tiny voice, she gave evidence that Cameron had not been in a car accident and had no visible injuries when she last saw him. On the morning he died, she said, he left the house around dawn while she was still asleep. She started to cry and dabbed her eyes with her kitchen wipe.

The next witness was Victoria Doomadgee, also in black, Cameron's alcoholic, monosyllabic sister. The coroner reminded her that she had to speak, she could not just nod. She said she'd spent the night at Cameron and Tracy's house. That morning her brother asked her to come and drink beer with him. He'd had no visible injuries. It was the last time she saw him.

Old Reginald Barry appeared next. He had lost an eye warding off a drunken son, and walked slowly to the witness's microphone. He'd spoken to Cameron around 7 A.M.

I was sitting at my home there having breakfast and he came
along and he sang out to me, "Hey, Uncle," he said, "I'm looking for a smoke." He came in and said, "I'm going to try and
get a loan of a boat to go fishing." And I looked at him and he
was cold sober. "Uncle," he said, "I'll leave you now. Would
you like me to bring you some fish?" and I said, "Yes, alright."

It was an hour or so later when Cameron first turned into Dee
Street. He stopped to chat to Edna Coolburra, an apple-cheeked
older woman with long gray hair. Edna now gave evidence that
they'd talked about her son, with whom Cameron had been best
friends. Her son had died nearly twenty years earlier after a diving
accident. Cameron was "just saying how much he missed him and
that." She noticed he'd been drinking, but he was "merry and in a
joking mood."

Leaving Edna's, Cameron went to drink more. When Edna saw
him next he was being arrested: "He couldn't resist cause Chris was
too tall for him . . . Chris is a big powerful person beside him." She
didn't hear Cameron swearing at Hurley, but in cross-examination
Steve Zillman suggested this was because she was hard of hearing.
Zillman questioned Edna in detail about the timing of events, but like
most Palm Islanders she did not wear a watch. She couldn't remember if it was ten minutes or two hours after they'd first chatted.

It was Gerald Kidner whom Cameron had been drinking with, at
Kidner's house, farther up Dee Street. When Gerald and his partner,
Verna Snyder, decided to go and get their welfare checks, Cameron
tagged along behind them on his way home to Tracy. In court, Gerald wore a black shirt trimmed with flames. He had trouble reading
his oath. "The only thing he was saying," he told the court, "was he
was singing a song, 'Who Let the Dogs Out,' after Patrick got locked
up . . . He just sang that song and he kept walking."

Boe stood up and said, "Gerald, you're a pretty good friend of
Mulrunji, aren't you? You were?"

Gerald Kidner: "Yeah."

Andrew Boe: "Does he sing it out a lot?"

Gerald Kidner: "Oh, yeah."

Andrew Boe: "And does he sing it out no matter who's around?"

Gerald Kidner: "Yeah."

Andrew Boe: "So he doesn't sing that song for a particular reason, does he?"

Gerald Kidner: "No."

Andrew Boe: "He just sings it?"

Gerald Kidner: "No, he just sing it."

Next up was Gerald's partner, Verna Snyder, emaciated, barefoot, shaking, apparently severely alcoholic. The coroner's clerk had to read out her oath and she repeated it in a slow, quiet voice. Her testimony was like a broken song: "Only singing along the road and the coppers come along . . . They put Cameron [in] back."

Terry Martin, counsel assisting the coroner, asked her who'd been singing.

Verna Snyder: "Cameron."

Terry Martin: "What was he singing?"

Verna Snyder: "Call the dogs out."

She broke down midtestimony and sat with her head in her hands, distraught and overwhelmed.

A stray horse put its head through the door. Wind rushed in and riffled the coroner's papers. Verna Snyder sat weeping. I can't have been the only person in court who felt sick, who felt the whole thing was hopeless. On this island the law didn't get any closer to the truth, it got further from it.

The day before, I'd driven with Elizabeth and Boe to remind witnesses not to drink too much. We stopped at a house shuddering with loud dance music. Teenagers, all of them wasted, started to crowd around the car. They were young, some no more than thirteen, and the closest things to zombies I've ever seen. One girl put her hand to the car window, staring in, clearly seeing no one. Beer cans lay all around; small children were underfoot. It was nine o'clock in the morning.

"Black man pretty hard to understand white man's language," a witness told me.

In this gymnasium, it was also plain the lawyers could barely comprehend the Palm Islanders' language. Most of them didn't want to be here. It was a case of "tippin' elbow"—the black term for white officials checking their watches, anxious to fly out.

Terry Martin addressed the coroner: "I'm sorry, Your Honor, I'm not getting any of this at all." Mayor Erykah Kyle went to Verna and put her arm around her. She was excused.

Gladys Nugent, the next witness, spoke softly, "under her skin." Terry Martin kept asking her to repeat herself because he couldn't hear. Gladys had been in the front of the police van when Hurley arrested Cameron. "[Cameron] was walking along quiet when I seen him . . . I never hear him swear." But Zillman asked how much she'd had to drink that morning and made the implication clear—she was too drunk to know if Cameron had sworn or not.

Nobie Clay had been sitting with her baby son on her veranda, watching when Cameron was arrested. She was in her early twenties, barefoot and in full bloom. She had been a heavy drinker as a teenager, but was now sober. Nobie was a champion local boxer, taking a break from her career to raise her son. Unlike the other witnesses, she was bursting to tell her story. She described what Cameron looked like when he walked past:

He didn't look sick. He wasn't limping or anything. He looked straight at me. He had no marks or bruises on his face. Chris jumped out of the driver's side. Uncle Cameron didn't say anything to him as he was coming down the road. All he said was the lyrics to the song "Who Let the Dogs Out." He was a happy drunk. As he was standing on the pathway, Chris jumped out of the driver's side, with his two hands grabbed him by the arm and pulled him towards the vehicle. And Uncle Cameron just said to him, "Oh mate, you're locking me up for nothing." And then Chris said, "Shut up, Mr. Doomadgee, I'm locking you up." Uncle Cameron didn't try to resist arrest. He didn't try to hit him. Didn't swear at him. Chris then grabbed him by the two arms, shoved him up against the back of the police paddy wagon. As Uncle Cameron went to turn to face him, Chris then grabbed his two legs and smashed him with like a spear tackle into the back of the paddy wagon. And that's when I heard a loud banging. And on my statement it said that I didn't actually see him hit his head but I know he's hit his head because his arms were still by his side and his legs were still in the air . . . He gave Chris no reason to rough handle him like the way he did.

Steve Zillman suggested she couldn't have seen all this if she was also watching her infant son. Nobie said she could and did. Then the PA system stopped working and the court was adjourned to fix it.

My picture of Hurley came in and out of focus: sharp and clear one moment, then a figure without edges, just a presence, a force hovering in the frame. I'd heard that he used to flirt with the island's women and that he'd pick up drunk men and drive them out past the airstrip and leave them there so they had a long walk back to sober up. That morning, the police commissioner had described the senior sergeant as a "very fine officer." But in the gymnasium, two mothers told me that their sons had returned from the watch house bruised; and I met a young woman who happened to be Cameron Doomadgee's niece, called Barbara Pilot. Barbara told me that one day Hurley had run over her foot and then left her lying on the ground.

In the tangled story of the morning Cameron died, Hurley was the good Samaritan one moment, helping Gladys retrieve her medication, and a brute the next, strong-arming Cameron into the van. Was he good cop *and* bad cop? Or in the morass of miscommunication and legal sophistry, had the real Chris Hurley got away?

From nowhere, Cameron's dog arrived and sat beside the Doomadgee sisters. (Later, Elizabeth claimed the dog had bitten a witness who gave bad evidence.) Other dogs were already lying in the shade. Children collected the empty water bottles the lawyers left on the floor. Cameron's son, Eric, was sitting with a friend. I had given Elizabeth some seeds and a set of tools for her garden. Eric had the red gardening fork tied with a bandanna to his calf. He was carrying it as a weapon, as if he had revenge in mind.

The court heard from Patrick Nugent, whom Hurley had been arresting when Cameron first walked past the police van. Pale and thin, an El Greco figure with a bandaged hand, a sleeveless football shirt, and no shoes, Patrick was beautiful and ruined. ("Does it smell of sour milk to you?" the island's white administrator had asked me earlier, wrinkling his nose at Patrick's acrid body odor.) On the evening of Cameron's death, Patrick had been interviewed by Detectives Robinson and Kitching. He told them he'd been taken to the station in a different vehicle from Cameron's, then placed in a separate cell. In other words, he'd seen nothing. When the Crime and Misconduct Commission interviewed him two weeks later, he claimed:

> I saw that Cameron was in the room outside the cells. He was lying on the floor on his back. Chris was on top of him . . . punching him in the ribs on both sides. At this time, Chris was telling Cameron to shut up and be quiet. He also said, "Do you want more, more Doomadgee?"

But the cell-surveillance tape showed Patrick was out cold, and couldn't have seen anyone do anything. When he was asked to read through and swear by his statement to the CMC, Patrick sat still.

Terry Martin: "If you look at your addendum statement, do you say that the contents of that statement are true? Please have a read through it before you answer that question. I want to know if the statement is true, do you understand?"

Patrick Nugent: "Yeah."

State coroner: "Mr. Nugent, do you read okay?"

Patrick Nugent: "No."

The coroner's clerk rose and, standing next to Patrick, read out his statement. The two men were probably the same age, but Patrick's English was limited and it was clear he had only a rudimentary understanding of what was going on. Even worse, he seemed to be trying to guess the right answer. Lawyers have a term for the tendency of Aboriginal witnesses to agree with whatever is put to them so as to be polite, avoid conflict, and get off the stand as quickly as possible—it's called "gratuitous concurrence."

Steve Zillman: "Now why did you make up those untruths and put them in your statement?"

Patrick Nugent: "Yeah."

Steve Zillman: "You in fact couldn't even stand up, I'd suggest."

Patrick Nugent: "No, I was sitting down."

Steve Zillman: "Mmm?"

Patrick Nugent: "I was sitting down and I got up."

Steve Zillman: "You were so drunk you were just about unconscious!"

Patrick Nugent: "No."

Steve Zillman: "In fact, you haven't got a clue about what happened that day?"

Patrick Nugent: "No."

Steve Zillman: "I've got nothing else. Thank you."

Patrick was followed out of the gymnasium by photographers who ran after him down the dirt road. As their cameras flashed, he held his bandaged hand over his face. That evening he went home and tried to set himself alight. His grandmother found him and saved him. Someone had just told Patrick that he'd been lying in the cell with Cameron when he died. He had not even known.

SIX HOURS INTO the inquest, the lawyers' business shirts were transparent and clinging to their backs. The women fanned themselves. Outside, cicadas hummed, party music throbbed, children chattered leaving school.

Now it came time for Roy Bramwell to give evidence. He was a slouch-shouldered young man with an old face—and the Palm Islanders' star witness. Down by the jetty one day, I'd asked Roy if he liked fishing. He pointed to an aluminum dinghy he hoped to buy and take beyond the reef to fish. He was born and grew up on Palm Island, leaving only to serve time in jail. He had been schooled to year nine and could read "a bit."

On the morning that Cameron was arrested and locked up for swearing at Chris Hurley, Roy, who had beaten three women, was allowed to go home. Local translation: it doesn't matter what you do to one another, just don't insult a cop.

Roy Bramwell was a drunk—a violent one—and hardly the rock on which to build a case; though Father Tony, who was watching the inquest, pointed out that he was at least honest about his bad habits. Roy had been looking through his police statement every day, trying to memorize it. "It's like a daily prayer for him," Elizabeth said. But Roy worried that the lawyers would "put it all together and twist it."

Terry Martin asked Bramwell: "In the assault on your de facto wife, Gladys Nugent, did you knock her out?"

Roy Bramwell: "Knocked her down."

Terry Martin: "Yes. I know you knocked her down, but did you knock her out?"

Roy Bramwell: "No."

Terry Martin: "Did you knock her down with a punch?"

Roy Bramwell: "Yes."

Terry Martin: "And after you'd done that, did you do anything else to her?"

Roy Bramwell: "I kicked her and whacked her with a chair."

Terry Martin: "You kicked her?"

Roy Bramwell: "Yes."

Terry Martin: "Whereabouts?"

Roy Bramwell: "In the face."

Martin led Bramwell to the moment he was sitting in the police station, and Roy testified: "What I could see—I could see just Chris. Because there's a big filing—gray filing cabinet around there. I saw Chris hitting him on the ground, when he was on the ground . . . see his elbow was going up and down and he yelled, 'More? You want more, Mr. Doomadgee?' . . . He went down on his knees. He's a tall man."

At first Roy had told police that although he hadn't seen where Hurley's punches landed, he assumed it was Cameron's face. Now he wanted to say they must have been to Cameron's ribs, where the fatal injuries were. He tried to convince Martin and the audience that in his first statement to Darren Robinson the day after Cameron's death, he was too frightened to say what he'd seen. He now looked at this statement and declared, "Every word what I said in that statement I didn't say."

The whole community had heard Roy's story and now they were watching. But under legal examination the story was slipping away. He could feel it. The lawyers could feel it. Those sitting watching could feel it. Roy was changing his testimony in order to—heroically, he thought—show that Hurley had caused Cameron's injuries. But in fact he was undermining the case.

Roy now said he'd stood up in his chair to see beyond the filing cabinet. He described Hurley's position: "Well, he had his knees on Cameron."

Terry Martin: "He had his knees on what?"

Roy Bramwell: "On Cameron."

Roy's frustration was palpable. He needed to do something to convince the coroner. Unbidden, he stood up and rested his knee on the ground, as he alleged Hurley had done, and punched toward the rib area.

Terry Martin: "And that's both knees on him?"

Roy Bramwell: "Oh, just one."

Terry Martin: "And where was the other knee?"

Roy Bramwell: "It was on the side . . . one on him and the other one just like on the ground."

For a moment everything went silent. Suddenly I could see it all clearly: a big tall man's knee pressed on the chest of someone pinned against a concrete floor. The knee pushing down.

IN COURT THE next morning, Boe was the first lawyer on his feet. He wanted to make an application for Aboriginal witnesses to be given more assistance, then he added, "I should place on the record, Your Honor, that Your Honor visited my quarters last night."

It was true. The previous night, in the motel, there had come a hard rapping on the door. "I have a warrant," a man's voice boomed. Paula, Boe, and I stopped in our tracks. It was Michael Barnes, in shorts and a T-shirt.

He and Boe greeted each other warmly. Boe invited him in and encouraged him to have a beer. The coroner looked pleased to have company. We all spoke of how depressing the day had been. (So this is how lawyers talk when they get together, I thought.) But at some point Boe must have had reservations about all this conviviality. It wasn't appropriate to be fraternizing. If the police in the barracks next door had seen this, it could have jeopardized the inquest.

Next, Peter Callaghan stood up in court and announced: "It is our submission you cannot continue to preside in this proceeding." The night before, he'd finally got to see a number of Hurley's complaint files, which had just arrived from Brisbane. In all of them, Coroner Michael Barnes—in his former job—had personally signed off in Hurley's favor.

This was bad enough for Barnes, but in a short adjournment Boe made it very much worse. He told Steve Zillman the details of Barnes's visit the night before. When the court resumed, Zillman and the police commissioner's lawyers joined the call for the coroner to stand down.

Steve Zillman: "I'm informed that you initially banged on the door of the quarters. That Mr. Boe came to the door. That you informed him that you had a warrant . . . That a beer was offered to you and accepted by you and drunk."

The coroner looked wretched. He looked like a man who'd come to work and found his head in a noose. Humiliated, Barnes had no choice but to stand down. It was March 1, 2005. It would be August before the inquest reconvened.

It says something about Andrew Boe that he was prepared to put the principle first. How much easier it would have been to remain on cozy terms with everyone. And it was going to cost him: it was going to make the inquest longer, and for him, especially—working pro bono—more expensive.

The inquest had collapsed. While the lawyers packed their wheelie bags with documents, the Palm Islanders asked one another what had happened. They were unsurprised by the hearing's dissolution. White law was like that. And yet there was a feeling on the island that something just might happen. With all this momentum, there was a chance.

At that moment, as if on cue, the Aboriginal activist Murrandoo Yanner arrived from his home in the Gulf country. The name Murrandoo means "whirlwind," and it's one he lives up to. A charismatic princeling, he walked into the hall of comatose reporters like a rock star. Murrandoo was the leader of a Ganggalida clan; Cameron's maternal grandmother, Lena Diamond, and stepgrandmother, Lizzy Daylight, were both Ganggalida women. The Doomadgee sisters, his distant cousins, clung to him as cameras flashed all around.

Murrandoo, thirty-four, was a hero to some, to others a thug. Since Cameron's death he had been advocating old-style payback, claiming resistance was honorable. "Deck that policeman hurting your brother, burn that station hiding a murderer. Stop bashing wives and start bashing racist coppers." It was a clunky reformulation of Malcolm X's "The time for you and me to allow ourselves to be brutalized non-violently has passed." Had Hurley been subjected to Aboriginal law, he might have been speared in the leg in retribution—or something worse, perhaps—and everyone else spared much pain, anguish, time, and money.

· · ·

MURRANDOO HAD COME to Palm Island to support the Doomadgee family and to lead a smoking ceremony—a kind of Aboriginal exorcism—outside the newly erected police station. It had been seventy years since anyone had seen such a ceremony on Palm Island; the missionaries had discouraged the practice. "The whole purpose of the smoking ceremony," Yanner told me, "is where people have suicided, or been murdered, or die in an accident, violently, and a lot of things were left undone, unsaid. They didn't know they were going on to the next life, so their spirit's extremely troubled. Then, it may linger." The smoking ceremony could relieve the feeling of being haunted, and stop the dead from visiting the dreams of the living. "It allows the spirit to go on to the better life, the afterlife, *ginggari* in our language. Heaven for us Ganggalida people."

Early next morning, the sky was overcast and cockatoos screeched as Murrandoo covered the arms of Cameron's friends and family with red ocher, symbolizing blood, to bind them with the dead man's spirit. The men in the group included Roy Bramwell, Patrick Nugent, and Eric Doomadgee. They took off their shirts. Then everyone circled around a bucket of coals and burning eucalyptus branches, before retracing Eric's father's last steps.

The group stood outside the glorified aluminum shed that was the new station. Tony Koch, some builders, the police officers currently posted to the island, the region's police superintendent, Andrew Boe, and I stood watching. Koch, who was close to Murrandoo, worried for his friend: a picture of him had been found on a rifle target used for practice by the SERT squad, the team that had arrested the rioters.

Murrandoo carried the bucket of coals inside the station; the assembly following as if magnetized. "The smoke purifies, cleanses, and it's a rebirth," he told me later that morning. "It's a genesis in that as the wood and timber is burning away, eroding, dying, a new thing is released, far purer, far lighter, far more able to move freely, almost as free as the wind smoke is."

People named after meteorological phenomena were traditionally believed to have the power to produce them. But Murrandoo struck me as caught in his own whirlwind. As leader of the ceremony, he was in an excruciating position. He was grieving with the Doomadgee family, but he also held in high regard the man they believed had killed Cameron. Murrandoo Yanner counted Chris Hurley as a friend. He knew him better than anyone on the island.

In 1998, when Hurley was thirty-two, he had been promoted to sergeant and posted to Burketown in the Gulf country. There he and Murrandoo became close. The policeman often visited the Aboriginal leader and his wife for dinner, and was much loved by their four sons. In December 2004, Murrandoo had spoken of their friendship in an interview with Tony Koch, titled "Yanner's Bitter Dilemma":

> "I have a real pain in my heart," Yanner told *The Weekend Australian.* "I am a proud Aboriginal man and I will never deviate from standing beside my people, no matter what the circumstances. But Hurley was the most decent copper I have ever known and he was definitely no racist . . . We got drunk together dozens of times and he used to come to my place and eat meals with my family. He was the only copper who ever got into my house without a gun or a search warrant in his hand. I trusted him. He used to give his own time to take Murri [Queensland Aboriginal] kids from Burketown on camps to places like Lawn Hill Gorge. Once he took my oldest boy. I wouldn't usually let any copper touch my dog, but I trusted this bloke with my son."
>
> Yanner has vivid memories of a conversation with Hurley in which the policeman told of the day he recognised and decided to confront his own inherent racism.
>
> At the time Hurley was stationed in the Torres Strait and was out searching at night for a fisherman who was lost. "Hurley said he was swearing and cursing about the black so-and-so but after a while he looked at the stars and listened to himself and said, 'I am a racist.' That was the turning point

for him. It changed him. They eventually found the Islander lad who was lost and later Hurley's sister came to that same island where the bloke came from and they treated her like a princess."

Murrandoo handed Carol Doomadgee, as Cameron's eldest sister, a cloth soaked in red ocher. The building now had to be raddled with an unbroken red line circling the walls, to symbolize that it had been cleansed. The ocher was not to be washed off. Carol wiped the cloth in a continuous line along the pristine aluminum of the police station, and of course it looked like blood.

TWO

Doomadgee

THE STORIES OF Chris Hurley and Cameron Doomadgee both led to the Gulf of Carpentaria. I decided to follow them there. It was a part of Australia I knew only by legend. The Gulf country is the Wild West in another guise, a lingering frontier replete with free-ranging cattle, rodeos, cowboys, and people of no fixed address. The arid plains shimmer in the heat and at night travelers on the primitive back roads are said to be mesmerized by Min Min lights uncannily hovering before them. Murrandoo Yanner's hometown of Burketown, on the Gulf waters, was where Hurley lived from 1998 to 2002. Sixty miles from Burketown is Doomadgee—the Aboriginal settlement Cameron's family came from, and where Hurley also sometimes worked. There had to be clues in both places. But if I turned up alone, would anyone speak to me?

Elizabeth and Valmae wanted to come along to visit their family. Elizabeth's eldest daughter had been living in Doomadgee for ten years, and Elizabeth wanted to see her grandchildren before they got too "rusty." Valmae was thinking of moving her family back to Doomadgee because, she said, the Bible shows one catastrophe usually heralds another: she worried Palm Island might be hit by a tsunami.

I met the sisters in Townsville. They were carrying their possessions in plastic bags. I bought them each a travel bag and we flew to Mount Isa—over the mining town's smokestacks—then boarded a smaller plane that stopped like a bus at different Gulf towns, including Doomadgee. The other passengers, about fifteen of them, were government workers and locals. Two young Aboriginal women were flying home from the hospital holding their newborn babies.

A private detective sat in the vinyl seat behind me. He was taking the flight to Cairns, the last stop. He'd been on a plane like this when it nose-dived after striking a kangaroo on the runway. In the old days, he said, men stood along the Mount Isa airstrip firing shotguns to frighten them away; now there was a PA system to replicate the sound of rifles. When we reached five thousand feet, we heard, over the hum of the engine and propellers, an alarmlike whirring. The copilot emerged from the cockpit, his face shiny with sweat, to listen. He joked to the detective it was most likely a vibrator going off in the baggage hold, then he leaned close to my face. "It's probably an *adult's* toy."

From the air, serpentine river trails were marked in green, and the land itself glowed raw red-purple. It was elemental, literally. The periodic table, inlaid under its surface—Cu, Pb, Zn, Au, Ag, Ni, U— was expressed in vast dusty mines stretching out beneath us. Elizabeth looked out the plane window. "Don't be surprised if you see a dinosaur bone," she said.

The earth was also marked by countless crisscrossing song lines, or Dreaming tracks, laid during the creation period, when Ancestral Spirits formed the land. "While creating this topography, they were morphing constantly from animal to human and back to animal again," "rather like the Greek gods," explains the writer Robyn Davidson. In the old days, when the Gulf Aborigines traveled, they remembered the layout of the land from song cycles about the Dreaming ancestors. This was akin to knowing *The Iliad* and *The Odyssey* by heart and then using that knowledge to make the land intelligible. Parts of the songs explained the natural features left by the spirits, and travelers followed these song lines like power lines that gave them their own spiritual charge. An Aboriginal man trying to explain this phenomenon in terms a European might understand told W. E. H. Stanner: "Old Man, you listen! Something is there; we do not know what; *something* . . . like engine, like power, plenty of power; it does hard-work; it pushes."

Murrandoo had told me that the Waanyi people—Cameron's mother's tribe—were freshwater people, river people, but the Ganggalida mob, Murrandoo and Arthur Doomadgee's people, who lived farther north by the sea, were both freshwater and saltwater. Ganggalida was the language spoken by twelve different clans, with Dreamings that included the Brolga, the Rainbow Serpent, the Hawke, the Dingo, the Dugong, the Groper, the Barramundi Devil, the Left-Handed Wallaby, the Shark, and the Bushfire.

Having grown up on Palm Island, Elizabeth considered herself a saltwater person. Being used to mountains, she found the land around Doomadgee too flat. The climate was also not to her liking. It is notoriously tough. To the European there are two seasons, the wet and the dry. The period in between is called the buildup: days of over a hundred degrees Fahrenheit and 100 percent humidity, when you walk outside and your shirt is soaked on impact; every bead of sweat is pulled from your skin as if the sun, despairing of the parched earth, turns to you. In the dry season, the Gulf country might be the plains of Sodom and Gomorrah: "The whole land a burning waste of salt and sulphur—nothing planted, nothing sprouting, no vegetation growing on it," as the Bible says. Then each year in late November come the rains.

The Waanyi define five seasons. The period from December to March is *wirrngil,* translated as "rain no stop now—can't walk around." In a good wet season, towns are completely cut off; roads are under water, airstrips flooded, sharks swim the perimeters of cattle stations. For three or four months these raw towns become lush islands.

We were visiting in late April, in *ngajirr*—"cold weather time"— the time of *wurrarra wala gulana* ("wind coming from south"). But if the baking heat was unseasonal, no one told me.

The vibrator went off again and we landed, skidding at a sick-making angle that turned the gum and bloodwood trees diagonal.

The private detective followed us out of the plane to stretch his legs. He told me he had been stationed in this community as a policeman in 1996, when the blackfellas rioted after a cop was suspected of running over a man.

He didn't connect me to the Doomadgee sisters, and asked if I was writing a report. I said yes. "Have you been to an Aboriginal community before?" I nodded. He warned me to be careful of the "young bucks, being a white woman on your own."

It was not the first caution I'd received. Another police officer, who knew Hurley and with whom I'd started corresponding, had once worked in Doomadgee and sent me this advice:

Just be careful where you tread as there is always hidden loyalties, mistruths, animosities between all the major players. As a visitor to Doomadgee you may find it on the whole a negative place. People don't smile much and a lot is placed on who can control the most gov't funding and have their clan employed. I personally have never seen the amount of negativity etc in any other community I have lived and worked in. But these are just my observations. Good luck.

I knew Doomadgee would not be Paradise Lost. It was another of the nearly twenty ex–mission communities set up around Queensland in the late nineteenth and early twentieth centuries to save the natives from the violence of the frontier and to civilize them. But I wanted to know where Cameron Doomadgee's family had come from, and whether life here was different than on Palm Island.

The Doomadgee Mission was established in the early 1930s by Len and Dorothy Akehurst. They were Christian Brethren, evangelical Anglicans, from Sydney. In the beginning, the Akehursts rode a cart around the district, gathering children by promising their parents they would be taught to read and write. ("A" stood for "Adam" and "All have sinned.") The original mission was on a site named Dumaji, on the Gulf waters, but mosquitoes, locusts, a cyclone, and the lack of fresh water—"Satan . . . strongly contending us"—drove the Akehursts and their mission south in 1936, to the town's present site. Troopers brought more children from around the region, in particular half-castes. Aboriginal mothers tried to disguise them with ash, but sometimes they had green eyes, and as one older woman told me, "when they bath time all the charcoal finished off them."

A 1950 government report on northern Queensland missions found the Doomadgee Aborigines were "the cleanest, the best fed and best housed," but also "the most severely restrained." Boys over the age of sixteen were sent out to work on cattle stations, and the girls attended to the mission's construction, gardening, and domestic work. "It is indistinguishable from slavery . . . Girls are forbidden to leave the mission compound unaccompanied during the day and are locked up overnight. No amusements, other than hymn singing, are permitted."

The Doomadgee missionaries ceded control of their settlement only in the early 1980s, at around the time the local clans were awarded land rights. The missionaries are still regarded by many Aboriginal locals with great affection, but they left the community ill-equipped to self-govern. Doomadgee's population of 1,500 is entirely Aboriginal except for the white staff. These public servants control the school, the hospital, the police force, and all the resources—they are nicknamed by some locals the KKK.

Doomadgee—or Doom City as it's called—consists of a bakery, a supermarket, a hospital, council chambers, a police station and courthouse, a school, and a war memorial, all laid out on a grid of red dirt roads. On the Saturday we arrived, the township was practically deserted. Most people were fishing, or had traveled hundreds of kilometers to watch the Doomadgee football team play Cloncurry.

The white administrator of Doomadgee—titled "the CEO"—a trim, bearded, ex–navy man, had lent us a car, but ordered that it be returned at night in case of vandals. We drove first to the house of

Elizabeth's daughter Rosie, where relatives rushed out to greet the sisters with hugs and tears, and new babies with chubby cheeks were passionately admired.

Nearby, women sat in a circle under a tree, gambling at cards. Children under the next tree were also gambling. Other kids played with toys they'd made by attaching strips of black plastic to beer cans. Later that afternoon, I saw kids spinning old bike and pram wheels down the dusty road while their friends threw beer cans and bottles, trying to knock them over. Broken-down cars were beached in most yards. Unless people were sleeping, their doors were always open. They sat outside on old car seats and office furniture, plastic crates, wheels.

"I never want to come here again in my life," a white-blond apprentice painter told me gravely, "not seeing the way they treat their cars."

The painters were in town to spray white lines on the airstrip. While the sisters stayed with relatives, the painters and I stayed in a house used by contract workers, alongside the white staff—teachers and nurses—and blacks who, because they lived near whites, were referred to pejoratively by other blacks as "flash."

In the doorway of the house lay a shriveled turtle that had lost its way and died. All was sun-blasted, stupefied—as if the town had sunstroke. Translucent geckos slithered along the walls, frogs were in the bathroom, ceiling fans burred. Outside, my white neighbors toiled in the blazing heat, dripping with sweat as they mowed their lawns, cleaned their barbecues, shifted sprinklers onto different patches of browning grass, willing themselves to be in the suburbs. I started to get a sense of what life might have been like for Hurley in these communities. In Doomadgee, claustrophobia battles with agoraphobia: it's a tiny, close community in the middle of nowhere.

The CEO—a driven, welcoming man who had self-published a book on the British aristocracy—invited me to the Anzac dawn service. I'd forgotten it was nearly Anzac Day, Australia's Memorial

Day, our premier display of patriotism, in which we honor those soldiers from Australia and New Zealand who died in unlikely numbers in the First World War. He gave me directions to the war memorial and told me to carry a large stick to ward off feral dogs. Across town was only a fifteen-minute walk, but the hospital treated three dog bites a week.

I rose before dawn and found two long sticks. Through the darkness I walked, as if with ski poles. Dogs barked as I moved along. Their barking set off more dogs. They were invisible in the shadowy dark, but in the moonlight I was not. My heart racing, I arrived at the war memorial. Four hundred Aboriginal men joined the armed forces in World War I, and five thousand in World War II, but those who came back to Queensland had their wages sequestered by the government and never saw them. The waist-high wall at the memorial had only a plaque bearing the names of U.S. servicemen who died in a nearby plane crash in World War II.

The CEO was the only person there. His grandfather had served at Gallipoli, his father in the next world war. Awkwardly, the two of us hung flags on top of the memorial, since the flagpole had been vandalized, then stood together in the dark for a minute's silence. He murmured, "Lest we forget." I felt like an intruder, and when he asked if I had lost any relatives, I did forget—my great-grandfather had been killed at Pozières. The CEO took down the flags.

At eleven there was another Anzac Day ceremony. The CEO now wore a suit, and chairs were set up facing the memorial on a patch of green lawn. A group of old Aboriginal people had been taken out of the nursing home by a white nurse and looked happy to be sitting in the sun. Except for a couple of female elders, the only others at the service were public servants—schoolteachers, police, and nurses, the modern equivalents of the "missionaries, mercenaries, madmen, and misfits" who had peopled the frontier. One wizened male nurse had a swag of medals pinned to his breast. The police were in uniform. We took off our hats. The sun stung our faces. The CEO made a speech about sacrifice. We all stood in the heat while a small black boombox played a tape of "The Last Post." The bugle call melded with the sounds of locals getting on with their day.

Most of the whites in this assembly had come to Doomadgee because they needed the experience to get a job back in "civilization." You could advance here much faster than you could in the cities, as Chris Hurley had discovered.

HURLEY'S STORY BEGINS in the most ordinary way; it begins 1,600 miles away in the heartlands, in lower-middle-class suburban Brisbane. He attended Saint Laurence's Christian Brothers College, a Catholic school perched on a hill in the once working-class suburb of Dutton Park. Jacarandas, poinsettias, and frangipani framed the grounds. In the quadrangle were old brown-brick Spanish mission buildings topped with crucifixes and dotted with shrines—white plaster statues of the Virgin Mary.

Chris Hurley's father had been president of Saint Laurence's Parents and Friends Association. The Hurleys were a "good strong Catholic family," "lovely, lovely, average people," acquaintances said, regularly attending the close-knit local church and very involved in school activities, particularly sports. Hurley played rugby, joining the world of chants and drinking games, but he did not overly enjoy schoolwork and he repeated his senior year. After graduating, he did a twelve-month stint in a bank; then, in 1987, like many Saint Laurence's boys of his era, and like his uncle and older brother Tony before him, he entered the Police Academy.

When Hurley joined the academy, police were still required to notify the commissioner before they married or divorced; fathering illegitimate children was cause for dismissal. Just over 5 percent of officers were women, despite an application pool that was 25 percent female. Tony Fitzgerald, in his 1989 report on corruption within the Queensland Police Force, wrote, "The tendency to select officers most likely to conform to present Police Force culture must be overcome."

Those who knew Hurley well say he came out of high school

with a point to prove. He had a sense of not having made it academically or socially, and he was going to find his way in the world by another route. He would show the old school network. Not that he turned his back on them. When he was looking for support for the Thursday Island youth sports club he founded in 1990, one of his many letters went to Saint Laurence's Old Boys Association. The college, according to its website, "exists primarily to teach its students about the God who loves them and . . . attempts to have the values of the Gospel and the message of Jesus pervade all that happens."

Hurley might not have enjoyed school, but all these years since, he had been living up to Saint Laurence's principles, fulfilling a Catholic notion of sacrifice, walking like Jesus among the poor and unwashed, acting as his brother's keeper. Policing was physical, but in this heat, in these badlands, Hurley had used his body to do good Christian work, fighting the power of evil. The Christian Brothers bred their boys tough, through prayer and liberal use of the strap, and Hurley could call on that if he wanted to. He had the stuff of a secular missionary.

Life in the Torres Strait, then the wild, remote Cape York, must have been confronting for a suburban boy. Where there was drinking there was also violence, both domestic and payback. Fights might take place on the sports oval, and the weapons were fists, rocks, sticks, pieces of steel, fence posts. One police officer who'd worked in Doomadgee told me: "It's hard for us to understand how three hundred people can start fighting over a fifth grader calling another kid's granny a slut." Vicious enmities exist between families and clans that seem part of an ancient revenge cycle.

In 1995, after five years in Cape York, Chris Hurley tried policing in Surfers Paradise, the beach town an hour's drive from his family in Brisbane. Now senior constable, he was still looking for ways to get ahead: he and another officer were accused of acting as repossession agents during work time without permission. Hurley spent three years in southern Queensland, but he liked the small-town feel of the frontier communities. In 1998 he answered the call of the wild by taking a promotion to Burketown. He went back to the wide streets, the red dust, the visceral intensity, the heat, the fights.

The posting was straight from a Boy's Own Adventure: speeding along dirt roads, dodging water buffalo and kangaroos, cruising down rivers past jabiru and brolgas and crocodiles, catching barramundi. He was in his early thirties, he was in control, and you didn't get this frisson in Surfers Paradise. In Cape York, he'd been given a "skin name," a traditional language name, so that the locals, whose relationships are all dictated by kinship structures, knew how to place him. The links between the Cape and the Gulf are strong: the name meant something to people here. And perhaps there was a force beyond the fast-track promotions that attracted him to these places. Perhaps the communities drew him with their power—the proximity to sex and death and beauty and horror; to song lines that are badly frayed but still give off some charge; to what is raw and ancient: our deepest fear that good and evil spirits make sport with us.

Hurley might have told Murrandoo Yanner he was a reformed racist, but a woman who knew Hurley well during his time in Burketown doesn't think he was drawn to the communities by a resounding desire to help Indigenous people. Once he was there, he went out of his way to mentor Aboriginal kids, although she says Hurley's manner could be paternalistic, as in "I like 'em on a case-by-case basis, but they need someone to look after them." "He was the daddy."

Do the things that draw a missionary to savage places also lure a cop? Does the cop get the same rush from lawlessness that missionaries get from the godless? Wild places prove who you are, slough off every comfort of a nice house on a nice street with a nice God-fearing family. Maybe some cops use the blue uniform the way the missionary does the crucifix.

And does that cop then face the same dilemma as the missionary? What if the sin is contagious? What if, I wondered again, fighting a war against savagery, you become savage yourself?

I stood in this Anzac Day assembly and wondered if it made more sense in the 1940s, when they sang "God Save the King" and war and the empire were recent memories. Now the boombox played "Advance Australia Fair" and everyone solemnly mouthed the words. The white staff went forward to bow and lay various wreaths upon the shrine. Everyone in these places, they say, knows everyone else's business. They say there are a lot of "pressure-cooker relation-ships" and "incestuous affairs," and in the buildup before the mon-soons they often overheat. The rains bring relief but they also mean there is no escape. People don't stay long. Most of these staff had never heard of Chris Hurley.

There were Australian and New Zealand flags on top of the memorial, alongside the Torres Strait and Aboriginal flags, but they kept slipping off and the CEO had to weigh them down with rocks. He talked about remembering those who had fought for our coun-try's freedom, those who had gone before us. Some sort of banging started in a nearby house. It wasn't *their* country set free, or *their* fallen memorialized. The CEO thanked the elders for letting us commemorate the day on this land. Then the group dispersed, the white staff to go to a barbecue at the Police Social Club, the Gee Spot. LEST WE, I noticed, had been scratched off the memorial. Now it just read FORGET.

THERE WERE NO Tall Man stories in Doomadgee. Here there were short men—*gurdidawa*. They were all around us, I was told at Blue Water, on the outskirts of the township, where I was fishing with Elizabeth Doomadgee and her relatives. We'd left Valmae sleeping through the heat of the day and had driven to a bend on the Nichol-son River that was Cameron's maternal grandfather's country—the country of Jack Diamond, known as Old Catfish, who came in spirit form to talk to Cameron's mother, Doris, when she was banished to Palm Island. Now Elizabeth and her older brother, Lloyd, sat on the riverbank. Lloyd had moved back to his parents' country from Palm Island, and lived here with his wife, Penny, and his kids, to whom he was trying to teach the old ways. Fishing with them was his Aunty Betty.

Aunty Betty, Arthur Doomadgee's younger sister, sat pulling baby catfish from the water. She had high, sculpted cheekbones, frizzy salt-and-pepper hair seemingly in a natural bouffant, and missing front teeth. She was a grande dame like her mother, Lizzy Daylight, sitting barefoot by the river in a cotton dress. On her hook the fish made squealing noises until she hit them on the head with a rock.

Before us the water, lined with tea-tree barks, was an intense jade green. A Catfish Dreaming track ran from the Northern Territory through Blue Water, and this was the section of the song line for which the family were custodians. The river also had a Bujimala (Rainbow Serpent) Dreaming, but at this bend at least it was not as potent. It was there that day, though. Aunty Betty showed me how the green water had the slightest red sheen, a sign that Bujimala—her mother's totem—was nearby. A sudden strong breeze arose, then stopped. "It's the serpent," she explained. "Rainbow can smell family." It could smell her and Elizabeth, who sat next to her aunt, enjoying hearing about the old days.

At Blue Water you must never swear or hit children, or the *gurdidawa* will punish you. The short men are believed to be mischievous creatures. They can act malevolently, especially toward strangers, making them lose their way. They can punish or reward by controlling the bounty of food. If you don't leave them an offering of food, Aunty Betty said, "they won't support you. They be greedy and horrid things." But the deed that most offends the *gurdidawa* is hitting children. "If you hit kids out here, you'll never see another part of yourself," she warned. In other words, you'd go blind, with "bunged-up eyes."

Victoria, Lloyd's five-year-old daughter, stood in comet-print underpants, spinning her line effortlessly into the water. She caught a small catfish, then twirled it around and around in the air, its head rhythmically smashing against the ground. Her parents shouted at her not to get too close to the water in case there were crocodiles. Lloyd's ten-year-old son, Cyril, was sitting by himself playing with three cars—a police van, a police sedan, and a fire truck—as if marshaling his own riot response. He was hesitant to talk to me.

Elizabeth once admitted that her parents had taught her not to like white people. Naïvely, I was surprised. "They treated our old people like dogs," she turned to me and said.

In 1911 the Northern Territory's government-appointed chief protector of Aborigines came across a cave near Doomadgee containing forty to fifty skeletons of adults and children. His local guide told him they had all been struck by a form of lightning—bullets, the European assumed. David Trigger, who first traveled to Doomadgee in 1978, has written that Aboriginal oral accounts of Wild Time

describe vicious killings of Aboriginal men, women and children by both Whites and members of the Queensland Mounted Native Police Force . . . smashing children against trees and rocks "so their brains came out" and after shootings, cutting up bodies, burning bodies and hanging up parts of corpses in trees where other Aborigines would later find them.

"I heard your grandfather was born in Wild Time and a whitefella shot him," I said to Aunty Betty.

She was surprised. "What, you read it in the paper?"

"I read it in the land claim."

In October 1978, the Waanyi and Garawa tribes lodged a claim to gain ownership of their traditional lands in the Nicholson River area. The 1983 government report, detailing the claim's success, quotes evidence given by Lizzy Daylight: "My father bin born in the wild time. White men bin scatter em, chase em. They ran away, they might get shot . . . my father bin shot in the shoulder."

A hundred years earlier, in 1883, a young Englishwoman at Lorne Hill Station in nearby Waanyi country noted in her diary that the station manager had "40 pairs of blacks' ears nailed around the walls collected during raids after losses of many cattle speared by the blacks." She also described seeing a woman who'd just been captured: "They brought a new black gin with them; she cannot speak a word of English. Mr. Shadforth [the manager] put a rope round the girl's neck and dragged her along on foot. He was riding. This seems to be the usual manner." The Aboriginal woman, who spoke only her traditional languages, was left chained to a tree outside the station, "not to be loosed until they think she is tamed."

Aunty Betty kept fishing. She told me her grandfather, whose name was also Murrandoo, ran over the Northern Territory border to his mother's country in the Gulf. "He was running away because whitefellas take the old girls for their sweethearts." One time Murrandoo ended up in a lagoon, with the troopers shooting on the banks. He is said to have survived underwater by breathing through a lily stalk.

Another relative told me that when Lizzy Daylight was a teenager she was shot at by men on a punitive mission. She fell to the ground, pretending to be dead, while the others around her fled or were shot. Lizzy survived. She was the youngest wife of King Peter— "King" being a title bestowed on tribal elders by Europeans.

To escape the violence of the frontier, Aboriginal men and women in the Gulf country began working on the vast cattle stations that from the late nineteenth century overlaid and cut across their Dreaming tracks. Station managers, unlike missionaries, usually allowed the practice of traditional ceremonies. Blackfellas refer to their ritual activity as "business," deliberately and cannily flagging its central importance. Aunty Betty told me her mother had been "a big businesswoman." Lizzy Daylight was in possession of sacred songs connected to the spiritual forces of the Rainbow Serpent, the Ancestral Spirit with the power to control the weather.

Lizzy and her brother Willy, who died in the early 1990s, were "the ones who sang the serpent so he won't get angry. They sing his head so he can feel heavy," Aunty Betty said. They sang the serpent's chin and his jaw, they sang his eyes to make him blind, they sang his tongue because "his tongue out—that's the whirlwind. They sang his back so he won't move. And they sang the tail so the wind won't get too strong. The head is dangerous and the tail." Their thrashing created cyclones.

People with particular Dreamings are believed to take on the physical characteristics of their totem. Just as the serpent needed to stay in water, Lizzy Daylight would wrap her feet in wet rags at night to keep her skin moist. She also had a depression in her scalp she called a "serpent hole." "If she pull one hair, all irons [the roof] would be off the house, the whole place would be all upside down," Aunty Betty said. Once, she was checking her mother's hair for *boobies*—lice—when she forgot herself and cracked a louse egg in the serpent hole. "Next thing we hear *Mmmmmmmmmmmmm!* Down the waterfall. Rainbow was singing. I killed an egg in her head in the hole. She just got up and she sang and the wind was stopped. She stopped it. She had the song for it."

Sitting at Blue Water, Aunty Betty was frustrated at not catching fat fish, only "bony, poor one." The baby catfish made squeaking sounds like plastic squeeze toys, while nearby on the bank lay the pale, scaleless body of a big fork-tailed catfish, its three pairs of fleshy barbels like whiskers around its mouth—her nephew Lloyd's catch. Aunty Betty told me that because she had not followed the correct protocol while visiting this country—the country of Jack Diamond, her brother's father-in-law—she'd offended this long-dead relative, "so he only gave me little, tiny, little skinny fish." According to her Law, she should have rubbed her hands and under-arms with mud, a custom described as "giving smell" to the Rainbow Serpent. Aunty Betty also said she should have asked the *gurdidawa,* the short men, for the fish properly, "in language," in Ganggalida.

"When you go for fishing you call that fish *yaguli.* We *ngamanda* for *yaguli, wugunggi yajuli,* we *ngamanda windiyaya yaguli,* and they give us plenty, when we ask 'em, they give us that thing. We tell them, *yilagadi ngida ngalaja yaguli,* it means 'go and get wood to cook your fish.'" Aunty Betty was asking the short men for permission to catch the fish and to gather the wood to cook it.

In the midafternoon heat, the green water was perfectly still and it felt cooler just to sit nearby. Dragonflies spun past us, and all around were birds, dozens of them, making strange, complex melodies—high, low, joyous, mournful, whole song cycles. It was totally, incredibly vital. Here all nature is believed to be sentient—every rock, every leaf, every bird, every fish has some spirit, and may in fact be closely related to you. Plants and animals are your kin. To me, too, Blue Water seemed somehow alive with an extra dimension.

Cameron was still a mystery to me. It was unnerving. I had approached Hurley through his lawyer to try to hear his side of the story. The senior sergeant refused to speak with anyone, but nonetheless he was becoming familiar. I could learn a lot from talking to people who knew him, and there were points of reference. In many ways it was easier to connect my world to Hurley's than to Cameron's.

It was galling to find myself thinking about Cameron's death but not about who he was. His sisters had involved me in their family but it was a world of children, of providing and worrying and holding things together. It was not Cameron's world. The men's sphere was separate. The Doomadgee men were not inclined to talk to me. They were friendly enough but seemed embarrassed if I spoke to them. ("White woman!" one of Valmae's nephews yelled to her when he answered my calls from Melbourne.) Cameron was two generations from Wild Time and he was one generation—or less, as his older siblings had been raised in the dormitory—from the stolen generations. He'd been sent to a Townsville youth detention center as a teenager for some minor break-ins, but his friend Lance Poynter told me Cameron had then stayed "on the straight and narrow."

Sitting with Cameron's family on their ancestral land, I felt closer to imagining what made him happy. In these communities, Aboriginal male culture has kept the traditional element of hunting and fishing that Cameron loved, and added drinking. Fishing is a balm, a respite. Cameron had set out to borrow a boat the morning he died, but in the last hour of his life all his worlds folded in. With Hurley he was back suddenly in Wild Time.

Aunty Betty believed, as did Elizabeth, that Cameron knew some secret about Hurley. "He must have had something on him. 'Who Let the Dogs Out'—that's just a song. It's on a record, eh? But he must have had something on him. That policeman had a reason. Because he was here. He was [at] Burketown. But there's no need to go all the way to Palm just to kill a boy for no reason," Aunty Betty went on. "For no reason at all! He must have played up in his mind. He must have played up in his mind and he was thinking, *That Doomadgee!* He's a Doomadgee mob! . . . But there's no need to take him in there and bash him in the jail and he singing out, 'Help me! Help me!' And now the little fella lying in his grave and the man still out walking about."

A story had emerged (and I found it was just a story, a mythical one) that Hurley had been run out of Burketown—or sometimes, the story goes, it was Doomadgee—by the local community, and Cameron, who was visiting relatives, had been a key player in this uprising. "Speak to X!" "Speak to Y!" Valmae and Elizabeth told me during my time in Doomadgee, claiming these people would prove the stories. But X and Y's connection to events was always flimsy and the main protagonists were in jail or dead.

Some past connection between the two men was not impossible. Hurley claimed to have had no idea who Cameron was, but Elizabeth believed Hurley had locked up Cameron for drinking in 2002 when her brother was visiting Doomadgee and Hurley might have been doing relief work there. There is no record of Cameron having been in the Doomadgee watch house, but not every drunk was put on the books.

Elizabeth and I drove back from Blue Water along a dirt road with wooden signs high in the treetops: JESUS SAVES! On the out-skirts of Doomadgee a row of men and women known as the riverbed people sat along the weir, drinking: thirty, forty people in a straight line, their feet cool in the water. Nearby, other drinkers sat or lay in the middle of the road. Life rolled over, each day like the last: limbo with alcohol. I thought of Aunty Betty pointing out Bujimala's red sheen in the green water. Here, Victoria Bitter beer cans lay by the river's edge, their red-and-green aluminum shimmering in the sun; a nightmare incarnation of the Rainbow Serpent.

Doomadgee seemed better and worse than Palm Island. People were closer to their traditional lands, but farther from opportunities to truly escape. A Doomadgee police officer told me he dealt mainly with alcohol-related crime and child abuse—not so much sexual abuse but neglect. He said there was a marked difference in the way parents treated their kids during the wet season, when the roads were inaccessible and people couldn't leave to buy grog in Burketown. The children were better fed and were more likely to be at school than fishing. This cycle played out weekly, too. Drinking and violence would peak, and fewer children attended school after welfare payments were made.

Aunty Betty did not believe alcohol was responsible for Doomadgee's social breakdown. "Nothing to do with grog, love. It's just the Dreamtime story dogs. We got it here."

A Dingo Dreaming song line ran near the township. Young Aboriginal men were illicitly touching a powerful, sacred ocher related to this Dreaming, which "turn everything upside down, back to front." In traditional times, the ocher was touched only by the initiated. It was believed to have strong love-magic properties, and women found themselves uncontrollably attracted to men who handled it. Elizabeth teased me that if anyone fell in love with me in Doomadgee, I would never be able to leave.

Aunty Betty said, "You look, young kids today about fourteen, fifteen, they all mum and dad here. Young fathers and young mothers who never look for the future." She sat staring in front of her. Lizzy Daylight had not taught her children her songs, had not wanted to pass them on to this broken new world. "This Law has been smashed like a chain smash. You know, when a chain break off your body."

Burketown

I SAID GOOD-BYE to the Doomadgee sisters and took the fifteen-minute flight to Burketown, where we landed on another red-dirt airstrip. I started walking into town with an Aboriginal man who'd been a health worker at Doomadgee until he couldn't take the suicides anymore, having to cut bodies down from trees or pull them out of the water. He'd worked alongside Hurley but never saw him hurt anyone.

A ute came along and we got a lift to the Burketown Pub, where I'd made a reservation. The town's "heart and soul"—as it's described in the guidebook—was straight out of *Crocodile Dundee*. Spears hung along the railing of the bar, and the bar stools were upholstered in crocodile skin worn to a dirty suede. Buffalo horns and spinning fans were mounted on the walls, alongside photographs of winners of the annual barramundi fishing competition—Burketown was a "fishing Mecca." My room, above the bar, had a single bed and an air conditioner.

I went to look around. Burketown's population was 235 people, but this toy town was the district's administrative center, and in contrast to the ex–mission community, all the buildings were bright and clean and neat. Sprinklers ran daylong and filled the gutters with water. All the lawns were uncannily green, but the broad deserted streets shimmered in the heat as if it were always high noon. I sweated in the humidity as if I were running a fever and the little white church with its little white cross and the park with its pagoda and benches were aspects of my delirium.

The Visitors' Center, a corner in the council chambers, offered racks of brochures advising on humdrum natural disasters: "Lightning Protection Action Guide," "Floods," "Preparing for Cyclones," "Crocwise in Croc Country" (*Never provoke, harass, or interfere with crocodiles, even small ones*).

Burketown was named for the ill-fated explorer Robert O'Hara Burke, who passed nearby on his overland journey to the Gulf of Carpentaria in 1861. (Burke expired from starvation, having shot at Aborigines who'd come bearing gifts of fish.) On the saltpans outside the town there was once a famous tree, the Landsborough Tree, which was inscribed by William Landsborough in the course of a fruitless search for Burke. Now there is just a sign and a little fence around a charred stump. The Landsborough Tree was burned down in 2002, it is rumored by blackfellas who were sick of the fanfare over white exploration. Not long after the tree had been inscribed, Murrandoo Yanners' great-grandmother saw her husband beheaded in a massacre.

The land around Burketown was traditionally owned by Yanner's tribe. He lived in the township with his wife and five children, and his siblings lived in adjacent houses.

Hoping to find Murrandoo, I went back to the pub. I wanted to ask him more about his friend Chris Hurley, but I'd been unable to reach him by phone before leaving Melbourne. At the pub door, blacks turned left, whites turned right. In the yellow glare of the strip lighting, the place was effectively partitioned, with the bar itself a kind of Switzerland. Sometimes the black elders crossed over to drink with the whites, but they would tell the young blacks to get back to their side. Some whites refused to drink there at all.

Patrons held their beer cans in polystyrene stubby holders, the regular drinkers keeping their own holders behind the bar. The regulars were mainly older white men, retirees, cattle station workers, council workers. They looked as if they spent their days in chains while eagles preyed upon their livers. Their organs restored by night, they returned to the same bar stools, faces slicked with sweat, to resume their stoic drinking. Their eyes glazed, their speech slurred, but they did not move from their bar stools until, without flourish, it was time to stagger into the night.

Meanwhile the young Aboriginal men and women played pool, singing, swaying, showing off their drunkenness, making theater of it. They drank to perform the passions; the old whites, to block them. Within moments of my sitting down, a wizened ex-commando, whose name was poker-worked on the back of his bar stool, told me he'd come here from down south after finding his wife in bed with another man. He also told me not to lend any money to the blacks.

A young white man came in: six foot four, broad, barefoot, with eyes very close together. Most of the buttons on his shirt were missing, as if he'd been in a fight. He asked if I would like some fresh crocodile meat. In his hand was a pink plastic bag bulging with soft contraband flesh. He'd just cut it up and didn't want it going bad.

One sunburned ex-miner, describing himself as "a nobody," wore shorts and a low-cut blue undershirt revealing swathes of white flab and an old-style tattoo of a bikinied pinup girl. His baldness was overtaking a crew cut. He looked around at the drinkers on his side of the bar and told me I wouldn't find this caliber of person anywhere else in the world. "No one here will bullshit you." Australia was two countries, he said. The south "was another country." Southern culture was good, northern culture was good. It worked fine as long as the south didn't try to impose its culture on the north.

Outside, a group of Aborigines sat drinking in a circle on the footpath. Forty years ago there were curfews. Blacks couldn't come into town between 6 P.M. and 6 A.M. But if the old miner yearned for those days, he didn't say it.

Murrandoo Yanner was out of town. I sat drinking a can of beer as slowly as possible and imagined Chris Hurley's arrival at the pub: the long shadow he would have cast, his bulk filling up the low doorway, everyone at the bar having to look up at him. Hurley had worked the place out. In a town where the population was 90 percent black, he figured his life would be much easier if he could be friends with Yanner.

During Hurley's tenure between 1998 and 2002, Murrandoo Yanner's was *the* face of radical Aboriginal politics. A month after Hurley's arrival, the activist's house was burned down by arsonists. At the time, Murrandoo was campaigning against plans for a local mine; he was calling for a treaty; he was meeting with the remnants of the Black Panthers on their 1999 Australian visit; he was in court appealing his prosecution for killing and eating crocodile (a protected species); he was encouraging black nations to boycott the 2000 Sydney Olympic Games. Yanner is a man of natural, deep, winning charm, but it still says something about Chris Hurley that they became fast friends. Others might have shrunk back and bided their time.

A sign outside Burketown's police station tells visitors which local roads are open and which are closed. The whites who turn up usually come in four-wheel drives looking for a remote hunting or fishing adventure. Next to the station is the cream-colored Queenslander—a high-set weatherboard house—shaded by a poinsettia, where Hurley lived for four years. From the Aboriginal Cooperative houses nearby he would have heard the sounds of breaking furniture and slaps; so Murrandoo Yanner had told me when I first met him. On duty Hurley wore very short shorts—"tiny one trousers," Murrandoo called them. Off duty he still wore shorts, plus a T-shirt and thongs.

In Burketown, Hurley was eight or nine hours' drive from Mount Isa, the nearest large town, along dirt roads that were underwater at least three months a year. To make sergeant at thirty meant he was doing well, very well. Hurley had a constable working for him and was away from the hierarchy. He was a small-town sheriff complete with a deputy. Hurley and Murrandoo Yanner came to an unofficial arrangement: they would sort things out man-to-man. What was the sense of getting a plane to come to Burketown to fly an offender out, or a driver making an eighteen-hour round trip, if Murrandoo could deal with the problem to the sergeant's satisfaction?

"Say someone bashed someone," Murrandoo explained to me. "He'd say, 'I want it sorted out. I don't want it growing into big family fights. If you can nip it in the bud now, I won't charge either of them.' Or if something was stolen from the caravan park, eight hundred dollars' worth of rods and lines, and he knew who it was, he'd come and say, 'Look, if you [can] get them returned, no names asked, I won't charge them and I get to write my books clean, otherwise I have to do a day's work.'"

Hurley did not much like paperwork, and with this arrangement "he got to go fishing, hunting, and chasing girls." But the deal made him territorial. Murrandoo said that if police from other Gulf towns arrived to drink at the Burketown Pub and they threw their weight around, the sergeant's reaction was "This is my town, you fucking know your place, don't mess with the locals."

Previously Burketown's police had booked people and stayed at arm's length. Hurley, however, was into everything. If there was a dance at the hall, or a gymkhana or a rodeo at the fairgrounds, Hurley would be there, drinking and joining in. He walked a fine line, maintaining his authority while mixing vigorously with the locals. At the Gulf town rodeos, he'd go inside the traveling boxing tent, the sweaty big top with its sulfurous lighting and roll-up drum, and watch Little White Lightning, the Cowboy, and the Friendly Mauler challenge men from the crowd, black and white, to fight. Hurley would roar along with everyone else. He sat on Burketown committees, including the rodeo committee. People remember the year he offered to ride a bull to raise money for the Flying Doctor. He got a swag of donations, but when the day came the bull threw him off and the Flying Doctor had to airlift him to Mount Isa, which left them thousands of dollars out of pocket.

He seemed to love the place. He told people he saw Burketown as a model for reconciliation. As he had in other communities, Hurley endeared himself to people through his kindness to their children. "He bent over backwards for our kids at the school, doing anything and everything he could to help," one of the Yanners said to me.

Burketown's school is small and neat and sunny, with thirty-five primary students and two white teachers. Hurley helped out with sports and recreation, and took the kids on camping trips. "All kids in town, he spent a lot of time with them," Murrandoo said. "On his weekends off, rather than chase the nurses and go drinking, he'd actually go along with the school trip, throw some kids in his car."

Children climbed on him as if he were a tree, and their adoration was easy to take, like standing in sunlight. "He couldn't do enough for us," a seventeen-year-old youth playing pool in the pub told me. He remembered Hurley taking his class camping to Lawn Hill National Park, showing them how to march in the Anzac Day parade, teaching them how to drive on the local oval, the police car stalling and hopping. He remembered Hurley taking the bullets out of his gun and showing them its workings. The sergeant even fingerprinted the kids—"for future reference," Murrandoo Yanner joked when I told him the story.

Murrandoo sent his youngest brother, TJ, to the pub to look after me. Around his neck, TJ wore a tobacco pouch he'd made from a kangaroo's scrotum. He had heard that a vicious nineteenth-century bushranger's testicles had been fashioned by his captors in the same manner; the idea struck him. A wallaby's balls, he explained, were too small, but a kangaroo's could hold an ounce of tobacco. Next to the pouch hung a snakeskin tobacco-paper holder. TJ showed me a snakeskin stubby holder, a snakeskin lighter, and a boomerang he'd made. (He told me he could also crochet but that if anyone poked fun, he'd punch them in the mouth.)

The next day TJ picked me up to go fishing with his wife, Sasha, and their three children. In a town where there was nothing much else to do, fishing was the highest form of hospitality. TJ was lean, handsome, athletic, and a heavy drinker. "I was born to drink beer, everyone in the Gulf is," he said. Beer transcended race. As he pointed out, the only place open after five o'clock was the pub. To buy furniture or clothes or a book was an eight-hour drive to Mount Isa, but "they made it very convenient to grog-face in the Gulf." "Grog-face" means to be alcoholic, as "money-face" means to gamble, and "tucker-face" means to overeat. TJ was unemployed but was about to start working at Century Mine, Australia's largest zinc mine, one hundred fifty kilometers south of Burketown. Murrandoo had mounted a campaign against its development in the mid-1990s for environmental and spiritual reasons. But TJ didn't want to go on just surviving.

We sat at a river bend surrounded by white-trunked eucalypts and paperbarks. White water lilies floated on the water. Sasha, a quiet, flawless Doomadgee girl, didn't want the kids getting too close because of crocodiles, or too far back because of snakes.

TJ strung a series of fishing lines in the water. They were baited with bright lime-green-and-yellow frogs he stored in a coffee tin. He moved lithely, stepping quickly on a network of eucalypt boughs to avoid the water, adjusting and checking each line as if playing some complicated song. He caught a large catfish and rebaited the line with a northern dwarf tree frog, *Litoria bicolor,* the type you see on tourist brochures. TJ's toddler son liked playing with the frogs, holding them by their slender legs until they escaped. He chased after them, crying, and was given others to play with.

"Wherever blacks are to be met with, the little boys indulge in aping the arts of war as practised by their elders," wrote W. E. Roth in 1906. In Burketown, Roth saw boys with toy spears, and in other places miniature woomeras, or spear throwers, and shields. "Natives regard the man according as he can hold his own in fighting and hunting."

I wanted to steer the conversation to Hurley but TJ was giving me a lesson in Gulf etiquette. In traditional hunter-gatherer communities, there are no Hurleys to go to; in broken hunter-gatherer communities, like Burketown, the Hurleys are obstacles to be maneuvered around—for the men, anyway.

"Like just say I have argument with someone at the pub," said TJ.

"You've got that mentality that to ring policeman, you're a fright-ened cunt, you're a yellow-bellied, lily-livered cunt and you can't deal with your own problem, you have to go and get *bulliman*. For a blackfella to get a policeman on another blackfella is just a down-right dirty thing," he explained. "If someone fucks around with your pride or dignity it's up to you to sort it out yourself. If someone stole my car I'd just wait till I found him, then I'd break his fucking legs."

Being on bad terms with the law was a Yanner family tradition. TJ remembered collecting his piggybank money to bail his father out of jail. His father was "a tough old cunt" and he would fight police if he thought they were bullying blackfellas.

Later, I met the simmering Vernon Yanner, taller than his broth-ers, a sleek mover with the same gruff charm. Vernon openly despised the police. He claimed that once when he was arrested he'd been given a beating by the coppers while he was handcuffed.

"Some lads out here accomplished fighters," he told me. "Half been to prison for four, five years, fighting every fucking week in prison, then they get out. In the pub, thirty, forty fights over a year, over two years, and no cunt's knocked them on the arse. Not nasty men, but just fucking brilliant pugilists." I got the feeling Vernon was talking about himself. "If someone's getting cheeky, they may be asked to step out into the street. People around here are brought up that way." This was in part a reaction to the mission days, when "girls had to lift their dresses over their heads so the old missionary could see if they had pants on." (On Palm Island, too, I heard that young women in the dormitory had to line up and lift their dresses to prove they were wearing clean underpants.) "People got tied up like a dog with a chain in the hot heat," Vernon went on, "because of hunting and giving too much feed to his sisters locked up in the mission. The older generation been beaten down and the younger generation brought up different . . . they're saying, 'I'd like to see the cunts do that to us.' So everyone's got a bit of aggression in them. Everyone's got to be able to fight, it's just a natural thing."

TJ Yanner didn't like police much, but he thought a lot of Chris

Hurley. The word he used was "charisma." "Because Hurley was charismatic it never gave you an inch to throw him out of the circle. He wasn't too hard to like. He didn't walk past without saying g'day, even if he didn't like you. If he didn't like you, there was all the more reason to come past you and say g'day, and find out what you were doing. He was fun. He'd get up and dance, and make a clown of himself, and come up with some jokes. He could make you laugh, that cunt."

Or make you cry. When one girlfriend left him, Hurley told the Yanners' mother, he'd found a message scratched in his saucepan—*Fuck You!*

Sasha, TJ's wife, said he was a womanizer. He liked white women and black women. In Murrandoo's words, "He'd screw anything that wasn't nailed down." At least one wife in the town had considered leaving her husband for him. Murrandoo said there was a rumor that the woman's husband offered "ten, twenty thousand for anyone stupid enough to knock him off."

"He was drunk there one time at the hall," Sasha said. "He was on the dance floor, he lift me up and swinging me around." He did the same at another dance and the girl hit her head on the concrete. He was "too bloody exuberant," the man who saw this told me. "Big people don't get it, they don't understand their own strength."

Chris Hurley was a man of large appetites. He was the life of the party. He was loud, raucous, opinionated—and with a lot of people, after fifteen minutes or so, the act wore thin. The girl working the cash register at the Burketown service station told me: "I thought he was a sleaze." In 1995, in the Cape York community of Kowanyama, and in 1998, in Surfers Paradise, he'd been the subject of formal complaints of sexual harassment from female police officers. The Crime and Misconduct Commission declared both complaints unsubstantiated.

Now by the river, TJ's children climbed a gum's diagonal bough, riding it. One child fell flat onto her back. She was shocked and her face crumpled into tears, and I rushed to pick her up. Shortly afterward TJ's toddler son plonked down on a chair that folded in on him and he too fell and wept. Again, almost without thinking, I rushed to steady him. TJ told me it was better to leave them. He wanted his children to be able to look after themselves, to be able to fight. His wife could give a man a black eye if she needed to. TJ had concluded it was better to be nasty in this world. Otherwise people made you their bitch. He quoted a Slim Dusty song:

> It's a hard, hard country
> It's a hard, hard land
> And to live in it you gotta be
> A hard, hard man.

TJ sat drinking, not catching many fish. He planned to swap the catfish for turtle with a relative. He complained about a man who had come fishing with money in his pocket, so no one had caught anything. I had a credit card in mine and wondered if it was my fault.

COPS, NORMAN MAILER wrote, "contain explosive contradictions within themselves. Supposed to be law-enforcers, they tend to conceive of themselves as the law . . . They are attached umbilically to the concept of honesty, they are profoundly corrupt. They possess more physical courage than the average man, they are unconscionable bullies."

Those contradictions find expression in all manner of ways. One white woman in her fifties told me that the first time she met Hurley in the Burketown Pub, he told her to sit on his knee, even though, as she put it, she was old enough to be his mother. When she declined he told her he was in charge of police and she'd have to do as he said.

If Hurley tended to conceive of himself as the law, it was partly because in Burketown he *was* the law. The white law, at least. And in Burketown, summary justice—cops doling out on-the-spot punishment with their fists—was not far removed from the Yanners' philosophy of payback.

As Murrandoo Yanner told the *Australian* journalist Tony Koch in his December 2004 interview: "Had he not been a policeman, him and me would have been identical in many ways . . . Like him, I will take on the black or white who talks shit to me. He was a thug and a mug. I am the same." Yanner continued, "He liked to give blokes a touch-up if they got out of line . . . He only had one fault—he couldn't keep his hands to himself."

If a man hits his wife in a place as isolated as Burketown, given the way the legal system works, it takes too long and costs too much to get him locked up. Then the man's released on bail, or the wife doesn't want to press charges. He hits her again. According to one school of thought, it's better to just give him a "touch-up." Teach him a lesson.

For Murrandoo, the Dirty Harry syndrome had a lot going for it. "[Hurley] was a good copper, but we have a twisted view of what a good copper is," Murrandoo told me. "A lot of people would rather have a fight with a copper, even if they're breaking the law. If you half win, or don't come off too bad, you'd rather that than a bunch of trumped-up charges where you got no chance in the legal system—a white jury in Mount Isa, this and that."

Murrandoo remembered seeing a young man with a bruised face who alleged he'd been assaulted by Hurley. "I went down the next day, banged on the police station door, and Hurley was pretty busted up, so this young fella had given him a bit of a hiding too." The sergeant had been driving past and seen the young man kicking his brother in the head. "His own brother!" Yanner said, disgusted. "Hurley got out to arrest him, so he give Hurley a touch-up. So Hurley give him a touch-up."

In September 2001, Vernon Yanner and Hurley also had "a big knuckle-up" when Hurley, after a session at the pub, decided to confiscate Vernon's new motorcycle. Vernon told me:

He was driving off on it so I threw my boot at him, crash-
tackled him off my bike, ended up wrestling there in the gut-

ter. He had my head underwater for a while, trying to drown me. Then I had his head under the water for a while, trying to drown him. I had his head underwater when the boys pulled me off him . . . We won't stop until one of us weren't kicking.

Murrandoo said to me after we had the fight, "Go and apologize to Hurley then you won't be charged. He wants you to apologize to him."

And I said, "Fuck him."

And he said, "Well, fuck him, but still he'll charge you with this and that. You don't have to like it, just go and apologize and you won't be charged."

I went up and apologized to him at the police station: "Sorry about that."

He just went off: "You little smart cunt! You should fucking take a leaf out of your brother's book, you cunt! I should just fucking take you to jail now!"

And I said, "Get fucked, you cunt! I'll see you in court."

"So you don't want me to drop charges?"

"No, not if you're going to speak to me like this. You can go fuck yourself."

And I walked out. I didn't like him full stop.

Hurley charged Vernon, but later, in light of the circumstances, the charges were dropped.

In the old days they would have said Hurley had gone native. Perhaps the authority he wielded and the town and the heat brought it out. The heat in the tropics attacks like a swarm of insects. It crawls over the skin. People wait for the storm, for the lightning to streak across the sky. Add booze and loathing and guns to the claustrophobia, add the habit of violence among men who don't put much premium on psychology but stand at the bar and compare the size of the snakes they've found in their gardens, and it does feel like a fever.

Or maybe Hurley was already wired that way, was—just as Murrandoo Yanner said—a thug and a mug.

After three years in Burketown, Hurley settled down with a bar-maid called Narelle. She was more than a decade younger than he was, a big-boned, blond girl. "She was an all right person," Vernon said, "pretty quiet, hadn't got too many bad sides even though she was with him." But how do you settle down in a place like Burke-town?

This town was full of old war veterans and crocodile hunters and missionaries who believed supermarket bar codes were the work of the devil. The wife of the gun-loving publican waitressed, wearing evening clothes and serving a rogue's gallery that included Murran-doo Yanner, the gentleman outlaw. The publican, Narelle's boss, did not get on with the Yanners. As the animosity grew, he installed barbed-wire fences, security cameras, and guard dogs. Some patrons reckoned he put something in an air-vent to get them out around closing time; they'd leave coughing and spluttering. The publican complained to Hurley's superiors that the sergeant was too close to the Yanners. Murrandoo claims that Hurley was warned by the police hierarchy to pull back, that he came to him troubled about what he should do.

The year 2001 was a crucial one for Hurley. There was talk among other police in the Gulf region about the sergeant's seeming lack of control, over both the Burketown locals and himself. He had applied for a promotion to senior sergeant of the nearby Aboriginal community of Mornington Island (population 1,200), seventy miles northwest of Burketown. When he missed out, the Yanners said, he was acutely disappointed. For a man with a plan like his, the rejec-tion was a major setback.

As Murrandoo saw it, rather than blaming the police hierarchy who had slighted him, Hurley seemed to blame the community—in other words, Murrandoo and his brothers. This was also how a local white cattle station owner saw it: "He'd come with the best of inten-tions; he tried to help and became compromised by the Yanners."

Hurley withdrew. He didn't go to the school to work with kids as much. He chose not to socialize at the pub. He had put up with all of them for three years and it had not paid off. Heeding the warnings of his superiors, the sergeant pulled back from the Yanners and soon had his eye on the prize again. One day a visitor to Burketown got trapped in a culvert. Murrandoo's uncle Johnny Yanner went to Hurley and told him if they did not act, the man would drown. Hurley didn't wait for the rescue team to arrive; he drilled into the culvert and they saved the man. For this, in 2002 he received a Police Commissioner's Certificate in recognition of his "intelligence, promptitude, resourcefulness and dedication to duty far exceeding what might reasonably be expected from a member of the police service in the execution of his duty." Hurley's career was back on track.

PEOPLE HAD BEEN kind to me in Burketown, but I had a constant sense that if I moved too far in any direction, something might go wrong. The rules were different from any I knew. It was hot in a different way. At night I'd leave the bar before ten and lie on my bed sweating, listening to people drinking and partying and fighting in the room beneath me. I knew it was melodramatic, but I couldn't help feeling I had to be careful to get out alive.

One morning, Johnny Yanner took me fishing in his dinghy on the Albert River. All along the muddy banks were the recent imprints of crocodiles. When he spotted two bulging eyes above the water, he started turning the boat around so I could get a closer view. I begged him not to bother. At the river's mouth, staring into the Gulf of Carpentaria, we dropped hand lines into the water and within moments both pulled out fish, the scales stunning in the sunlight.

At the end of my stay, the publican—different from the one in Hurley's time—dropped me off at the airstrip in his truck and I waited to board the plane to Cairns with the passengers who'd just flown in from Doomadgee. On board I met a fresh-faced woman dressed in pink who waved a silk fan and held her jacket over her nose against the rancid smell of sweaty, unwashed bodies. She claimed Aboriginal, Torres Strait Islander, and "white Australian" ancestry.

This woman, a Doomadgee police officer flying home for a holiday, was young and burned out. She'd seen so many women with punched-up faces and so many children hurt, too. She'd just seen a child killed in a drunk-driving wreck. I remembered a Townsville cop telling me that he'd carried a knife ever since being unable to cut down a suicide in time to administer CPR. It was also useful, he said matter-of-factly, for cutting seat belts after crashes. The young officer on the plane said she'd reached a stage where she couldn't stand any more. She would say to herself, I don't care, I don't care. She was hoping for a transfer back to "civilization," where she wouldn't have to care. I remembered the sign on the Doomadgee war memorial—FORGET.

The policewoman made me think of Chris Hurley's leaving all this and returning to Brisbane to see his family. Reentering mainstream society, he could slip back in with an invisible cloak of whiteness. *Forget, forget,* said all the bitumen roads, neat houses, manicured lawns. But Hurley was like a man returning from a war—a war he couldn't get out of his system. In November 2002 he was promoted to senior sergeant, and soon after arrived on Palm Island.

THREE

The Inquest Resumes

T HE MAIN STREETS of Townsville are lined with palm trees and emblems of colonial prosperity. Ornate urns and columns and wreaths swathe Victorian shopfronts that are still marked TAILOR, STATIONERY, BANK. Hot-pink bougainvillea grows weedlike up wrought-iron lace to balconies with French doors flung open to the breezes. The city was settled in the early 1860s as a place for boiling down the carcasses of sheep and cattle for tallow. A sugar industry developed around it, and to work the cane fields the planters imported (some say stole or enslaved) nearly fifty thousand Melanesian men and women from the South Pacific Islands—a practice known as "blackbirding." Townsville is named for such a blackbirder, Robert Towns, an entrepreneur who in 1865 wrote from the fledgling settlement: "I never felt so unhappy from home in my life what from bites and blight." He left the next month and never returned.

Townsville's courthouse is a flat-roofed modernist building of weathered concrete. It rises amid more palms and tropical fruit trees, with small square windows staring out from its façade.

It was Wednesday, August 3, 2005, eight and half months after Cameron's death, and Chris Hurley and the other police officers were only now being required to give evidence. Coroner Michael Barnes had stood down and the inquest was being heard by the deputy state coroner, Christine Clements, an attractive woman in her midforties whose manner gave nothing away. Clements had spent the past two days on Palm Island hearing evidence from the Aboriginal witnesses who'd earlier appeared before Barnes. This time they testified in a much smaller room at the island's Police Club Youth Center, with the aid of an interpreter. Now the court had reconvened in Townsville, where, it was argued, the police witnesses would be safe.

Erykah Kyle and a group of Palm Island women had traveled to the mainland for the hearing. Some of them looked much older, twenty years older, than they were. All of them were mothers with lost sons: sons in custody, sons who'd died in custody, sons who claimed to have been beaten by the police. Some had sons who had rioted, and although these men were now allowed back on the island, they were still awaiting trial. To enter the courtroom the women had to show ID, before being electronically scanned, then patted down. In the airless room they emitted a low drumbeat of heartache. I could feel their desperation for any tiny victory. "You long for it, long for it," one of them said to me. Their heightened expectation was the antithesis of the police officers' attitude. The same squad that had kicked down the rioters' doors was on security and sat outside the courtroom, flicking through magazines. They all looked upward of six foot four and they all had crew cuts. "This inquest is an example," one sergeant told me, "of people trying to look for the worst in a situation."

Tracy Twaddle and the Doomadgee sisters sat in the front row. Elizabeth's eyes gleamed with *now*: *now* it's happening. She had been praying for this moment, and these lawyers—Boe, Callaghan, Moynihan, brimming with bravado and hot for the sport of it—were here to answer her prayers. The legal teams remained unchanged. Hurley's lawyers—Zillman and Cranny—had an irritated air: this had already gone on longer than anyone had imagined. Terry Martin, counsel assisting the deputy coroner, examined the witnesses. The jurors' seats were filled with court reporters.

The first witness was the head electrical engineer at Queensland's Department of Public Works. He sat in the witness box as a section of the cell-surveillance tape was played, showing Cameron and Patrick Nugent stretched out on the floor. We stared down at the men, splayed as if at the bottom of a deep box. We could not see their features, just the outlines of their bodies, and one—Cameron's—writhing. Patrick Nugent patted his head drunkenly. The tape was silent apart from the wretched, distorted sound of Cameron calling, "Help me! Help!"

The tape went for a long time. Hurley's lawyers were murmuring and smiling about something. Tracy's lawyer seemed to be trying to stay awake. Behind them Tracy sat quietly weeping.

After Hurley discovers Cameron is dead, he and the other police can be seen on the tape talking. Then, when the ambulance officers arrive, Hurley speaks to them in an animated style. None of these conversations are recorded. The only sounds loud enough to register were the dying man's cries.

Palm Islander Gordon Johnson had given evidence that he heard Doomadgee calling for help as he walked past the police station that morning. And now the engineer testified that it was unlikely Cameron's calls would not have been audible throughout the police station. "[The police] would have heard on the intercom master what we hear on the tape."

The ambulance officer who'd been captured on the video was up next. He'd entered the cell at 11:25 A.M. and tried to resuscitate Cameron. He said he believed Doomadgee had been dead for at least twenty minutes, and he had a pronounced black eye. The video reveals the officer having a heated conversation with Hurley, but he told the court he could no longer remember what was said. He was excused.

The next witness was the one everyone had been waiting for: Police Liaison Officer Lloyd Bengaroo. Boe and Callaghan were especially keen to hear his evidence. Other than Hurley himself, Bengaroo would be the last eyewitness to the arrest to testify. In the video interview he gave police investigators the day after Cameron died, Bengaroo had reenacted the events of the arrest but stopped at the moment when Cameron was taken inside the police station.

Bengaroo claimed he had stayed by the doorway. "I stood here," he said to the police investigators, "because I was thinking, um, if I see something, I might get into trouble myself, or something . . . the family might harass me or something, you know . . . ?" The "or something" he had referred to was, Callaghan believed, most likely police intimidation. Bengaroo, who had spent twenty years working in some capacity for the police, also had to observe "the code." He was a man caught between two tribes—the blackfellas and the coppers—and both tribes had means of exacting revenge. Callaghan and Boe believed he knew more than he was saying. Under cross-examination he might reveal what it was.

Somber, heavyset, Lloyd Bengaroo walked to the witness box wearing his police uniform. His long socks were pulled tight to his knees, and keys jangled in the pocket of his shorts. His hair was shaved close, his face pockmarked, his brow furrowed. When he sat down, fat rolled at the back of his neck. In a surprisingly soft voice he swore on the Bible, although he went on to admit he wasn't a Christian. Nearly twenty years ago, I'd been told, his eighteen-year-old son was murdered one night on Palm Island over a cigarette. This son had been to school with Cameron Doomadgee.

A fierce cough plagued Bengaroo as he gave evidence.

> Cameron come. He walked past. He said to me, "Bengaroo, you black like me. Can't you help us?" I told Cameron, "Just, just walk down the road or you'll get locked up" . . . I said that for his own safety. Soon as me and Chris Hurley's put Patrick in the back of the police vehicle, both of us jumped in the front . . . We heard Cameron sing out from down the road, distant down the road . . . Cameron sort of said a few words . . . I knew he was saying some swear words but I couldn't, didn't hear what he was speaking out . . . [Chris said,] "We'll drive down to lock him up."

When they got to the police station, Bengaroo now claimed, he *did* witness the two men tripping through the doorway. He told the court he'd seen them falling side by side, and confirmed that no "part of Hurley came into contact with any part of Mulrunji." Bengaroo also testified that he'd then gone inside the station after all, and that Hurley had not assaulted Doomadgee.

Peter Callaghan wanted to show Bengaroo the crime scene photograph of Cameron's black eye. The police lawyers protested that this would be culturally insensitive. The deputy coroner put white paper around the photograph of the dead man's face so only the wound was visible.

When Callaghan showed Bengaroo the photograph, the officer admitted that Cameron did not have a black eye when he was arrested. He could not explain how the injury had happened.

The courtroom was tense. I could hear Erykah Kyle and the older women at various points booing, moaning, or whispering encouragement: "Yes, yes."

It was hard to know if Lloyd Bengaroo was trying to mislead or genuinely didn't understand the lawyers' questions. When asked directly whether he saw or heard anything improper, he made no grand revelations. But in an exchange with Peter Callaghan he said something that had an honest ring.

Callaghan: "You told [Cameron] to walk on down the road for his own safety—what did you mean by that?"

Bengaroo: "I told him to walk down the road or he's getting locked up. For his own safety. I just told him to walk down the road or he'd get locked up."

Callaghan: "And the reason you did that was 'for his own safety'?"

Bengaroo: "Yes."

Callaghan: "And a safe place is somewhere away from you and Senior Sergeant Hurley?"

Bengaroo: "Yes."

Callaghan: "It wasn't safe being near the two of you, for him?"

Bengaroo: "It wasn't, no."

Once or twice Bengaroo seemed on the verge of saying more, but each time, by chance, someone in the court coughed or shuffled and some spell was broken. Callaghan was worked up, aggressive, in a kind of fury. Bengaroo crossed his arms, then briefly put his head in his hands. I wondered what he had thought of Chris Hurley— whether he had trusted him, whether he'd noticed something about the mood Hurley was in that morning. And I wondered what Bengaroo had thought of Cameron.

Callaghan: "Why was he being arrested?"

Bengaroo: "Creating a disturbance."

Callaghan: "Who was disturbed?"

Bengaroo: "Myself and Chris."

Callaghan: "And how were you disturbed?"

Bengaroo: "By the way he was calling out to us."

Callaghan: "But you don't know what he said."

Bengaroo: "No, got no idea."

Nor did Bengaroo know what legally constituted a public nuisance. He had never been trained in the matter.

At the end of the day in court, Lloyd Bengaroo stood down a hallway, surrounded by six police officers. They were all smiling. The scene was collegiate, even congratulatory. They picked a moment when the hallway was clear, then Bengaroo and his escorts stepped into the elevator. At the last minute, I found myself joining them.

"Safest lift in Townsville," one young policeman said. It was Constable Kristopher Steadman, who'd waited outside the police station that morning while Hurley was alone with Doomadgee.

"Not if you swear," I answered.

Steadman laughed. The doors opened and Bengaroo was spirited away.

Outside the courthouse, Erykah Kyle told me that Lloyd Bengaroo made her think of the Native Police, who until the late 1890s were the subordinate allies of white police and involved in blood-curdling killing sprees. The system had used Lloyd, she felt, and she wished her council had tried to reach out to him. "I feel sorry for him, truly I do." Lloyd had spent his policing years being the white

cops' errand boy, holding the van doors open while other blackfellas were arrested. Cameron had shamed him that morning, but it
wasn't like he hadn't been shamed before. In his twenty-one years as
a community police officer, he'd heard similar things during most
arrests. It was just that, this time, Cameron Doomadgee was dead
forty minutes later.

AMID MUCH EXCITEMENT the next morning, Senior Sergeant
Chris Hurley arrived at the courtroom—and I felt I was glimpsing
some figure from myth. After nearly nine months of intense specu-
lation, and legal proceedings in which he was the absent subject of
witness accounts, here he was—tall, dark, classically handsome.
Flesh and blood. He came in through a back door so he could not be
photographed. His uniform was so carefully pressed each crease was
visible. He was clean shaven, tanned, calm, polite. It went to making
him a good witness. He sat very straight and referred to Doomadgee
as "Mulrunji" or "the gent" or "the gentleman." He called Terry Martin "sir" and looked him directly in the eye. His accent was unpol-
ished, but not particularly broad. He told the court of his years of
volunteer work with Aboriginal youths.

Martin: "Do you have friends who are Aborigines?"

Hurley: "Yes, sir."

Neatly dressed in jeans and shiny shoes, Murrandoo Yanner sat
in the courtroom, leaning forward, attempting to be seen by Hurley.
Murrandoo had traveled from Burketown to try to confront his old
friend. "We know each other too well and have too much respect for
each other," he had told Tony Koch, "for him to be able to look me
in the eye and not tell me the truth."

Martin: "Do you have anything against Aboriginal people?"

Hurley: "No, no. I wouldn't have, I . . . I wouldn't go to these
communities if I had something against Aboriginal people, I . . . I
couldn't serve in those communities."

Hurley sat very still in the witness box and told the court how,
on November 19, 2004, he had been waiting in the police van on Dee

Street with Lloyd Bengaroo while Gladys Nugent collected her medication. "We had the windows up and I could hear some yelling going on. And Lloyd asked, 'Are you hearing what he's saying?' . . . Patrick Nugent was yelling out abuse toward Lloyd and myself."

The senior sergeant had got out of the van to arrest Patrick, and that was the moment Cameron Doomadgee walked past and spoke to Bengaroo. When Hurley returned to the van he could tell his colleague was upset. "His pride was hurt. He's a very proud man," Hurley told the court in a sincere tone, "and Lloyd takes his job very seriously." In the 1980s, Hurley explained, Bengaroo had been in charge of thirteen community police officers and was entrusted with the power to arrest. By 2004, the system had changed and he had "no actual authority." Lloyd's only role was to liaise between the Palm Islanders and the police.

Hurley said that he'd looked over at Cameron, farther down the street, who yelled out, "'Fucking cunts. You fucking cunts!' or something similar to that." But it was the insult to Lloyd that concerned him. Lloyd, Hurley told the court, had said, "'He shouldn't speak to me like that, mate.' And I said, 'Well, who is it?' And he told me Mulrunji's correct name."

Doomadgee.

The day before, Lloyd Bengaroo had told the inquest that Chris Hurley knew Cameron and "knew the Doomadgee family, where they came from." Hurley maintained that he did not remember Cameron, but even so, the very surname must have brought to mind the red-dirt town. It must have had a smell to it, a feel. All day long, blackfellas in old cars drove up from Doomadgee to the Burketown Pub and loaded up with cases of beer and bottles of rum. Young men from Doomadgee would go up the road and slash the tires of whites at the local trailer park. The Doomadgee men had broken noses, scarred faces, do-it-yourself prison tattoos; the Burketown whites could feel the tension in the air.

Steve Zillman stood up and asked for a brief meeting with his client. The rest of us sat waiting in the courtroom, suspended in the moment when Hurley reversed thirty meters to arrest Cameron. One man had seen a black drunk, the other a white demon. The next step was pure ritual. It was hot, it was clammy. It was, to quote Norman Mailer, "carnal." "At the moment of the arrest, cop and criminal knew each other better than mates . . . an arrest was carnal. Not sexual, carnal—of the meat, strangers took purchase of another's meat."

When Hurley returned to the courtroom he announced, "I take the opportunity to claim privilege."

Christine Clements directed that Hurley was required to "answer questions and provide evidence to this inquest." She had the power to order him to speak, but any evidence he subsequently gave could not be used against him in a criminal proceeding.

Hurley now told the court he'd decided to arrest Cameron "in support of Lloyd, because Lloyd doesn't have the power of arrest . . . my view is," he added, "that we give one hundred percent support to Lloyd. Our job is difficult over there but it was nothing compared to Lloyd's." The senior sergeant sat in the witness box telling his story confidently, as if no one could fail to see how reasonable he'd been. The suspicions around this death were all due to a terrible misunderstanding. A mix-up. He had actually been supporting Aboriginal people that day. In fact, the arrest itself was a brotherly, protective arrest to help a black subordinate—Cameron's offense was "public nuisance."

"But why would being rude to Lloyd justify that offense?" Terry Martin asked.

Hurley's face changed minimally. "Well, my point being, sir, is that I believe if Lloyd had the power of arrest, he would've arrested the gentleman himself."

Martin: "For what, though?"

Hurley: "For public nuisance."

Belligerence flickered just beneath the senior sergeant's poise. Experience had taught him, he told the court, that if he didn't arrest Cameron that morning, chances were he'd reoffend. Hurley wanted to take him back to the station and check if he had a criminal history.

But Terry Martin wondered, in a place where drinking domi-
nated life, why did Hurley not say, "Look, mate, you've had too many,
you're yelling out in the street, come and we'll give you a lift home."
Doomadgee, after all, was not known for being a troublemaker—
Hurley said himself he had never met him.

The senior sergeant claimed that, having just arrested Patrick
Nugent, he wanted to be evenhanded.

Martin asked what had happened back at the station. "How did
you get him out of the vehicle?"

Hurley: "I asked him to get out at first and then placed a hand on
his leg or his arm to assist him, and when I say assist, whether I had
to drag him I can't recall, but whilst he was getting out I was punched.
It was a shock." It was a shock because Hurley believed the community knew that he was tough but fair. "One of the reasons I like being
in the communities [is] because you could build up that rapport, you
weren't just a number on the street, people knew who you were." As
for the punch, he wasn't angry, just annoyed: "I was a bit fazed by
it . . . a bit annoyed by it, yeah, but not angry. Anger is too strong a
word." In this state, he said, they struggled to the station door.

Martin: "And you fell down?"

Hurley: "Mulrunji fell down before me."

Martin: "And did you also fall to the floor of the police station?"

Hurley: "Correct, I fell to his left."

Martin: "You didn't land on top of him?"

Chris Hurley: "Well, I now know that medical evidence would
suggest that. That I landed on top of him. If I didn't know the medical evidence, I'd tell you that I fell to the left of him . . . I mean, life
doesn't unfortunately go frame by frame, and if it did, I would've
been able to give a hundred percent accurate version. But the version
I gave was my best recollection and the most truthful. It was the
truth that I thought."

Murrandoo Yanner moved to a seat in the gallery behind Terry
Martin, directly in the senior sergeant's line of sight. Hurley's face
flashed with recognition.

Murrandoo's brother Vernon had told me that at the Burketown Pub, Hurley sometimes stood by the jukebox daring blokes to come outside and rugby-tackle him. For four long years he'd been out of sight in Burketown, keeping the peace in ways that did not always bear mainstream scrutiny. He didn't carry a gun, his brawniness was a kind of protection.

But in the courtroom Chris Hurley was controlled, urbane, inscrutable, with none of the aggression Vernon Yanner described. If Hurley was rocked to see Murrandoo, his mask hid it well. Here at the inquest Hurley was the good Catholic boy, all manners and discipline, grown-up. He was like T. E. Lawrence back from the wilderness, smooth and upstanding at the London club.

Hurley denied assaulting Cameron. And he was utterly convincing. Put aside the parts of his story that didn't add up and there was no reason to doubt this man. His arrest of Cameron had been heavy-handed but his sincerity was compelling. The courtroom felt his self-belief, his conviction. I wondered if it were possible to feel innocent of a death that you had caused but that you did not intend. Could you be mechanically responsible but humanly guiltless? Any one of the police guarding the inside and outside of the courtroom could have been in Hurley's position. Was it possible, then, for Hurley to convince himself that, since he'd behaved much as anyone else would have in the circumstances, he was no more guilty than anyone else?

Terry Martin reminded Hurley that in three police interviews—on the day of the death, the day following, and the week following—he had said he fell to the left of Cameron. There would now, Martin claimed, seem to be only two possible explanations for Cameron's black eye and massive internal injuries: either Hurley had indeed fallen on top of him or he had assaulted his prisoner. Since he had repeatedly denied the former—until knowing the medical evidence—could the latter be possible?

Martin: "Just think back: Was there a flash of anger whereby you got up first and drove your knee into him, and said something like, 'Have you had enough, Mr. Doomadgee?'"

Hurley: "No, that's not correct."

Martin: "Clip to the jaw and then, you know, with all due respect to the Court, you fell arse-over-tit through the doorway, but it didn't make you angry enough to get up and . . . ?"

Hurley: "No. No. I wanted him in the cell."

Martin: "I beg your pardon?"

Hurley: "I wanted him in the cell. I was trying to pick him up after that."

By "pick him up," the senior sergeant was referring to standing over Doomadgee and pulling: this was his alternative explanation to Roy Bramwell's claim that Hurley's elbow had been moving up and down in a series of punches. Was Hurley now telling the truth, or was he covering himself against Bramwell's allegation?

It would be seven months before these questions could be put to Hurley in cross-examination. His testimony was literally interrupted due to another legal battle taking place. The deputy coroner, Christine Clements, had decided to allow Hurley's prior-complaints history to be used in evidence. His lawyers were appealing and the inquest was again adjourned until the appeal was heard.

Hurley slipped out a side door to again avoid photographers and disappeared in a waiting car. Giving evidence, he had been the model of a virtuous cop. If it was Roy Bramwell's word against his, who would believe Roy? I tried to look at things from every angle. I took each doubt I had and tried to explain it away, then put it back in to test whether Cameron's death could have been just an accident. Was it possible that Hurley was innocent?

ONE AFTERNOON—months after the August 2005 inquest had been interrupted—an officer invited me inside the police barracks on Palm Island. It was the wet season and water lay pooled on the ground. Plants looked close to drowning. Vines entwined fences as if intent on suffocating them. Out in the bay the rain had filled a boat and sunk it. The officer unlocked the heavy padlock, I entered the barracks through the Cyclone-wire gates, and he locked us back in. He led me to the social area, a tight garage space where the cops had retreated during the riot. There was now a half-size pool table, a stereo, old office chairs, and a television playing *Video Hits*. Two dilapidated couches had been given over to one of the police-woman's dogs.

The officer offered me a drink and went to a fridge filled with budget colas and beer. There was a notepad that he marked to pay later. He wanted companionship. He wanted to talk about music and travel and the things young men talk to young women about everywhere. I felt the whole building vibrate with loneliness. Out-side, one of his colleagues had been gardening in the narrow beds alongside the barracks, the plants meticulously, lovingly tended. On the walls above were windows covered in protective screens.

This officer had been at the riot, but could not talk about it because Lex Wotton's trial was still pending. Do you think Hurley is innocent? I kept wanting to ask, but since I was drinking his beer, it seemed unfair.

I thought of what I had learned. Chris Hurley could be a kind man and he could also be tough and uncomplaining, in ways that a good cop has to be. When a plane crashed not far from Burketown, Hurley and his deputy were first on the scene. They waited all night for the rescue crew. Later, he told a friend that he dropped off to sleep and woke horrified to find himself among the eight incinerated bod-ies. Hurley could endure the most confronting experiences, but lit-tle things would wind him up, this friend said, and then compared him to a Vietnam veteran: close up, he could be alarmingly moody, unpredictable, easily irritated—and very intent on control.

I had heard some Palm Islanders say they thought Hurley started acting differently after his girlfriend left him. Narelle had followed him from Burketown. But early in 2004 she left the island. No one I spoke to knew why she had gone. I wondered if being on his own made Hurley more vulnerable to his tormentors.

One police officer I met in Doomadgee who'd also worked on the island told me that while he hated to talk down Aboriginal communities, the island had nearly broken him. It was physically stunning—mountains, white sand beaches, shimmering waters—but one day, when he was sitting with another officer in the police barracks, a missile in the form of a full can of beer flew over the fence and just missed the other officer's newborn baby. And one night, they got a call to an area known as the Farm, near the mission's abandoned farmland, and along the way came upon a roadblock. It was dark. Getting out to clear the road, they knew they were in danger. People began pelting them with rocks. Such incidents weren't uncommon. The police were threatened constantly; their windows were broken, their cars rocked. Once, as the officer was unlocking the barracks gates, a passerby said to him, "What do you think you're doing? You're not allowed out!"

The most recent craze for the island kids was to cut the power cords off people's main appliances, then fray the plastic coating at one end to make a whip. People couldn't use their washing machines, but boys and girls of all ages were wandering around the streets swinging the cords with the skill and grace of stockmen. All the petals on the white spider lilies that had come out with the rain had been lopped off. At night you could hear flowers being beheaded with whip cracks that sounded like rifle shots. So many people were complaining about their missing cords that the police had started confiscating the whips.

In the Palm Island barracks, the officer and I finished our beers and he walked me back to the wire gates, releasing me, then locking himself back in.

"Here was I, the white man with his gun, standing in front of the unarmed native crowd—seemingly the lead actor of the piece; but in reality I was only an absurd puppet pushed to and fro by the will of those yellow faces behind." So wrote George Orwell in "Shooting an Elephant," an essay about his time as a British Raj policeman in Burma. "I perceived in this moment that when the white man turns tyrant it is his own freedom that he destroys. He becomes a sort of hollow, posing dummy . . . For it is the condition of his rule that he shall spend his life in trying to impress the 'natives,' and so in every crisis he has got to do what the 'natives' expect of him. He wears a mask, and his face grows to fit it."

I thought of Hurley's inscrutable face at the inquest. I thought of all the ways he'd tried to "impress the natives" with acts of kindness and of force. He even looked like a lead actor, and no one calls the lead actor a "fucking cunt" and gets away with it.

Hurley had told the inquest: "I wouldn't go to these communities if I had something against Aboriginal people, I couldn't serve . . ." But who knows if, like Orwell, who was hooted at wherever he went, Hurley's life as a policeman wasn't "one long struggle not to be laughed at," and if it did not sometimes "get badly on his nerves"? Black communities can morph into the opposite of white communities on purpose. If Doomadgee kids were teased by their peers for not washing, they'd retort: "I'm no white man!" Junk was strewn in people's yards in part because neatness was seen as a white ideal. It was as if the locals were saying, "You think we're all abject— well, here's what abject is. Here is chaos and self-destruction, unreason and cruelty. Here are all the things you accuse us of, all those things you're frightened of. This is what they look like." Hurley went straight in. But it would take a truly exceptional person to serve in these places and *not* develop feelings like Orwell's.

Like the British police in Burma, cops on Palm Island were still "doing the dirty work of Empire at close quarters," feeding good intentions into a broken machine and watching them come back in other, twisted forms. Were these cops also caught between a feeling of contempt for their countrymen who didn't know the realities of life in these places, and a feeling that it would be, as Orwell put it, the "greatest joy in the world" to do violence to those who laughed at them, those useless, abusive men throwing rocks while their children didn't have enough to eat?

ON FEBRUARY 27, 2006, seven months after the last adjournment, the inquest resumed yet again. It seemed to Tracy Twaddle and the

Doomadgee sisters that they were forever waiting for something to happen. "This just drag, eh," Valmae said, but she believed her brother was watching over her. "It's like he there telling me to keep pushing, don't give up."

Behind the scenes a protracted fight had been playing out. In the course of the inquest, lawyers for the Queensland police commissioner and Hurley twice tried to prevent the senior sergeant's twenty or so prior-complaint files from being seen by the opposing lawyers and used in evidence. Trial courts always seek to ensure that the burden of proof is greater on the prosecution than on the defense. Inquests, being fact-finding missions, are not bound by the same constraints, but nevertheless neither Hurley nor the Queensland Police Service wanted his records released.

Andrew Boe and Peter Callaghan had had to go to the Supreme Court to win permission to see the files. The police lawyers then claimed that, even though Boe and Callaghan could see them, they should not be able to use them in evidence. Boe and Callaghan went back to the Supreme Court and won the right to use the prior complaints in evidence, but only those that indicated negligence on the part of Hurley, or a propensity toward violence in arrest situations, and only those that related to Palm Island.

Deputy Coroner Christine Clements called two men to appear at the inquest who both claimed they'd been assaulted by Hurley in the Palm Island police station. The inquest also heard from a woman who alleged Hurley had driven over her foot and left her lying on the ground. Hurley was called back and cross-examined.

Over a period of five days, more than a dozen police—all of whom were white—also testified as witnesses to these incidents, but they had seen no evil, heard no evil, and would certainly not be speaking of any evil.

Police commonly feel they are subject to malicious false complaints: it is one of the justifications for "the code." A Brisbane police sergeant told me he'd been accused many times of things he'd never done. He said there was a "culture of complaint" among those who were arrested—claiming they'd been assaulted gave them a sense of having a win, and a certain credibility among their mates.

But people in remote communities have good reason *not* to complain. First, there's the perception that nothing will be done; second, they assume they'll then be targeted by the police for minor things, such as their car's roadworthiness, and by other white service providers friendly with the police. "You've got the hospital turn against you. You have the school turn against you," said a man in Doomadgee whose son, the Crime and Misconduct Commission found, was beaten by police. "You have them all turn against you."

The stories told by the three complainants at the inquest were, on one level, mundane. All three had been drunk at the time they came into contact with Hurley, and perhaps as a consequence it was virtually impossible to work out who was being honest. This had been the problem with Cameron Doomadgee's case all along. Almost everyone had a strained relationship with the truth. Often the police seemed less than candid, but so did the blackfellas. With this level of drunkenness, the facts blurred, and were almost impossible to locate.

The first Palm Island man to give "similar fact" evidence was Noel Cannon. He had come forward after Cameron died and made a sworn statement to the Doomadgee family's lawyers. In that statement he claimed he'd been picked up on July 8, 2004, for public drunkenness. He was in his brother's front yard, sitting on a trampoline, talking to his three-year-old grandson, Gerry. He claimed:

> Mr. Hurley, the police officer, came past and was talking to Georgina, my partner, she was next door. I was talking to Gerry saying to him, "Don't jump in the police van, if they see you, they'll lock you up." I was not using any bad language. Mr. Hurley thought I was talking to him but I was talking to my grandson. I had been drinking. I would have had a six-pack that morning and then a few more during the day.

What Noel Cannon had neglected to mention was that Georgina was actually his ex-partner, and she had called the police because he was outside her house, drunk, stoned, and flouting a domestic violence restraining order.

After Hurley arrived, Cannon went into his brother's yard nearby and sat on a trampoline with his grandson. According to Georgina, who testified at the inquest, he started calling, "Piggy, piggy, piggy, piggy!" Senior Sergeant Hurley got Cannon on his stomach against the trampoline and handcuffed him; the child watched on.

At the inquest, Noel Cannon claimed that he was taken to the police station and Hurley "put me in the cell. He took all my clothes off. He left me in my shorts." There was no mattress in the cell. Cannon says Hurley told him to wait for twenty minutes so he could do his paperwork. Cannon waited for what he thought was twenty minutes before calling out. Hurley "came in with a temper." If Cannon was "going to keep singing out and kicking the door," he'd be made to wait another half hour. Cannon waited, then started calling again. The next time Hurley came in, he "grabbed me by the throat, squeezed my throat, squeezed it . . . kept squeezing and squeezing until I wet myself." Cannon claimed that while Hurley had him by the throat, "he sticked me up the guts," meaning that Hurley had his knee in Cannon's abdomen, winding him. "He threw a mattress in for me then."

The senior sergeant denied the entire story.

The second man to give "similar fact" evidence was Douglas Clay, a twenty-five-year-old with a medical history of drug-induced psychosis. Clay is the son of Tracy Twaddle's half sister, another Elizabeth, and the nephew of Lex Wotton's older brother. He was drunk and having an episode when, on August 14, 2004, he walked into the Palm Island police station with a beer in his hand to ask for help. Chris Hurley told the inquest he'd been sitting with five other officers, including Darren Robinson. "I saw Dougie walk in the back door drinking a can of VB. And of course I thought that was unusual, just walking in the police station . . . he stated something along the lines of, 'You fucking police cunts.' I'm thinking, What's going on here? I said to Robbo, I said, 'Who's this bloke?' He said, 'It's Dougie Clay. Don't you know him?'"

Hurley thought Clay might have been one of Darren's informants, but in fact he was wanted just then for "touching up the nurse at the canteen the other night." Hurley stood up to tell Clay to get out, and, he claimed, Clay lunged as if to head-butt him. Clay said Hurley gave him a "flurry of punches," something Hurley denied: "I mean, a man's first instinct's survival. I reacted. I pushed his face away. I struck out at him basically. I slapped him. I pushed out hard in his face and I slapped his face hard and pushed it over towards the wall."

Clay was dragged to the cells, his mouth bleeding. After he'd been locked up, Darren Robinson told Hurley, "Mate, he's a nutter. He's been over in Townsville in ward 10B." That was a psychiatric unit.

The most damning evidence against Hurley involved the third complainant, Barbara Pilot, a round, soft woman of thirty. Barbara is the daughter of Cameron Doomadgee's elder sister Victoria, and on the night of May 19, 2004, she was drunk. So was her partner, Arthur Murray, who pushed her down some stairs and hit her hard on the head with a screwdriver. An ambulance collected Barbara, and while she was at the hospital, Senior Sergeant Hurley arrived at the Murray house to perform his usual thankless task. (In the right light, Hurley can seem like Everyman walking through a landscape where the characters are Death, Drunkenness, Violence, and Despair.)

He arrested Murray and put him in the back of the police van. As he was driving away, Barbara returned. She approached the van, remonstrating with "Big Chris," who told her to go away. When she did not, she claims, he reversed over her bare foot. "She made the exclamation that I'd run her over," Hurley told the inquest. "She was singing it out. I can't recall whether she was screaming in pain but she was singing out, 'You run me over!'" It was dark. Hurley opened the door, looked Barbara Pilot up and down, and apparently seeing no injuries, drove away. He went back to the station, put Murray in a cell, then left him unsupervised and went to the hospital to drink tea with the nurses.

Before long, Barbara Pilot arrived back at the hospital. According to the attending doctor, Clinton Leahy, "the bone [was] clearly protruding from her foot in a very unusual manner." Dr Leahy, who testified at the inquest, claimed that while he examined Barbara, Hurley was waiting for him. The two men were friends. Hurley asked Leahy if he thought the injury was caused by a car tire, but to the doctor "he seemed interested, to me, to find out that there was another cause for it." Hurley ran through some different possibilities.

Dr. Leahy testified: "I told him that I'd never seen an injury like this before, and in my opinion, it required something quite profound to push a bone, not only out of its joint, but through the skin and out into the open. And I told him that such a great force would be well explained by a car tire."

The coroner called a bone specialist from Townsville, to whom Pilot went subsequently for surgery, and a forensic pathologist on retainer from Hurley's lawyers. They both told the inquest that the woman's injuries were consistent with her having been run over. In fact, even Hurley—albeit under legal privilege—admitted the possibility: "I'd be ignorant to do that; to exclude it 100 percent."

Yet the night it had happened, that is exactly what he tried to do. He called his superior and family friend Inspector Gary Hickey to report the incident. At the inquest, Hickey read from a bound book the notes he'd taken of their conversation: "More consistent with kicking ground but possibly from car [according to] Dr. Clinton Leahy. [But] Hurley claims not possible from position near driver's window." Then, of the victim: "Intoxicated, playing up." Hickey ordered Hurley to start investigating Barbara's allegation.

This relatively minor episode might be the Rosetta Stone of the death in custody. The senior sergeant proposes an alternative story: Barbara Pilot was kicking the ground. (The equivalent in Cameron's case: he tripped over a step.) He gets involved in the investigation himself. Then his supporters step in. In the case of Pilot, Warren

Webber, who would later head the investigation into Doomadgee's death, commissioned Hurley's close friend Detective Darren Robinson to look into her complaint. Robinson waited a month before he began. By this time, although her foot still ached, the visible wounds had healed. Robinson did not try to access Barbara's medical records, or even to interview Barbara herself. Instead he questioned her partner, Arthur Murray. The interview went like this:

Robinson: "Is it fair for me to say and do you accept that a lot of people on the island do 'drunk talk'?"

Murray: "Yeah."

Robinson: "All right. You know, well, you've known Barbara, you know her better than me. When she was speaking to you the next day, did she tell you this was just drunk talk?"

Murray: "Yeah."

Robinson: "Do you know why she said it?"

Murray: "Drunk."

Robinson: "She was drunk. Okay. So she actually said to you that, 'Hey, the police hadn't run over my foot.'"

Murray: "No. She said, 'The car just run over my foot.'"

Robinson: "Do you think she's just trying to stir trouble?"

Murray: "Yeah."

Robinson: "All right. Is it like her to stir trouble?"

Murray: "Yeah. Liar."

Robinson: "She lies?"

Murray: "She lies all the time, she's so drunk."

Robinson: "Have you asked her or has she told you how it happened?"

Murray: "Yeah, she told me next day the wheel ran over her foot."

Robinson: "Yep. All right, a wheel ran over her foot. It was drunk talk that the police ran over her foot."

Detective Robinson reported to senior police that Barbara Pilot's claims were "fictitious."

On October 21, 2005, the Crime and Misconduct Commission questioned Robinson about his previous investigations into Hurley's conduct. Robinson's own chance of promotion had been jeopardized due to this investigation, and in the meantime he was stuck in Townsville, a place he found ugly. It seems the thirty-two-year-old thought he'd teach the CMC detectives a lesson. The transcript of Robinson's interview contains two closely typed pages of a lecture on alcohol and memory that he delivered. It reads like a student's plagiarized term paper: "Today I wish to talk about the dangers for investigators when relying upon a person's memory . . . This brings me to advise yourselves about a condition in which memory is disturbed known as amnesia."

He told the CMC that the Aboriginal witnesses had memory loss through alcoholism and their evidence against Hurley and himself—theoretically Robinson could have faced charges for perverting the course of justice—needed to be treated cautiously. The witnesses, he recommended, should each have an electroencephalogram, a brain-function test often used to assess brain death, and a computerized tomography scan to identify structural damage. They should also undergo analysis by a psychologist. Finally, he warned the commission against "bias-ism": "Your investigation is to be an accurate reflection of the truth in all matters."

Even among Cameron's family there were some who had been critical of Boe and Callaghan's pursuit of Hurley's complaint records. It meant more waiting, more delays. But each witness's story suggested a way to decode what had happened to Cameron. Douglas Clay's claim that he had been knocked across the room in front of five officers made me wonder what Hurley might do to someone who actually struck him, especially if there was no one around. Noel Cannon's story suggested that a knee to the chest—a common police "settler"—could have been part of Hurley's modus operandi. The case of Barbara Pilot seemed to show that he was capable of duplicity. And it also showed something else: even if Hurley had no recollection of Cameron, Cameron knew exactly who Hurley was. His niece claimed that this man had run over her foot and left her lying in pain on the ground.

The Funeral

HUNDREDS OF PALM Islanders had followed Cameron Doomadgee's coffin on the narrow road from the Catholic church to the
cemetery, a journey of several kilometers on a blisteringly hot day.
Cameron's sixteen-year-old son, Eric, had led the funeral proces-
sion, holding a white wooden cross to place on his father's grave. A
year and a half after Cameron's death, Eric had his own white cross.
On July 31, 2006, he was discovered hanging from a tree in bushland
on Palm Island. The family friends who found him cut his body
down and carried it into town.

In the Aboriginal diaspora, people regularly pool money and
travel hundreds of kilometers to bury their relatives. For Eric's
funeral, Elizabeth's daughters Rosie and Doris drove from Doomadgee with their small children. Distant cousins came from farther
north. Claudelle Doomadgee, Eric's homeless aunt, a "street lady" as
she calls herself, took the ferry over from Townsville.

When I arrived, the day before the funeral, the island seemed
quieter than usual, strangely peaceful in the blue-green refracting
light. I'd read that the coastal people of Arnhem Land believe they
can see their unborn children in the pattern of the waves. Eric had
died two weeks earlier.

Andrew Boe flew in the day I did. We found Valmae in the council chambers, sleepless but happy to be busy finalizing the funeral
program, organizing poems and messages to go inside it. We went
to look for Elizabeth, who was in one of the island's gambling circles, trying to get some money together for the wake. She was vague

and remote, embarrassed perhaps about playing cards. I guessed she wanted one win to wipe out all the losses. It had been hard for the Doomadgee family to find money to pay the Townsville undertaker for the funerals of Cameron and their mother. The added cost of Eric's funeral would be crippling. Boe had sent an e-mail around his legal circle, and several barristers and a magistrate donated funds. Boe now told Elizabeth there was enough to pay off the debt and to erect three headstones. It did not seem to penetrate. When she returned to the circle, he handed her $10 and asked if she'd make a bet for him.

The next morning, Eric's body was laid out in a small outbuilding of the hospital, where people could say good-bye. His friends, Palm Island's young men, had dressed in long-sleeved maroon shirts and black trousers. Others wore maroon, yellow, or white, the colors of Eric's favorite rugby team, the Brisbane Broncos. His cousins had pinned ribbons in these colors to their clothes.

Inside the building there started a terrible keening. The queue filed past Eric. In his coffin he had white silk around his neck. People touched his face and hair. In front of him sat his aunts and his stepmother, Tracy, all of them weeping. Grief had taken them somewhere far away. Eric's parents' relationship had broken down in the year after he was born, and he was raised by his grandmother. His aunts Elizabeth and Claudelle breast-fed him because his mother, Lyn, had a drinking problem. Lyn still lived on the island and now sat, devastated, with the other women.

As the hearse drove to the Catholic church, people stood outside their houses, bowing their heads. Drivers pulled their cars over and did the same. It was a larger church than the one I'd visited with Elizabeth a year earlier, but still it was overflowing. Mourners stood outside, staring in through the Cyclone-wire windows. Inside, plastic flowers were attached with masking tape to each pew.

"Jesus said, 'Let not your heart be troubled,'" this Aboriginal pastor announced. She did not address the circumstances of Eric's life, or why he may have ended it, or his father's life and why it had ended. Recognizing Jesus as the Way, the Truth, and the Life was enough to ease a troubled mind. As the service was ending, someone played "He Ain't Heavy, He's My Brother" on a tape deck and there was a sudden howling from Eric's aunts.

Palm Island's young men reckon they can hear the Hairy Man urging them to kill themselves. In Doomadgee they say they can see the hangman. But no one spoke of sorcery at Eric's funeral. And no one thought he had been drunk or stoned when he hanged himself from the tree.

Although there are no reliable statistics, health experts estimate young Aboriginal men are two or three times more likely than non-Aboriginal men to commit suicide. The sociologist Colin Tatz concedes the impossibility of ever truly understanding why someone takes their own life. But he has created a "typology" of Indigenous suicide, which includes the existential suicide, the person who "sees no horizon and . . . no means of altering such horizons as they have"; the grieving suicide, the person trapped in a cycle of mourning dead friends and relatives; and the political suicide, who, according to Tatz, has a score to settle, particularly with the police, and makes a "rebuke and a stand against authority." Eric's death fits all three.

The service over, I looked around the churchyard for Erykah Kyle, but I could not find her. Erykah was soon to retire from the mayoralty to write a book. I recalled what she'd said on my first day on the island, when we passed a group of youths with shoulders hunched: "Who knows their potential?" Eric was seventeen. He'd left school and had few prospects. On Palm Island, to reach puberty is for many to reach the edge of the abyss. The young inherit a community in which they have sovereignty over nothing but their own bodies—a sovereignty many willingly and rapidly relinquish. "Nothing to do and every day the same faces," Claudelle's seventeen-year-old son, also named Cameron, told me the night before the funeral. "This face and that face and that face."

The women outside the church carried hand towels to wipe their eyes. Their clothes were bright and yet seemed blanched of color. Young men stood very still, crying. None of Eric's friends would consider visiting the hospital's counselor, just as he hadn't after his father died. Eric had been grieving for his father and his grand-mother. Like other people on Palm Island, he was still mourning one death when the next occurred: compound grief. One woman told me she'd gone to three relatives' funerals in two weeks; another that she went to her mother's and sister's funerals on the same day.

According to Eric's cousins, Eric wanted justice for his father and was making a stand. More than nineteen months had passed since Cameron Doomadgee's death and still no charges had been laid. No decision had been reached about what had happened in the police station. The inquest had finished hearing evidence in early March 2006, but four months later the law remained silent.

As the hearse left the church, Elizabeth, who had stayed com-posed and stern during the service, pressed her hand to the car and followed it down the driveway. She blamed her nephew's death on a television crew that had come a few days earlier and filmed Eric talk-ing about his father. His other aunts had thought he should speak, that it would do him good to express his feelings. Elizabeth said she'd tried to stop him, believing it would stir up too much pain.

The Palm Island cemetery was a field of white wooden crosses against a backdrop of mountains. Most of its graves were carefully tended and adorned with colorful plastic flowers; on older graves, frangipani trees twisted in full fragrant bloom. Eric's friends had jostled so intensely to be pallbearers along prearranged routes—from church to hearse, from turnoff to last coconut tree, from last coconut tree to grave site—that the wooden coffin almost broke open. They passed around a shovel to fill the grave, covering the maroon, yellow, and white flowers that swathed the casket.

As at his father's funeral, hundreds of people had gathered and most of them seemed to be sober. The Queensland government had just introduced an alcohol-management plan on Palm Island, ban-ning full-strength beer. Only light and midstrength beers could be sold at the canteen. Hospital staff and elders told me they had noticed an immediate difference.

Lex Wotton, who had not yet been tried on the charges of rioting and arson, was out on bail. He stood in the graveyard along with the other alleged rioters who'd been banned from the island at the time of Cameron's funeral. Lex had entered a plea of not guilty. His trial had been delayed while his lawyers, the Sydney firm Levitt Robinson, argued it should be moved from Townsville to Brisbane. A Townsville jury, they claimed, was likely to be racist.

The trial was now scheduled for early 2007. Lex was not nervous. His sense of destiny gave him a peculiar calm. He told me that immediately after the riot, when he was locked up, a voice came to him urging him to see himself as "God's vessel" and a leader of his people. Off the island, Lex was now celebrated by activists and sympathizers as a great warrior, a prophet. His lawyers had given him works by Nelson Mandela and Martin Luther King to read.

Also standing at Eric's grave site was David Bulsey, who had warned people on the day of the riot that their own child might be next. Tall and thin, wearing a sapphire silk shirt and black trousers, Bulsey was a close friend of the Doomadgee family. When the riot squad had kicked down his door that night, his pregnant wife, Yvette, was made to lie on the floor with their children, rifles pointed at them. Their daughter (another Cameron) was induced prematurely, and David and Yvette believed it was because of the raid. Now a year and a half old, Cameron was on heart medication. When she became upset, her mother could hear an irregular heartbeat. This child was Eric's goddaughter.

I noticed Elizabeth standing away from all the other mourners, at the edge of the cemetery. Sometimes she was so regal, holding herself ramrod straight, giving orders to the lawyers with such authority, I would forget she'd been born into an island jail, leaving school in her early teens to help her mother do cleaning work. She was the bearer not only of her grandmother Lizzy Daylight's legacy of power and resilience, but also of the hard-line Christian tradition in which she'd been raised. During the first phase of the inquest, Elizabeth had suspected Eric of breaking into her house for money or food, possibly because his other relatives were drinking and there was nothing to eat in their house. Elizabeth summoned the police, and when they arrived she asked them to give Eric a warning. It seemed odd to be calling on the cops at such a time, but she embodied both strict traditions, including all that was contradictory about the resulting hybrid, and somehow it worked in ways that astonished.

With her youngest child, Sylvia, now at boarding school in Cairns, Elizabeth cared for four foster children aged under ten—three girls and a boy. I'd seen them running around her house looking for food, for attention, for fun. One of them was Elizabeth's great-niece. Elizabeth told me that her mother had used the girl as a shield against the girl's father when he violently attacked her. Despite her own tribulations, Elizabeth planned to take two more boys to keep the other company. Hanging in a broken frame on one of the walls in her house was a government certificate commending her work with children.

Now she stood away from the crowd, arms tightly crossed, holding herself. Andrew Boe walked over to her, and when he put his arm around her shoulders she began to cry uncontrollably, bending toward him as if in physical pain. She was saving all these children but she had not managed to save her own nephew.

The endless legal inquest, with its undertones of moral outrage, real and feigned, was supposed to prevent more deaths. But somehow it had missed the dead man's son. That was the sickening part. Whatever the legal system decided about Cameron's death, nothing would change for Eric, whose grave now lay alongside his father's.

After the burial, the young men who were Eric's friends all posed for photographs in front of the fresh white cross: first a group shot, then they took turns for single shots. They crouched close to the newly formed mound, touching it tenderly. I thought of young martyrs posing for the video camera before blowing themselves up.

Elizabeth had long since left the graveyard, but Boe and I waited with the rest of the family, who we were driving in a van lent to him by the council. Valmae wanted Eric's friends to have as much time as they needed.

My past twenty-four hours on the island had been strained. I would talk to Eric's cousins and find them staring back at me as if I were speaking a different language. The most basic phrases sounded utterly foreign. Boe told me that something similar had happened to him: he'd been driving Eric's aunts and at one point it was as if they were talking in tongues—as if people who live without hope could not be understood by people with hope in abundance.

When the boys were finished, Valmae handed me her camera. She stood in front of the grave with Cameron's elder sisters and his nephews and nieces, including Barbara Pilot with her foot that still ached from having been run over by Hurley in the police van. They wanted separate shots of Eric's aunts, cousins, in-laws—the husbands and wives of Eric's aunts and cousins. Then everyone gathered behind the grave for a group photo. "Smile! Smile!" called Dwayne, Eric's burly, mentally disabled cousin. "Smile!" he called to me, becoming upset. It was the photographer, he believed, who was meant to look happy.

The Submissions

FOUR DAYS AFTER Eric Doomadgee's funeral, on August 16, 2006, the inquest into his father's death sat for the last time. It was hot in Townsville, the sun bit the skin. In the bright light everyone looked older.

All the evidence having been taken, the lawyers were making their final submissions, summarizing their arguments before the deputy coroner went back to Brisbane to compose her findings. Normally, final submissions are presented in writing, but this was now a high-profile case and there was seen to be a need for transparency. Tracy Twaddle and Cameron's sisters were in court, but not many Palm Islanders had traveled to Townsville. The community's interest in the inquest seemed to be waning; it had dragged on and on and people with their own haul of problems had to focus on surviving day to day. This moment in court was largely for the local media—the Townsville reporters—who again sat in seats usually reserved for the jury.

Paula Morreau had taken up a scholarship at Harvard Law School, but before leaving she had, along with Andrew Boe, painstakingly prepared a tightly spaced, hundred-page document. For Boe, this fight was personal. He had defined himself by it. He'd fought it as if he were fighting for a man he'd known and loved, and in a way he was: his Aboriginal foster son had been in trouble with the police and had spent time in custody; this young man might have found himself in a situation like Cameron's that morning on Palm Island.

The case had driven Boe for nearly two years and cost him well over a quarter of a million dollars in forgone fees. Few could have afforded to pay him for the hours he'd put in. He was offended when he saw signs from other lawyers that to them this was just a job. Boe was exhausted and frustrated and emotional. He thought the deputy coroner would rule that Cameron's death was an accident, and all this effort would be for nothing.

Two days earlier, the local news had run stories about a professional white footballer accused of saying "fucking cunt" on the football field. Should he be suspended? Reprimanded? In Townsville the controversy created a minor furor. Now Boe addressed Deputy Coroner Christine Clements for the last time:

> Police arrest people for street offenses, language offenses, frequently. The statistics show that most of those people are poor people who live on the streets. Most of them happen to be Indigenous. There's an awful irony that the newspapers in the last forty-eight hours are dealing with what might happen to a football player using the very same words that Mulrunji was arrested for. The Palm Island community cannot understand why it is that the law is applied differently to them.

"A mustard seed can move a mountain," Elizabeth had told me as we walked to the courthouse. She was thinking of Jesus's telling the disciples, "If ye have faith as a grain of mustard seed, ye shall say unto this mountain, Remove hence to yonder place; and it shall remove." I wondered if her faith now felt that small—and this fight that great. To Andrew Boe, the mountain was the legal game. The inquest was a mountain of legal precedents and sections and codes, of closed-rank police and rival personalities along the bar table, of one-upmanship, adrenaline, and ego.

At a coroner's inquest, unlike in most court situations, members of the deceased's family have a statutory right to voice their distress. It's part of the fact-finding. Elizabeth had planned to speak but after

Eric's death chose not to. Tracy Twaddle now walked to the witness box, her eyes cast down. With bobbed curls and no makeup, she had the same fine features as the Doomadgee women. Her large body was hunched in old clothes—widow's black with a print of white flowers. The year before, she'd gone to hospital with pneumonia after sleeping at night on Cameron's grave. A teacher's aide, she'd found it hard returning to work after his death and was now unemployed. In her living room the walls were covered in photos of Cameron. Tracy often sat there playing solitaire. She had wondered if she wanted to continue living.

"Can I sit down?" she asked the deputy coroner, keeping her eyes low.

"Yes. Please," Clements answered.

In a soft voice, Tracy read out a statement she had written. She was articulate but she said her piece modestly and without a hint of guile:

> I met Cameron, Mulrunji, in 1994 and we lived together soon after that. We had a simple but happy life together. He was unselfish, and he was caring, and he tried to do the right thing by the people. He'd help anybody. He didn't—he didn't care what color they were. He wasn't mean. He was always caring. He was always there for me and his Mum and his family.
>
> And Cameron was always joking and ready for a laugh, you know, he always lifted our spirits. I think he saw the good and right in life. And he never sat around and brooded over things. And in a way he was an inspiration to me, because I used to watch him and, you know, think gee, he knew how to enjoy his life. He was content. It was a simple life and happy.
>
> Cameron was a hunter and he was proud to carry on that tradition. He was a proud hunter. He was always proud that he could provide food for us: goat, possum, fish, and share it out amongst his family and friends.

Cameron was, you know, more or less in his prime when this happened to him—when he lost his life. He was still a young man, and he had a lot to look forward to. He was especially proud of his son, Eric—he meant the world to Cameron. He was a proud father, and to watch his son grow and to be there when Eric became a man was something Cameron always talked about, but that's never going to happen now.

Cameron wasn't violent or troublesome in the community. We had our little ups and downs. He wasn't a saint or anything, but he was a real and genuine person, and he was a good person. He was saying to me, you know, we've been together for a decade, I've made up my mind we're going to grow old together.

My life is on hold. I get frustrated because everything's dragging on slowly. I think about if we're ever going to get real justice for him. Everything is still up in the air.

Eric was even more in a state of anguish than I was and tragically, Eric killed himself just a couple of weeks ago. In spite of this, you know, I'll always try to be positive, because of Cameron. He's never far from my mind. That's all I can say.

People in the courtroom cried.

Everyone on the island described Cameron as happy-go-lucky, as the last person to look for a fight, as a peaceful man to whom they would never have imagined this happening. But it was hard to reconcile the picture of the Cameron who "saw the good and right in life" with the Cameron who drank methylated spirits, or with the man whose hospital records showed he had suffered knife wounds and alcoholic seizures. Tracy had delivered a eulogy, and eulogies smooth away sharp edges—but this also seemed to be a question of perspective, or of degree.

It was one of the problems of looking at the island from the outside. A few days after her partner's death, Tracy had told investigators that Cameron wasn't usually aggressive when he was drunk; he was more often silly, goofy. If there was a problem, she said, she would lock herself in the bathroom. This was ordinary life up and down every street. And for her, it was a good life, a happy one. From the outside, Palm Island often doesn't make sense. From the inside, perhaps it does.

Anthropologist Peter Sutton, who has for many years studied and lived with the Wik people of western Cape York, writes that in Indigenous communities, outsiders' "compassion fatigue" is matched only by locals' "tragedy tolerance." Palm Islanders are infuriated by people who criticize their island and the way they live. White people do all the same things in the suburbs, Elizabeth once complained. Another woman told me that whites in Townsville called her people niggers, adding with outrage, "But we try to live peacefully here, not like them negroes who always shooting each other."

That all this is contradictory is the one constant in the story. Cameron's grandfather's family, the Diamonds, who fled from the Northern Territory during Wild Time, came from a place called Nguyjburri. *Nguyjburr nguyjbul* translates as "meat that's gone rotten," and the area had a Rotting Meat Dreaming. The Dreamtime encompasses all the phenomena of the world, good and bad, the Dreamings that provide and the Dreamings that take away, the Dreamings of the Rainbow Serpent and the Catfish, but also of painful and unpleasant things. One can, for instance, have a Diarrhea Dreaming, or Cough, or Itchiness Dreaming, or a Dead Body Dreaming.

These Dreamings are many-layered, a metaphilosophy, their details only for the initiated. In the early 1960s, W. E. H. Stanner described the Aboriginal view of life as "a joyous thing with maggots at the centre." Decay is part of the world. And in the midst of what is rotten—the history of Palm Island, addiction, the hopelessness of early deaths—there is the ongoing human attempt to find joy.

Tracy Twaddle might have been romanticizing in her statement to the court, but she was still being genuine. She meant every word. In all this tragedy there was love. There is love on Palm Island. There is happiness on Palm Island. And contradiction is in the matter of being alive.

The Findings

WOULD ANYONE PAY for Cameron Doomadgee's death? Would anyone be held responsible? Finally, the morning of September 27, 2006, Queensland's deputy state coroner, Christine Clements, handed down her findings as four armed police officers stood outside the Townsville courtroom and another waited inside with a gun, pepper spray, and handcuffs—the full utility belt. The Doomadgee family was not feeling optimistic. Chris Hurley was nowhere to be seen.

Christine Clements had been Sphinx-like, but occasionally she would regard the male lawyers as a dismayed headmistress might regard foolish schoolboys trying to impress. Now she started reading from her thirty-nine pages of findings and, as she did so, dropped a series of grenades. She found that Senior Sergeant Hurley, "the ultimate figure of power and authority on Palm Island," had arrested Cameron Doomadgee on a public nuisance charge, the public being the senior sergeant, who said he had heard him swear. She found the arrest "completely unjustified." She also found: "Police Liaison Officer Bengaroo must surely have seen more than what he has told this court . . . His accounts vary to such an extent regarding factual matters that he must be considered unreliable." She felt "some sympathy" for Bengaroo, "powerless to exert influence on the unfolding tragedy," but noted "he was careful not to see or intervene in a situation where he knew he had no power to influence what happened."

She found that the senior officers who investigated the death—

Detective Inspector Warren Webber and Detective Inspector Mark Williams—had been "as willfully blind as Bengaroo chose to be." She found it was "unwise and inappropriate" for Detective Robinson to investigate Hurley, and for Hurley to pick up Robinson and the other investigators from the airstrip and socialize with them during the investigation. It was "a serious error of judgment" for the investigators to share a meal with Hurley at his home that evening. The investigation was "compromised" by Hurley having the chance to discuss the case with the other police witnesses. It was "reprehensible" that Detective Senior Sergeant Kitching had not passed on Roy Bramwell's allegation of assault to the pathologist at the time of the first autopsy.

The deputy coroner found that at least one of Cameron's cries for help as he lay dying must have been heard by Hurley, and that his response had been "callous and deficient." Then she turned to the cause of Cameron's death. Those present said her voice quavered.

Despite a steady demeanor in court, Senior Sergeant Hurley's explanation does not persuade me he was truthful in his account of what happened. I reject Senior Sergeant Hurley's account that he simply got up from the heavy fall through the doorway and went to assist the man who had just punched him and caused him to fall over. I find that he did respond with physical force against Mulrunji while Mulrunji was still on the floor.

I am satisfied, on the basis of Roy Bramwell's account of what he saw and heard, together with the immediately preceding sequence of events, that Senior Sergeant Hurley lost his temper and hit Mulrunji after falling to the floor.

I find that Senior Sergeant Hurley's repeated clear statements that he fell to the left hand side of Mulrunji are in fact what occurred.

I find that Senior Sergeant Hurley hit Mulrunji whilst he was on the floor a number of times in a direct response to himself having been hit in the jaw and then falling to the floor.

It is open on Mr. Bramwell's evidence that the force was applied to Mulrunji's body rather than his head. This is also consistent with the medical evidence of the injuries that caused Mulrunji's death. It is also most likely that it was at this time that Mulrunji suffered the injury to his right eye.

After this occurred, I find, there was no further resistance or indeed any speech or response from Mulrunji. I conclude that these actions of Senior Sergeant Hurley caused the fatal injuries.

The police lawyers shook their heads. The Doomadgees all burst into tears. "About time they realize we're people, too," Valmae told me on the phone the next day, her words ricocheting.

It was the first time in Australia's history a police officer had ever been found responsible for a death in custody. The deputy coroner did not have the power to lay charges, but she had written to Queensland's director of public prosecutions, Leanne Clare, recommending that her office consider charging the senior sergeant with manslaughter.

The police closed ranks immediately. Within hours, the president of the Queensland Police Union, Gary Wilkinson, had given a press conference in Brisbane. Tall, red-faced, and heavy in the gut, he appeared on the evening news, an old-school cop full of righteous outrage. The deputy coroner, he said, had "conducted a witch hunt from the start that's been designed to pander to the residents of Palm Island, rather than establishing the facts. Clearly she approached this inquest as a foregone conclusion despite the mountain of evidence in support of Chris Hurley that she deliberately overlooked."

An invitation subsequently appeared on the union's website:

Send you [*sic*] support to Chris Hurley—click here
All messages of support are appericated [*sic*] and will be
passed onto Senior Sergeant Hurley.
supportchris@qpu.asn.au

The next day, September 28, the Queensland police commissioner announced that Chris Hurley would not be suspended or stood down. He would be taken off operational duties and given a desk job. The state premier, Peter Beattie, backed the decision and added, "I regard our police service as one of the best in the world." He looked grave, harassed, nervous.

Beattie's government had to maintain public confidence in the police, but in supporting Hurley, the premier and police officials appeared to be saying that Doomadgee's unfortunate death was not unfortunate enough to ruin a young officer's career. And in that moment it seemed a screen was pulled back on something very ugly. "We're people, too," Valmae had told me and I'd been taken aback by her need to even say this, but now I wondered if she was right to point it out.

A little over a week later, Hurley put an end to the imbroglio by announcing that he'd decided "reluctantly" to stand down on full pay. Boe thought he did this on the advice of his lawyers, who wanted to keep their client off the front page.

They had no idea how many front pages Hurley was about to appear on. Two and a half months later, on December 14, Queensland's director of public prosecutions, Leanne Clare, appeared at a press conference. Impeccably made up and wearing a white suit, she announced that she would not be pressing charges against Senior Sergeant Hurley. "Mr. Doomadgee," she said, "died from internal injuries caused by a crushing force to the front of his abdomen. The evidence suggests that in this case, this could only be the result of a complicated fall . . . Mr. Doomadgee's death was a terrible accident."

Her decision caused outrage. Cape York Aboriginal leader and newspaper columnist Noel Pearson, well known for his impatience with Indigenous people who refused to take responsibility for the failings of their own communities, was especially blunt: "The last time the world was told equivalent nonsense about the death of a black man being an accident was when Steve Biko was bashed by the apartheid South African police and thrown out of a multi-storey building."

Tony Koch did not buy Leanne Clare's decision. He had never bought the story of the fall. The day after Clare's announcement, his *Australian* opinion piece began:

BLOODY DISGRACE: State's Worst Injustice

The question giving most discomfort to the Queensland Government following the violent cell death of Mulrunji Doomadgee two years ago is a simple one. If the scuffle in the watch house had ended with the police officer lying on the floor with four ribs broken and his liver torn in half—and it was the Aboriginal man who got up and walked away—would two years of investigation have found that the Aboriginal man would not face any charges?

On December 19, five days after Hurley's reprieve, the Melbourne *Age* ran a story on thirty-one-year-old Alyssa Norman, who ten days earlier had been sentenced to eighteen months' jail time for throwing a rock at a police officer during the Palm Island riot. The mother of four children, including one just eighteen months old, had pleaded guilty. Her original sentence, a twelve-month intensive corrective order to be served in the community, had been appealed by Queensland's attorney general as too lenient. She had no prior convictions, but in revising her sentence the state's chief justice, Paul de Jersey, took into account the police officers' victim impact statements, noting that their lives—and often, he claimed, "career paths"—had been "seriously disrupted."

On December 20, Premier Peter Beattie took the unprecedented step of going to Palm Island to explain the director of public prosecution's decision. The Doomadgee family refused to meet him. In newspaper photographs Beattie looks sour, beaten. The community faces him holding placards: PALM ISLAND WANTS JUSTICE FOR MULRUNJI. STATE SANCTIONED MURDER. When I spoke to Peter Beattie a year later, on December 17, 2007, he recalled the trip. "I can't say it was easy," he told me. Days like these were the low points of political life, he said, especially for someone who prided himself on his efforts to engage with Indigenous issues. And Tony Koch's articles, in particular, were preying on him.

Beattie could not instruct Clare, but he told me that he had hoped she would send her files to a director of public prosecutions in another state for review. He thought she'd made her decision in a "high-handed way without explaining it." Beattie, who is married to the daughter of an Anglican missionary from Pormpuraaw, said to me: "The test of your government, the strength of a democracy is shown in how you treat the weakest citizens, the most fragile people. The police cannot be above the law."

In Queensland the DPP shared the right to prosecute with the state attorney general, but attorneys general very rarely exercised it. On December 22, two days after Beattie's visit to Palm Island, Attorney General Kerry Shine asked for Leanne Clare's files, and next day he announced he would be seeking an independent review of the evidence.

Many senior lawyers believed such a review would undermine the DPP's independent prosecutorial discretion, that it amounted to a disgraceful political intervention in the legal system, and that Beattie and Shine had set a dangerous precedent. For those who took this view, Chris Hurley had had a suspended sentence for two years, with infringements to his liberty, constraints in the way he worked, and intense public scrutiny. But Leanne Clare had a history of controversial decisions, and just as many lawyers felt that as Doomadgee's death had primarily been investigated by the main suspect's friends,

Hurley's civil liberties had to be balanced with the disregard shown for Doomadgee's.

On New Year's Day, the attorney general appointed former New South Wales chief justice Sir Laurence Street to review the evidence. Sir Laurence was a southerner. His famous mother, Jessie Street, had been a key campaigner for Aboriginal rights. A senior Brisbane barrister, Peter Davis SC, was recruited to assist Street. Davis was cerebral and careful, the barrister other lawyers consulted if they needed to check a point of law. Street and Davis went to Palm Island twice to look around and to interview the protagonists. The Palm Islanders called the two men "sir" and "Boss Man."

Soon after their first visit, on January 15, Cameron's cell mate, Patrick Nugent, hanged himself. Police, I was told, had taken Patrick from a scene of domestic violence and driven him a distance away to cool off. His body was found somewhere between that place and his home. Local people threw rocks at the police officers who cut him down. Street and Davis called on the Nugent family to pay their respects.

After studying the transcript of the inquest, the two lawyers took issue with the deputy coroner's findings that Doomadgee had been fatally punched. Street and Davis thought it was more likely Hurley had kneed Doomadgee in the abdomen, a backroom police technique used to subdue difficult prisoners. They decided that neither Lloyd Bengaroo nor Roy Bramwell were reliable witnesses: no one knew what Bengaroo would say, and they believed the defense would destroy the drunken Bramwell. But even without their evidence, Street and Davis said, Hurley had a case to answer.

> The case against him is circumstantial. In interviews between investigating police and Senior Sergeant Hurley in the days following the death, Senior Sergeant Hurley denied falling upon Mulrunji and denied assaulting him. The interviews contain no explanation as to how Mulrunji while in the cus-

tody of Senior Sergeant Hurley was so seriously injured. A jury could well find that the only rational inference that can be drawn as to the fatal injury is that it was inflicted by Senior Sergeant Hurley deliberately kneeing Mulrunji in the upper right abdominal area immediately after the fall while Mulrunji was lying on the concrete floor.

On January 26, 2007, Australia Day, Attorney General Shine announced that he had taken advice from Street and Davis. "In light of Sir Laurence's opinion, and having given careful consideration to the matter myself, I have decided it is in the public interest that this matter should be resolved in court. Furthermore, Sir Laurence believes there is a reasonable prospect of conviction." Chris Hurley would be charged with assault and manslaughter—the first policeman in Australia ever to be charged over the death of a prisoner in custody. His trial would begin in mid-June, five months away. If convicted he could face ten years in jail.

Now that the Crown was prosecuting, Andrew Boe's role in proceedings finally ended. Neither he nor Peter Callaghan would have any official involvement with the trial. I had the sense that on some level Boe was relieved, not that he stopped agitating from the sidelines. He did not gladly suffer fools, or people who didn't share his passionate convictions, but he had been unfailing in his generosity, clever, incisive, and never less than tenacious. He'd gone for the police's throat and had not relaxed his grip. The case would never have gone to trial without him.

The day after Hurley was charged, Boe received this letter:

Dear Andrew,

I have been a QPS [Queensland Police Service officer] for over 20 years. I have just read the findings of Sir Laurence Street and recognise this as a huge achievement for all the Aboriginal people.

*Not all police are racists and liars—many are. I have
witnessed this for myself first hand.*

*It is time the community, the government and the QPS
executive saw for themselves that some QPS officers actually
support and respect the Aboriginal people. The public need to
know that not all police in the union support the hysterical
claims of the executive.*

Good luck—at least one police officer was on your side.

The Queensland Police Union had a new acting boss. Denis Fitzpatrick, the vice president until now, took over from the raging Gary
Wilkinson, who had been charged with contempt for his criticism of
the deputy coroner's findings. Fitzpatrick brought much the same
style to the job. After the Palm Island riot, he'd called for the rioters
to be charged with attempted murder. Now he said, "If they don't
want the police there, get them out. Let tribal law take over, let them
police their own communities."

The charging of Hurley had woken a flexing, thundering giant:
the union planned to march on Queensland's Parliament House,
and in early February began touring the state's northern cities—
Cairns, Rockhampton, Gladstone—holding rallies with the Queensland Police Service's 9,200 officers. Fitzpatrick threatened a strike—a
not-unprecedented action, but one with civic consequences that he
had almost certainly not considered.

To his legal team of Glen Cranny and Steve Zillman, Hurley now
added a big gun, Queen's Counsel Robert Mulholland. In his early
sixties, Mulholland was a senior criminal barrister who had made
his name in the late 1980s prosecuting Queensland's police commissioner, Sir Terence Lewis, on twenty-three counts of perjury, corruption, and forgery. Peter Davis, coauthor of the Street report, would
act as Crown prosecutor at the trial. Although he would produce no
eyewitness to manslaughter, he'd argue that the only reasonable
conclusion to be drawn from the facts was that by his actions Hurley had deliberately caused the death of Cameron Doomadgee.

Most of the police officers who were to give evidence at the trial refused to cooperate with the prosecution beforehand, and did so only after receiving written orders from the police commissioner threatening them with disciplinary action. Even then, they were accompanied to their depositions by as many as three police-union lawyers. A Crown lawyer described to me the lack of police cooperation: "When I took statements from police in preparing the case, I experienced resistance, interference, and in one case threats." As Robert Mulholland had once remarked in the wake of prosecuting Commissioner Lewis, "Police officers will at times, even generally honest police, turn a blind eye to the misconduct of their colleagues."

The Rally

FOR THE POLICE Union this was now war, and the war room was the palm-lined, twenty-million-dollar Brisbane Broncos Leagues Club. I followed a group of police officers through the club foyer past a lush tropical water feature with a bronze bucking horse, and walls covered with blown-up action shots of mighty men in maroon, white, and gold; men whose heads seemed to be fused with their necks as they rammed one another with elbows, knees, and shoulders, their faces contorted by the effort; while the whole building rang with the whirring and clanging of the poker machines in the gambling hall, Cauldron of Champions. Up a ramp walkway, a neon sign marked a pair of double doors: AUDITORIUM.

On February 1, 2007, five days after it was announced Hurley would be charged with manslaughter, this room was filled with two thousand police officers in blue uniform, all gathered to protest his treatment. They were mainly men, white men in tight clusters, insignia on their shoulders indicating rank. What was most striking was their height. Until the late 1980s, an officer had to be at least five foot ten. This was a room of tall men, big men with tans or sunburns and close-cut hair. And they looked athletic. The venue was not a random choice: the Brisbane Broncos' famous coach, Wayne Bennett, an ex-policeman, was for a long time the Police Academy's fitness instructor; he had been when Hurley did his training.

The air was close, clammy with sweat and testosterone. The officers held their hats, some using them as fans, and chatted and laughed. More police poured in and a speaker told the crowd to get in tighter. "I'm doing my part," said one policeman, nestling in close behind a giggling policewoman. Somewhere a baby was crying. We were in a pack. We could feel one another's animal warmth and sweat and breath—and it made me shiver.

One sergeant, himself six foot four, told me that the inquest had not considered all the evidence. He repeated the now common myth that Cameron Doomadgee had been hit by a car the night before his death. He also claimed that Andrew Boe had tried to become a cop but was knocked back, hence his relentless pursuit of Hurley. This sergeant was in his early fifties and ran a suburban police station. He spent his days, he said, going to people who had been beaten and raped, telling them there wasn't enough evidence to lay charges. "That's our life. Here's one of ours and suddenly the rules have changed . . . This is a witch hunt . . . We acknowledge that he could have, there's no two ways about it. I haven't heard one person say, 'Look, Chris is innocent,' no one's saying that. It's just the process hasn't followed (a) the evidence and (b) the normal conventions."

He went on: "Let's be philosophical—if for those ten thousand times [black drunks were arrested], 9,999 times it prevented further offenses being committed . . ." His voice trailed off. The man was a fundamentalist Christian. He saw his role as akin to the Good Samaritan's. "I've never lost my patience. I believe it's my God keeping me that way."

It was hard to know whether the Police Union truly saw Hurley as an innocent man trapped in a legal maze—Kafka in the tropics— or their stance reflected the old-style police belief that rough justice in tough conditions was justifiable.

The stage at the front of the auditorium had black velvet drapes and theater spotlights with tinted gels. A moral drama, a passion play was about to begin. Ross Musgrove, the dapper media officer for the Police Union, came to the microphone. Cameras flashed; reporters were sitting at the front.

"As you know, this is the third of the mass meetings held by the union around the state," Musgrove announced. "This is just incredible. Well done. I mean it, really well done, thanks for turning up. It's very important that we're all here to send a message to the Beattie government that we're not happy about what's goin' on, and we want some changes made! And we want some changes made now!"

The hall filled with a radio advertisement, funded by the union, that was about to hit all the commercial radio stations on high rotation. The tagline was "Mr. Beattie, our police deserve justice too!"

A few days earlier, 450 officers had gathered at a Townsville rally in support of Hurley. Detective Sergeant Darren Robinson, who had warned the Crime and Misconduct Commission investigators against "bias-ism," urged the crowd to move a motion against "blatant political interference in the case" and for "the government to respect the separation of powers." In a few days' time, Hurley's older brother, Senior Sergeant Tony Hurley, would address another five hundred police on the Sunshine Coast. The union was calling for twenty-four-hour surveillance in all watch houses, a recommendation, as Denis Fitzpatrick pointed out, of the 1991 Royal Commission into Aboriginal Deaths in Custody that had never been implemented.

Denis Fitzpatrick now arrived on the Broncos' stage. In his suit and police-union tie and glasses, he looked like a schoolboy with an aged face. He had a tough-guy swagger and a dry, outraged manner. Fitzpatrick had spent all but a few months of his twenty-four years as a police officer in the wilds of Far North Queensland. He called his fellow officers "brothers and sisters." Some were. A lot of recruits follow their family members into the force, as Hurley had. And they often marry fellow officers. Cops know what it's like for other cops; they can sympathize, understand, offer protection. They watch one another's backs.

Some of the assembled officers had worked with Chris Hurley in Cape York or the Gulf country or Surfers Paradise. If you were a cop and didn't know Hurley personally, there was a good chance one of your relatives did. There was a good chance one of your family had gone to school with the Hurleys, or gone to the same church, or played rugby on the same team.

"This roll-up is spectacular! Thank you for your attendance!"
called Fitzpatrick. "I particularly also want to thank our minister,
Judy Spence, who's made the time to come and listen to our con-
cerns today." Spence, Queensland's elegant police minister, was
police royalty: the daughter of a cop and the great-niece of Frank
Bischoff, another disgraced police commissioner. Known as the Bag-
man for his corruption, Bischoff had ended up in a psychiatric asylum. Because the minister steadfastly supported the Police Union,
Elizabeth Doomadgee had been praying for her to be purged of evil.

Fitzpatrick stood staring at the crowd, microphone in hand:

Right across this state, Queensland, police officers are *disgusted* with the unfair treatment of Chris Hurley. Chris is
being singled out for special treatment by the government
in this state. He is being treated differently from any other
Queenslander in our history. Legal conventions and centuries of established law are being cast aside so that Chris
Hurley can be charged. All of us in this room know only too
well that what happened to Chris Hurley could happen to
any one of us!

Members, Queensland taxis have better video surveillance
currently in them than our watch houses, that's the truth . . .
Well, maybe then, Premier, we should keep our prisoners in
the back of cabs!

The applause was thunderous. This felt like a revivalist meeting. Just
as Cameron Doomadgee had become a martyr for Aboriginal Australia, Chris Hurley was now a martyr for anyone who felt blacks got
too much from the system. Hurley was Gulliver, suddenly gigantic
and tied to the ground, with all "the noisy minorities," as Fitzpatrick
put it—the civil libertarians, the bleeding hearts, the blackfellas—
running riot around him. This was no longer about justice in the
abstract, or the law according to governments and courts—the purpose of this meeting was to establish that the police were the vic-

tims. It was they who suffered the injustice of the law, they who suffered the manifestations of dysfunction, violence, and addiction. Measured against two hundred years of Aborigines' dispossession and abuse, the idea is fantastic, but no one in that hall was thinking about historical relativities. This was real-life über-Australia up against insipid, politically correct, bullshit Australia. It was North against South. It was the cops, huddled close together, against those besieging them.

Fitzpatrick's skin had begun to shine in the heat of the stage lights. "Members!" he called. "I'm proud to report we have the majority, the vast majority of community support . . . Our phones haven't stopped ringing. E-mails are flooding into the union office, and letters containing donations of support for Chris and his family . . . In fact, yesterday, and I kid you not, yesterday, a former Queensland police officer donated and pledged," he slowed down for emphasis, "*fifty thousand dollars* for Chris's legal expenses!"

There was the caterwauling whistling you hear at concerts. These people clapped with strength. They had strong arms, strong hands. They put their bodies into their clapping. Fitzpatrick's tribe—underpaid and undervalued, perhaps—was a far more intact, more homogeneous, more powerful, and more privileged tribe than Cameron's. And it was far more able to defend one of its members.

"The clear message for you, Mr. Beattie, is the silent majority are about to get noisy. If we do need to march on Parliament, members, I predict Queenslanders in their thousands will come out and support us. They will welcome us!"

Fitzpatrick now changed his tone: "There's been an incredible amount of pain, angst, and sorrow caused to all parties involved in the death of Cameron Doomadgee over the last two years. If there had been video surveillance at the watch house entrance on Palm Island . . . there would have been an indisputable record that could have avoided all that pain." He had a point, of course—and there could hardly be a more opportune time to make it.

Trevor Pope from Traffic Branch stood to read the first motion:

"The motion is that this meeting support Senior Sergeant Chris Hurley for any form of legal assistance to defend the charge of manslaughter and any other charge that may arise."

Fitzpatrick said, "I will now put that to the membership. Those in favor."

"*Aye!*" the crowd roared, raising their hands.

"I'd say that's carried unanimously," Fitzpatrick said, deadpan.

The second motion was raised by Sergeant Bill Earnshaw from the Drug and Alcohol Unit. "Might need your assistance after this," Fitzpatick quipped, to much laughter, as the sergeant made his way to the stage.

"Motion number two," Earnshaw read, "that this meeting support the union's stance for the immediate upgrade of watch houses and staffing in Queensland so that the recommendations of black deaths in custody [the 1991 Royal Commission] are met."

Again the motion was carried. When the crowd voted they didn't put their arms straight up, but held them out at a forty-five-degree angle. It was surreal.

"This third motion," announced Senior Constable Mick Carmody of General Duties, "is that this meeting endorse the executive to organize a mass meeting and march on Parliament!"

"Again, all in favor!" Fitzpatrick called.

"*Aye!*"

"And who'll turn up and march!" he called again.

"*Aye!*"

"And who won't stop marching!"

"*Aye!*"

The applause was tidal. All this was for Chris Hurley. His presence hovered over the proceedings though he was nowhere to be seen. Nowhere and everywhere. Around me, the man I'd watched at the inquest—tall, dressed in righteous blue—was multiplying. I was surrounded by him.

Civilians and the media were then asked to leave. I walked back through the Broncos complex and thought of Eric Doomadgee, who loved this team so devotedly that his family had buried him with maroon, yellow, and white flowers on his coffin.

Outside the building, I waited until the police left the auditorium, their shirts doused with sweat. Three protesters also waited, one holding a sign saying NO MORE DEATHS IN CUSTODY. The other two had a painted sheet: POLICE SERVICE NOT FORCE. They were drowned by a wave of blue uniforms. The car park being full, many cops had parked illegally. While their colleagues stopped traffic on a busy road nearby, they swiftly made their getaways. Then the sky opened up. It rained hard and fast and the lower ranks got caught in the downpour.

I wondered how many of these officers were aware that they couldn't in fact march in protest, that such action was regarded by the union's own lawyers as being in contempt of court, and might affect Hurley's receiving a fair trial. Behind the scenes, the union was working on another campaign. Before the week was out, the *Gold Coast Bulletin*'s cover showed a policewoman raising her clenched fist to display a navy blue wristband. A phalanx of officers surrounded her, all in the same pose, all with the same wristbands, which were stamped with Hurley's police registration number, 6747. "They are a silent protest," explained Denis Fitzpatrick in the article, "a sign of solidarity plus a fund-raiser for Senior Sergeant Hurley's legal costs." Soon Queensland police were selling blue wristbands on the streets and in community newspapers and advertising them on regional television news.

The wristbands were supposed to be available for $5 at most police stations, but at Townsville Police Headquarters, a doughy young constable manning the desk told me that five thousand had sold out before they reached the north. "We get everything last in Townsville," he complained. He intended to buy one from the next batch, for the good cause, but he'd never wear it. It was too much like a bracelet. He thought he might put it on the gearshift of his car.

As you go farther north, the constable told me, you understand the problem of Aborigines better. It was easy down south, where you don't see many blackfellas, but up here it was different. Over the border, he said, police in the Northern Territory were buying the wristbands too.

I WAS TRAVELING north to Laura to see the tall spirits. I flew to Cairns then drove until the red-dirt road was lined with old mango trees. Laura's shopkeeper sat outside her store to keep cool. Otherwise the tiny town seemed deserted, asleep in the sun, and yet like a Greek village among ancient ruins, Laura was surrounded by drama. In rock art galleries on cave and cliff faces were paintings of the *quinkans,* the tall spirits, who were said to inhabit the surrounding hills.

I hired a guide to show me around and, when I told him I was following the Palm Island case, he said he knew a gallery I'd find interesting. We drove away from Laura and, near a creek, turned and headed straight into bushland. "Trees!" he exclaimed, with an aftertaste of irritation, having run down another sapling. We parked and started walking across a river, then uphill through long grass with dartlike seeds until we came on walking tracks that led us to the gallery. On a cave wall stretched a sorcery painting from the end of the nineteenth century: two white policemen, horizontal, rifles by their sides. A snake stretched farther along the wall, biting one of the men's feet. Beyond the snake were the figures of two naked black men with round white eyes. They too had rifles. The guide believed these were self-portraits of the men who'd painted the police; that they had painted themselves with guns so they might by magic obtain them. Drawn as if from the core of the country's history, this was a drama of revenge.

FOUR

The Trial

CHRIS HURLEY HAD to bow his head to fit through the doorway of the Townsville courtroom. In a dark-gray pinstriped suit, he looked like a man from another era, a handsome 1940s figure with a granite face. It was as if he were made of material too hard to sculpt very deeply, leaving a bullish neck, broad nostrils, a big brow over mournful dark eyes, and a high forehead accentuated by oiled hair parted just off center. He sat in the polished-timber dock, the giant who'd been brought to the fair.

The courtroom was a grand wooden box with ultramarine carpet, high ceilings, and a wall of small square windows. A relief featuring a British lion and unicorn hung above Supreme Court Judge Peter Dutney, who was in white-collared red robes. It was Tuesday, June 12, 2007. Outside on the pavement, Aboriginal dancers wearing body paint and laplaps had performed with clap sticks and bouquets of gum leaves.

"Christopher James Hurley," read the judge's clerk, "you are charged that on the 19th day of November 2004 at Palm Island in the state of Queensland you unlawfully assaulted and unlawfully killed Cameron Francis Doomadgee. Christopher James Hurley, how do you plead? Guilty or not guilty?"

"Not guilty, Your Honor."

The security was fit for a visiting head of state. Extra court guards stood outside next to uniformed police. Inside, plainclothes officers sat in each corner, handcuffs visible under their jackets. The first rows of reserved seats were marked DEFENDANT'S FAMILY AND

SUPPORTERS. Sitting here were Hurley's two brothers—olive-skinned men of similar bulk but more average height—his kind-looking mother, and his girlfriend, a petite, curvaceous brunette with pale blue eyes, wearing gold earrings, bracelets, rings, and a tiny crucifix around her neck. Interspersed among the family were the police chaplain, a police psychologist, and the Police Union officials, including Gary Wilkinson and Denis Fitzpatrick. When the officials crossed their arms they revealed their blue wristbands. As stony-faced as men at a funeral, they wore matching ties and shiny shoes and had the tight swagger of those who carry guns.

In a high-tiered gallery, as if floating above the court, sat the Doomadgee family. A Justice Department employee had warned me not to go upstairs if I was scared of heights. The gallery was vertiginous, and the air close with body odor. "It's easier if you're drunk," a plainclothes officer said, gesturing to Cameron's sister Claudelle, who lived in a local park. She sat with Elizabeth, Jane, Valmae, and their brother, Lloyd, who had traveled from Doomadgee. Tracy Twaddle had woken and not been able to face coming.

Elizabeth looked wary and tired and thin. It was eleven months since Eric's death, and her hair had started graying in streaks around her forehead. She and her siblings wore yellow wristbands that a supporter had produced, stamped MULRUNJI 19–11–04 JUSTICE NOW!

From the gallery, the family looked down on the tops of the jurors' heads—four men and eight women, all white and mostly middle-aged. They looked down on the lawyers. They looked down on Chris Hurley, grave and shifting in the dock—the tall man captive in his waist-high pen.

The two legal teams were lined up along the bar table. The defense comprised Hurley's original lawyers, Glen Cranny and Steve Zillman, plus the steely old-school barrister Robert Mulholland QC. The Crown prosecutor, Peter Davis SC, was assisted by barristers David Kent and Jonathan Horton. Twenty journalists from around the country were gathered in a second courtroom down the hallway, where the inquest had been held. The trial was being shown on closed-circuit television and they could move around, type, field calls. I chose to stay in the first courtroom.

In his late forties, Peter Davis was tall too, but stooped, pale, and thin, with glasses and fair, bowl-cut hair. A self-confessed "cold fish," Davis prided himself on remaining emotionally aloof from his work. But this time he had not succeeded. He was shocked by the conditions on Palm Island, a slum on a lush tropical island, and the case had gotten under his skin. In a soft voice, he began:

> The story is this—Mr. Doomadgee, we know, was a resident of Palm Island. On the 19th of November 2004 he was on the island and he was walking down a street called Dee Street, and the evidence will tell you that Mr. Doomadgee was drunk. The accused arrived in the police van in Dee Street. The accused then proceeded to arrest Mr. Doomadgee. The van was then driven to the police station. Mr. Doomadgee struck the accused. A short time later, the Crown say, the accused then struck Mr. Doomadgee. Now that assault is count one of the indictment.
>
> Mr. Doomadgee, though, continued to resist and the pair of them then struggled. As they got toward the door of the police station there's a step. It seems likely they tripped on the step and fell into the police station.
>
> The Crown says that the accused man then killed Mr. Doomadgee and he did that by administering some force, most probably with his knee, but with such force as to cause Mr. Doomadgee's liver to be virtually cleaved in two across his spine. . .

Davis projected onto a screen a CAT scan showing the profile of someone with a healthy liver. On the black image, skin and viscera were a light gray, framed by the spine—a curving white exclamation mark. Cameron's abdomen, Davis told the court, had been squeezed so hard his liver was pushed back against the spine, which had almost torn it in two. He would "have died ten minutes after receiving such an injury."

Davis then played a segment of the video reenactment Hurley had made with his investigators the day after the death. The senior sergeant stood in the dingy police station, his head nearly touching the ceiling, and claimed he fell next to Cameron Doomadgee on the linoleum floor.

Hurley sat fidgeting. He straightened the fabric of his trousers over his thighs, pulled at his cuffs, adjusted the knot of his tie. He looked like a man unused to wearing a suit, one brought to heel. His mouth had become a line. He'd been to court countless times, but always on the other side of the dock, always for someone else's trauma and mess. Now he was the accused, and it was in his hands that the stress showed. He knitted them. He rubbed one hand with the thumb of the other. He balled his hands into fists, tight fists, and sat bracing them on his knees, as if asking the court to guess which one held the key, the truth.

Throughout Davis's opening address, the Police Union's president, Gary Wilkinson, played with his watch, which emitted a sharp beeping. He was chaperoning Hurley's mother. Wilkinson knew what it was to have trouble with the law. In the late 1980s, he was found to have given false evidence at an inquiry into a stolen-car scam involving police. He had also been charged with attempting to obtain a five-thousand-dollar bribe, but at trial was found not guilty. *Mbeep. Mbeep. Mbeep.* As he sat fiddling with his watch, Gary Wilkinson was about to face a Crime and Misconduct Commission investigation for allegedly selling a Police Union car to his wife at a discount of several thousand dollars.

Only when the defense barrister stood did Wilkinson place the watch back on his wrist, next to the blue wristband.

No-nonsense Robert Mulholland QC gave the defense's story: Senior Sergeant Hurley had fallen on top of Cameron Doomadgee. Hurley was a big, heavy man—253 pounds to Cameron's 163. Subsequent traumatic events had "eroded" the senior sergeant's memory, hence his initial claims that he and Doomadgee had fallen side by side.

Mulholland, cultivating a practical, sensible demeanor, leaned forward, elbows on his lectern. His tone was "Let's not get carried away." By the end of the trial, he assured the jury and everyone else assembled in the courtroom, we would have no doubts about his client's innocence. But he added a cautionary note: "When you listen to the evidence, members of the jury, you're not expected to throw your common sense out the window. You came here with your common sense and experience of the world, and we would say to you, please use it when you listen to the evidence."

I looked at the jury: a platinum blond with a double chin chewed gum and never stopped writing in her court-issued notebook; two senior men, with short-back-and-sides hair and the familiar scars of old sunburn, wore carefully pressed short-sleeved shirts in tropical tones of mango and papaya. In Townsville, it is safe to say, the jurors did have a rather particular experience of the world. Among other things, with the highest number of defense personnel in Australia, it's a promilitary town. It's also a town with considerable racial tension.

During June and July 2006, the Sydney law firm defending Lex Wotton had commissioned a market research firm to conduct a poll establishing a statistical profile of the Townsville community. The results helped them get his trial moved to Brisbane. More than four hundred people were randomly telephoned and asked about their perceptions of Aborigines and Torres Strait Islanders in northern Queensland. They were told there were no right or wrong answers: "We are interested only in what you actually think." Under "negative-themed comments" were listed the following responses:

- Ha ha—there are no wrong answers?! Well something needs to be done—they have no respect, they want everything for nothing and most of them are better off than me.

- In my opinion they are a protected species. You can't touch them. You can't kick them.
- I have a pretty low opinion of them. I know there must be some good ones—but I have only come across the scumbags.
- I'm tired of people being beat up due to being white.
- They use the parks and bushes as public toilets.
- They drink too much and they smell.
- They are mongrel dogs.
- Pass. I don't have an opinion except to shoot them all.

The "negative-themed comments" accounted for 42.7 percent of all responses; 43 percent were "unsure," "neutral," or "ambiguous." The remaining 13.3 percent were deemed "positive":

- They are all right.
- Pretty good footy players.
- They are just normal.
- They have a right to be here.

When those surveyed were asked what they thought of Palm Islanders, 63.7 percent of the comments made were "negative-themed":

- My father-in-law works there and says it is like a dump— the people are pigs.
- The same story—they get too much.
- Leave them on the island.
- Glad they are over there.
- It's disgraceful that they are given an island and can trash it the way they have.

Tony Mooney, Townsville's mayor, did not dispute the poll's findings: "Townsville is no different to any other community and if you did that survey around the suburbs of Cronulla or Redfern, you'd find the same outcome." (In 1989, then Deputy Mayor Mooney allegedly drove away after his car hit an Aboriginal pedestrian. A witness chased him down but the police, it is further alleged, let him go without even a breath test.)

The jury for Chris Hurley's trial was drawn from a population that, racist or not, saw every day the ugly and pathetic signs of chronic dysfunction, dependence, and despair. According to the poll, Townsville's white population was at best indifferent to Aborigines, but more commonly angry and contemptuous. When people live beyond the pale it is hard to see in them anything of ourselves. It is likely that those jury members *wanted* their streets vigilantly policed; they wanted to be kept safe from "mongrel dogs." Peter Davis had had the opportunity to indict Hurley seven hundred miles south in Brisbane, to set the trial in a more neutral environment. Andrew Boe had told him he should. But Davis told me after the trial he felt it smacked of game playing and took too cynical a view of Townsville jurors.

THE PROSECUTION'S FIRST group of witnesses was the Palm Island residents who had seen Cameron Doomadgee being arrested and taken into custody. Peter Davis wanted to prove that Cameron had not done much "to deserve being arrested" and that Hurley's strong-arming him into the van was "the spark" that ignited the fatal events. But in the trial's opening days, these witnesses, who had all previously testified at the inquest, did not do the prosecution's case any favors.

Penny Sibley, who claimed Hurley had punched Cameron outside the police station, was gravely ill with a weak heart and diabetes. The prosecution lawyers collected her from the hospital and made sure she had the right medication while she waited to testify. As she gave evidence she shook as if in a storm, her whole body shivering. In each hand she held a white washcloth to wipe away sweat or tears. On her wrist was a plastic hospital ID band. Looking

down, she told the court, very softly, that she'd been standing outside the police station when she saw Cameron, drunk and swearing,
hit Senior Sergeant Hurley. Hurley, she said, then gave him a quick,
hard jab to the ribs. She told the jury she had started crying, worried for Cameron. She sounded vague, hesitant.

Next to appear was Doomadgee's friend Gerald Kidner, who had
been walking with Cameron the morning he was arrested. In his
oversize gray down jacket and dirty high-top sneakers, Kidner
looked as if he'd just stepped in from the Perfume Gardens opposite
the courthouse, where blackfellas sat in the pagoda among the tropical plants, drinking and hassling for money. Kidner was overwhelmed and sat very still in the witness box, speaking in short
sentences as if unable to make longer connections. He told the court
he and Cameron were drinking together at his house, with Verna, his
partner. The three of them set off down Dee Street, where Cameron
"keep singing the song, 'Who Let the Dogs Out' . . . Chris pull up and
locked him up then."

Steve Zillman asked Gerald about the day before the death. Did
he remember going to the mainland in a dinghy to get cheap cask
wine and beer with Verna, Cameron Doomadgee, and Patrick
Nugent? Gerald said he'd been too drunk to remember. But he did
recall waking the next morning—the morning Cameron died—and
seeing his friend watching a kung fu movie, *Enter the Dragon*.

Zillman: "And Cameron was then drinking from a cask?"
Kidner: "Yeah."
Zillman: "That was Moselle?"
Kidner: "Yeah."
Zillman: "And he also had some goom, didn't he?"
Kidner: "Yeah, methylated spirits."
Zillman: "That's right. Just for the record, *g-o-o-m*, goom?"
Kidner: "Yeah."
Zillman: "Metho and water?"
Kidner: "Yeah."
Zillman: "And you had a bit of a drink yourself, too, didn't you?"

Kidner: "Yeah, there was only a bit was in it."

Gerald's partner, Verna Snyder, took the stand next, wearing shorts and a filthy jacket of balloon material that hid her emaciated frame. She had been walking with the men when Cameron was arrested. At the inquest in February 2005, she had broken down in the middle of her testimony and the coroner had allowed her to stand down. Now she spoke with her hand over her mouth, covering her face as if she'd just been hit. She, too, was shaking from what might have been DTs. When Zillman got to her, it was hopeless. Asked how much Cameron had drunk, she shook, thinking she was the one on trial: "No. I don't drink. Never!"

Then came Gladys Nugent, big and shy, with a double chin, her hair tied back. As one of the victims of Roy Bramwell's assault, she had the misfortune of being the reason Chris Hurley was in Dee Street in the first place. Gladys told Peter Davis that Hurley had taken her to Bramwell's house to get her medication. While he was there, her nephew Patrick started abusing him and was locked up. Then Cameron came past. She didn't see him do anything but he was locked up, too. Both men were now dead.

Steve Zillman rose. His melodious voice issued from a tight mouth, which he pursed when asking certain questions. "How much did you drink, Ms. Nugent?"

Gladys Nugent: "I drank all night."

Zillman: "You drank—well, you started at about eleven, half past eleven in the morning on the Thursday. Do you agree with that?"

Nugent: "Yeah."

Zillman: "And you drank . . . ?"

Nugent: "All night."

Zillman: ". . . Through the rest of the morning, all through the afternoon, and all through into the night?"

Nugent: "Yeah."

She sat perfectly still. Zillman stood with his hands on his hips, a small gut protruding from his thin frame. He seemed to eke her hopeless story out of her, extracting it with relish. Having been in the backseat of the police van when Doomadgee was arrested, she did not see the actual arrest, admitting, "I don't remember anything much." Zillman, with what looked very like a leer, still suggested she was unreliable.

Zillman: "Tell me, were you affected by the alcohol that you'd had? You'd had a fair bit if you'd started drinking at 11:30 in the morning the day before?"

Nugent: "Well, when I got outside, it was a hard hit and I started sobering up a bit."

Zillman: "When you got hit?"

Nugent: "Yeah, I got hit. I got knocked down, kicked . . ."

Zillman: "Mmm?"

Nugent: "Hit by chair."

Zillman: "Kicked and what, sorry?"

Nugent: "Hit with a chair."

Zillman: "With a chair?"

Nugent: "Yeah."

Zillman: "Yes, that sobered you up a bit?"

Nugent: "Yeah."

Gladys didn't flinch as he went at her. She answered without emotion, looking back at him. She'd been beaten before and would be again. Hunched slightly in her faded clothes, rolls of fat on her back, Gladys Nugent stood for everything white Australia doesn't want to know about black Australia. She was alcoholic and diabetic, and she had heart trouble. She told the court about drinking all day and night, being bashed, binging on methylated spirits; about her partner, Roy, being in jail; about her nephew Patrick sniffing petrol and hanging himself. She had a kind of plain, obstinate dignity. And fleetingly it was not clear who was more abject here—Gladys or the lawyer paid to hector her.

Chris Hurley, statuesque in his good suit, looked like a banker watching a play about lives in some far-flung ghetto. But at the end of the first day, as he was whisked into a waiting car, a barefoot black drunk stood on the side of the road yelling, "You're a killer! You're a killer! Who let the dogs out?"

That evening I ran into Aunty Betty sitting at a bus stop with her pillow and a plastic bag of clothes. I had last seen her fishing for catfish by the river outside Doomadgee. Now she was traveling to a funeral. Borrowing a pen, she drew a picture for me on her hand to explain how Hurley had definitely not fallen on Cameron. She stared at her skin, satisfied this proved the matter conclusively.

THE NEXT MORNING—and on every one of the seven mornings of the trial—Aboriginal activist, nurse, and lecturer Gracelyn Smallwood, whose grandfather and father had been sent to Palm Island, organized a small demonstration on the footpath outside the courthouse. Witty, feisty, and one of nineteen children, Smallwood had done her homework on a typewriter her brothers pulled off a rubbish heap. It had no ribbon: she would type indentations onto a sheet of paper and then fill them in with a pencil. When she began her nursing training in northern Queensland, black workers in the state's health department had to tie string around their coffee cups so their white colleagues did not drink from them by mistake. In 2000 Gracelyn intervened when she saw police hassling an Aboriginal youth. She was arrested and taken to a watch house, where she was strip-searched and had police dogs set on her. When the police saw her identification, showing her to be a professor, they asked whose wallet she'd stolen.

Outside the courthouse, Gracelyn wore a T-shirt emblazoned STOP BLACK DEATHS IN CUSTODY. Surrounded by a scraggly group of twenty or so supporters, she made a spirited speech appealing to mothers—white and black—for their help. Then three Aboriginal dancers in body paint and with feathers in their hair danced, calling on the Ancestral Spirits for backing.

The Doomadgee family stood holding hands with Gracelyn and the other supporters. Among them was a South African woman in full traditional dress: bright orange robes, a stiff, bright orange hat, ropes of beads. She held hands with Claudelle Doomadgee, who looked like she'd dressed from a Salvation Army bin, wearing a huge checked coat over a floral dress over track pants, completed by a beanie in Aboriginal colors.

We were all now sorted into our respective castes—blackfella, copper, lawyer, journalist. A murmur went around the watching media pack that the South African woman, a friend of Gracelyn's, was a distant relation of Steve Biko.

"Who's Steve Biko?" a blond newsreader asked me. She was the girlfriend of one of the cops at the riot.

After the demonstration Elizabeth told me: "They trying to make out Cameron a short man." She seemed offended by the suggestion that her brother was felled by Hurley's height.

Lloyd Doomadgee suggested he could stand up in the courtroom and show everyone how tall he was. He reckoned he was the same height as his brother, and Lloyd was over six foot—taller still in his black Akubra hat. "They'd get a surprise," he said. He'd brought along his young children, who couldn't stop staring at Townsville's buildings, all of eight stories high; after Doomadgee, these were skyscrapers.

In the courtroom, on day two of the trial, the prosecution called the pathologist who conducted Cameron's first autopsy, Dr. Guy Lampe. Lampe had been a pathologist since 2001. Tanned, with his dark hair parted at the side, he wore a gray suit, light blue shirt, navy tie. His manner, earnest and oddly genial, was the same as it had been two years earlier when he testified at the inquest. Suddenly, eyes crinkling, he would burst into awkward mirth. He might have been discussing his favorite restaurant, rather than what he'd found on November 23, 2004, when he cut Cameron open.

This man with a black eye had died not of a head injury, but from massive internal injuries, Dr. Lampe testified. "His liver was ruptured and there was a hole in the portal vein that supplies blood to the liver, and that had led to a considerable amount of bleeding into his stomach cavity." Lampe explained that without enough blood circulating to his vital organs, Cameron would quickly have died. His blood-alcohol level was at least five times the legal driving limit, but, Lampe revealed, his liver was not cirrhotic. It was no more vulnerable to injury than anyone else's.

Dr. Lampe, along with the two doctors Davis called after him, claimed that Cameron must have been close to flat on his back, pressed hard against the police station floor. The fatal force was applied to his front. Since his liver had all but cleaved in two, it must have been pushed down violently against his spine. The injury required some kind of projection and a "squeezing mechanism." Hurley's knee, being round and smooth, wouldn't leave external markings and was therefore a likely candidate.

Dr. Lampe noted that he didn't encounter such injuries very often:

> In fact the times that we see it, it's usually involved with high speed motor vehicle trauma, motorbike accidents, some air-craft injuries . . . You know, high speed trauma, or falls from heights, or people having sporting injuries—so falls from horses, injuries coming down ski slopes and hitting trees, things like that.

But the pathologist had never seen a liver split "this big with a rupture of a portal vein." Usually, he said, a portal-vein wound would be caused by a stab or gunshot.

Lampe said he had no way of distinguishing whether Cameron's injuries were the result of an assault or of a fall in which Hurley's knee happened to land in his prisoner's abdomen. But this didn't stop his broadcasting his view in court. He had concurred with the police at the time of the autopsy (while unaware of the assault allegations against Hurley) that the injuries were caused by a fall, an opinion he now repeated: it was, he said, "his best guess" that the fatal injuries had been sustained in a fall, during which, "I suspect . . . one of Senior Sergeant Hurley's knees has contacted Mr. Doomadgee's abdomen."

Cameron's black eye and bruised jaw could have been due to them "sort of banging onto things."

In an adjournment, Valmae told me she was feeling sharp pains herself, listening to the doctor. "Every time he speak like getting wind knocked out of me. Just broke down outside. Them talking about his insides." Tracy Twaddle, next to her, was silent. She had forced herself to make it to the courthouse. Valmae asked me to wait for them at the end of each day to explain what was happening.

It had been the announcement of Dr. Lampe's initial findings on November 26, 2004, that started the Palm Island riot. The state coroner had then called in Dr. David Ranson, an English pathologist based in Melbourne, to review those findings. Bearded, bespectacled Ranson was the next witness. He had an extra fourteen years' experience on Lampe, in Australia and overseas. He had a law degree; he had various diplomas and fellowships. When he reeled off these qualifications in court in his clipped, serious voice, I noticed the police chaplain and the police psychologist both laughing.

"Ever heard of FIGJAM?" the chaplain asked me later, explaining what they had found so funny. He was referring to the acronym for "Fuck I'm good, just ask me."

Dr. Ranson told the court about the further bruising he'd discovered on Cameron during the second autopsy on November 30, 2004, which Dr. Lampe had also attended. (Earlier in court, Lampe had admitted he hadn't comprehensively searched for bruising in the first autopsy: "I was a bit pressed for time.") Ranson found bruises on Cameron's right eye and eyelid, his forehead, the back of his head, the upper part of his back, along the right side of his jaw, and on his right and left hands. This pathologist was not prepared to speculate as to how any of the injuries were sustained. They could theoretically have been caused by a deliberate assault or a complicated fall. Ranson would, however, agree with Lampe that "forceful pressure" had squeezed the liver, "pushing it up against the front of the spine so it was nearly split in two." On one medical scale, liver injuries are graded one to six. Ranson believed this injury to be "at least a five and it could be higher." There were no external markings on Doomadgee's stomach, and for this reason Ranson favored Hurley's knee as the cause of the damage.

The Police Union's president took off his watch again and started fiddling with it, producing more high-pitched beeping that eluded the judge, perched high at the opposite end of the courtroom.

Next, the prosecution called a liver surgeon, Steven Lynch, who gave evidence that a "massive" force had killed Doomadgee. Dr. Lynch said that he would not usually treat patients with similar injuries because they were fatal.

But the damage to the prosecution's case had been done. Peter Davis had not realized how detrimental Lampe's evidence would be to his argument. The jury had heard this doctor say that he, with all his training, thought Cameron had died in a fall. "If he's a prosecution witness, I'm an astronaut," said the Police Union's media officer, Ross Musgrove, with glee.

The tightness around Hurley's mouth was gone. He subtly moved his neck from side to side, stretching out the tension.

WHILE THE COURT heard from the police officers who'd been in the station when Cameron died, their colleagues kept a vigil outside. Around fifteen officers, some on duty, some supporting Hurley on their own time, stood in the hallway. They stared at passersby in ways that made them wonder what their own crime was. Intimidation had become second nature. Anyone not a cop was regarded as suspicious. These officers, the police chaplain told me, had "mongrels" of jobs. Recently a young officer had been spat on by an Aboriginal offender "known to have hepatitis A, B, C, D." It was a week before the officer's wedding and he was warned not to kiss the bride. The chaplain said the police were trying to do all that was "good and true and lovely in the world. They are men trying to lead moral lives."

I thought of the cell-surveillance video of Cameron dying. It was the next witness, Sergeant Michael Leafe, who had come in and kicked him. Leafe had been living on Palm Island for three months at that point. Sitting in the witness box in his pressed blue uniform and helmet of brown hair, Leafe's manner was now slightly robotic. He might have been nervous: he was testifying in front of the power-brokers of the Queensland Police Service.

Sergeant Leafe recalled the fatal morning. He told the jury he'd heard Hurley call, "Oh shit, he's hit me!" Leafe went to open a cell door. When he came back Hurley was standing over Cameron Doomadgee, who was on the floor inside the station door. Hurley was "trying to lift him up." Doomadgee was "just lying there" limp. The two officers each grabbed Doomadgee by a wrist, Leafe said, and dragged him on his back into the cell.

I remembered TJ Yanner telling me about a night at the Burke-town Pub when a local, drunk and aggressive, tried to hit Chris Hurley, "to put the bomb on him." Hurley, TJ alleged, "grabbed him by the scruff of the shirt and then he tripped him, and as he tripped him, and [the man] went down, he put his knee into his throat, sat on his chest, put his knee into his throat and still had him by the scruff of the shirt, pinned him down with his knee in his throat and held him there until he passed out. Yeah, and only took about five or ten seconds." Noel Cannon's "similar fact" evidence at the inquest had suggested that this squeezing to the neck, this use of the knee to subdue his prisoners, could have been Hurley's modus operandi.

Sergeant Leafe, who had previously claimed he'd left Hurley alone with Cameron for ten seconds, now revised his assertion. It had been only six seconds.

Peter Davis was considering declaring the police "hostile wit-nesses." Only if he followed this convention would he be able to cross-examine the officers with the same force Steve Zillman had the Palm Islanders. But he believed the inconsistencies in their testi-mony needed to be more glaring.

Leafe testified that later in the day on which Cameron died, he and Hurley discussed the death. He said Hurley told him "he'd fallen

beside Cameron. He also—he also said that he had dirtied his knee
or his trousers," meaning he had landed on the floor. After Hurley
was charged, Leafe wanted to swear an affidavit claiming he'd been
mistaken, and that Hurley had never told him he'd landed to
Cameron's side, but it would not have been admissible in court.

Hurley was facing eight to ten years in jail. He sat on the edge of
his seat in the dock, then he sat right back. He twisted and shifted.
It seemed hard to keep that body still. All that flesh and bone, all that
weight and strength. In that suit, his body was a painful burden. It's
a mixed blessing, being so big. The strongman is a kind of freak.
Hurley's hands were flat on his knees, then balled to a fist in an
instant. He rubbed his fingertips. He wiped at his nose, sniffing like
a boxer, his nostrils flaring. The sniffing set off an involuntary facial
twitch on his right cheek, the side turned to the jury, the side
Cameron had hit, the side on which Cameron was bruised.

ON THE THIRD day of the trial, young Constable Kristopher Steadman testified. His trousers were pulled high and padded by his shirt-
tails. He took deep breaths, and when he inhaled he appeared to be
squeezed into his uniform. His stiff police cap sat upturned in front
of him on the witness box. Steadman had arrived on Palm Island
fresh from the Police Academy on November 18, 2004, the day
before the death. Asked at the inquest if he'd received cultural-
awareness training, he said he'd been told about the barbed wire surrounding the barracks.

The morning of November 19, Steadman had arrived at the
police station as Hurley's van was pulling in. He walked into the
garage and stood waiting, unnoticed, in a dark corner. "I heard
the van open and what sounded like a scuffle." He saw the two men
struggling toward the doorway. Chris Hurley was standing behind
the prisoner, holding him by the shoulders. Then "one—or both of
them—have tripped and they've fallen through the door . . . It was
hard and it was loud. I heard them hit."

Steadman was about a meter from the doorway, but he didn't

move. "All I could see after that was feet, two pairs of feet." The feet were just inside the doorway: a pair in police-issue black boots and a pair of bare black feet. "The black boots were on top of the other feet." He could not see the position of the bodies. Hurley was shouting something at Doomadgee, and these shouts "sounded angry." Seconds later, the black boots disappeared. Five or more seconds later, the bare feet were gone too.

This was a world away from the Police Academy. The new constable waited in the garage until whatever was taking place inside was over. When Steadman finally walked in, Hurley was farther down a hallway with Cameron, but, Steadman said, "I didn't look down the hallway." In his peripheral vision he saw "something," and "there was blue in that, so that would go along with his uniform." He did not check to see if the struggle was continuing, if Hurley was winning the struggle, or if he needed help. Steadman had told the Crime and Misconduct Commission: "I didn't see it as my business to stick my nose in."

Hurley was yawning now, and scowling. His collar was irritating him. He sat forward, almost glaring at Steadman, and clearing his throat. Behind him sat his girlfriend, with whom he shared a house near Surfers Paradise. His girlfriend had a friend. The friend had a hole in her black pantyhose, and long, shining, dark hair. When the friend turned quickly, her mane flicked the face of the plainclothes officer sitting behind her. They both smiled. The two women sat behind Hurley chewing gum.

Constable Steadman was considered the defense's most important witness because, they claimed, the two pairs of feet proved that Hurley had landed on top of Doomadgee.

Now Judge Peter Dutney made a crucial point. He sat back, casual in his red robes, his hands clasped. "I'd just ask you this, just to make it clear in my own mind, Mr. Steadman. You told Mr. Davis that Mr. Hurley was holding Mulrunji by the shoulder?"

Kristopher Steadman: "Yes."

Peter Dutney: "Was he going in frontwards or backwards?"

Steadman: "He was going forwards . . . they were facing forwards."

Hurley's lawyers glanced quickly at one another. Constable Steadman frowned, but his young brow barely creased. When he walked out he was followed by the union president. I followed too. Steadman was taken to a small room, where I saw him being spoken to by Wilkinson and their scowling solicitor. His testimony had raised a difficult question: if Cameron Doomadgee had been walking through the doorway facing forward, and Hurley was behind him, how could Hurley's knee have landed in the middle of his prisoner's abdomen?

The Accused

BY THE FRIDAY of the trial, day four, the courtroom was still divided like some disastrous wedding. The two strained families had been waiting nearly three years for this. And now time stood still; it bent and stretched and both sides waited for the seconds to pass.

Robert Mulholland had spent the morning arguing for the case to be thrown out. "If Your Honor pleases, on the evidence, no jury, no reasonable jury, properly instructed, could convict Mr. Hurley of either charge." Mulholland had in part been playing to his employer—the Police Union—and in the hour he took to fight the point, he seemed to have taken on their bullying tone. Peter Davis sat through it all slowly shaking his head. Judge Dutney finally said, "There must have been some contact, otherwise he'd still be alive." He ordered that the senior sergeant had a prima facie case to answer.

The prosecution's case now rested. It was the defense's turn to call witnesses, and Mulholland made a shock announcement: he called Hurley. The ripple of surprise that runs through courtroom dramas ran through this court. Davis had assumed Hurley would not give evidence: How, under cross-examination, would he explain his early vehement denial of landing on Cameron?

"Through it all, Mr. Hurley has remained silent," Mulholland said, standing still with his arms by his side. "He has had to remain silent. Now, finally, he has his opportunity to give his side of things." The barrister sounded like an impresario about to pull back the curtain. And it *was* dramatic. Hurley, the main act, sat in the dock staring straight ahead. Mulholland asked the jurors to listen to the senior sergeant's evidence with "open hearts and open minds . . . Assess him, we invite you," he pleaded almost tenderly. "Assess him."

Hurley stood and walked to the witness box. He towered over the bailiff, a Bible raised high in his hand, swearing truth to "our sovereign lady the Queen." Sitting, he gripped the seat, his knuckles white. His brow was in a permanent knot, his deep-set eyes looked as if it had been a while since sleep came easily, but his skin was remarkably smooth.

Thin, ruddy Steve Zillman had smoker's gravel in his voice, but he spoke softly to the accused: "Now, is your name Christopher James Hurley?"

Hurley: "Yes, it is."

Zillman: "And you are the accused man in these proceedings?"

Hurley: "I am."

He spoke plainly, without flourish. He gave evidence in the precise, unemotional tone of an officer reporting to a superior: "Correct." "Yes sir."

The morning of November 19, 2004, had been "hectic," Hurley testified. He'd visited the hospital, where the three Nugent sisters were in casualty, having just been beaten. "One of the sisters was to be medevaced out. She had a broken jaw." The other two came to the station to be photographed, but Hurley decided the extent of their wounds would be more visible the next day. Gladys asked for a lift to pick up her medication. He refused because he had work to do. But Gladys said Roy Bramwell might beat her again (he had not yet been arrested) and so Hurley finally agreed. He had never seen Cameron Doomadgee before that morning in Dee Street when he heard him call "you fucking cunts."

His supporters bristled. I could feel the electric charge of indignation shoot through the room.

Hurley said he drove toward Cameron and asked: "What's your problem with the police?"

The plainclothes officers in the court, some of whom had been at the riot, some of whom were Hurley's friends, were moved by this. The insult was not just to Hurley, but to all of them. They felt it and he knew it. His chin jutted.

Cain's self-defense was "I am not my brother's keeper." For years Hurley had been playing the role of brother's keeper, but now it seemed to me that this had been an act. His attitude suggested that, yes, Cameron had died on his watch, but it wasn't his responsibility. And his real "brothers" were sitting in the courtroom wearing blue armbands, keeping *him*. They understood his existential moment, they'd been there.

Describing his efforts to get Doomadgee into the cage of the police van, Hurley was frank:

> He didn't initially want to go in, so I took hold of his left arm . . . basically somewhere around the biceps area. And I just led him around to the back of the car, using the car as, you know, support. And perhaps the cage was open when I got back there because all I had to do was put him into the back of the cage. And how I did it was I used my hip and I bumped him and he sat down on his backside in the car. And then I said, "Get in." And he still wouldn't get in and I just upped his, upped his legs, the quickest way to get him into the car.

Hurley no longer fidgeted. He was now perfectly calm and strangely matter-of-fact. He went on to describe the arrival at the police station. When Cameron got out of the cage he struck Hurley "to the side of the face with a backhand fist." "The effect was it surprised me," Hurley said. "It shocked me. I don't think I'd been assaulted over there in the two years."

Zillman: "Well, what did you then do?"

Hurley: "Well, like I would have done anywhere else, I . . . I reached out to the neck or the collar area of the shirt and pulled him toward me fast . . . I didn't want any other chances for him to assault me."

Zillman: "And I want to know how strong he appeared to be?"

Hurley: "He was strong, he was actually surprisingly strong for a fellow of his size."

Zillman: "Did you at any time jab him or hit him, strike him or punch him?"

Hurley: "No, I did not."

The day before, the court had listened to an audiotape of Hurley's police interview, made a few hours after Doomadgee's death. If Hurley had been remorseful or traumatized that afternoon, he'd hidden it well. He had spoken in a big, confident voice, the voice of his old life.

In that interview, Detective Senior Sergeant Joe Kitching said: "So you tripped over a step, is that right?"

Hurley: "Over the step as we came in—there's a step there."

Kitching: "How did you manage to fall on the ground?"

Hurley: "I fell to the left of him and he was to the right of me."

Later in the interview, Hurley's friend Detective Sergeant Darren Robinson asked: "And you didn't land on top of him?"

Hurley: "No, I landed beside him on the, ah—what do you call it?—the, ah, lino."

After the jury had heard the audiotape, they then watched the video reenactment Hurley made the day after Doomadgee's death. In old Westerns, doorways were built small so that the heroes looked taller. That's how it appears in this video: Hurley as John Wayne in a doll's house. Again he tells the investigators that he fell to the left and Doomadgee to the right. But what is remarkable about the video is that there is no fall. There is an approximate description of a fall but no attempt to reconstruct the fall itself. The very thing the reenactment is meant to explain is the one thing it most patently ignores: how Cameron Doomadgee sustained the injuries that killed him.

Sitting in the witness box, Hurley now broached the fall. He said this was "the grayest area" of his memory: "I mean, when I say 'gray' it's not black, it's not white."

Zillman: "How quickly did you fall?"

Hurley: "In an instant."

Zillman: "How rapidly?"

Hurley: "In an instant. We, we fell very fast to the floor . . ."

Zillman: "And you know that in the course of those interviews, you essentially said that you fell beside him?"

Hurley: "Yes, I know that."

Zillman: "What do you say about that?"

Hurley: "I would say to that, that if I did not know the medical evidence that came to light out of the postmortems, if I . . . if I had not sat in the court for the past week listening to what the witnesses have said, I would sit in this box today and say that I still fell beside him."

Zillman: "What confidence do you have in that recollection as you expressed it in those interviews?"

Hurley: "Well, it's not correct, obviously. It's not correct."

Zillman: "What do you say to the proposition that after the fall, you in some unspecified way deliberately applied force resulting in the fatal injuries to Mr. Doomadgee?"

Hurley: "I say that's not correct. I can say with a hundred percent certainty and honesty that I did not do that."

For forty minutes an invisible string connected Hurley to his barrister; there was a rhythm to their back-and-forth, and together they played a *We know what the real world is like* chord. A few phrases Hurley repeated had the subtlest air of rehearsal, but if he was lying, he was brilliant at it. He seemed grave. He seemed sincere. He really could have been an old screen idol from a time when men had grit and did not go to a gymnasium to get it. A figure before black voting rights, before black land rights, before Reconciliation.

After Cameron was found cold in the cell, Hurley said, he and the other officers were "just tossing thoughts in the air about why he was dead." A heart condition, choking on sputum, an aneurism, food poisoning—these were some of the "ideas" they'd been "throwing around." Lloyd Bengaroo had wept. Hurley told the court that during the first two interviews, he too had been "emotional." "I just felt very distressed about it. I knew he had a partner because she had come up to the police station and she had a little one with her at the time and that was what was upsetting me." Also they were the same age, thirty-six: this coincidence unnerved him.

"There's been some evidence you're a big man," Steve Zillman said, and he asked Hurley for his dimensions.

"Six foot seven or two meters, a hundred and fifteen kilograms," Hurley replied. His hands were big hands, his knee a big knee.

PETER DAVIS MAY not have expected Hurley to give evidence, but he'd prepared a cross-examination just in case. Standing with his arms folded, Davis rocked back and forth, leaning over the bar table, inclining toward the accused.

This would be Hurley's great test. He sat with his legs apart. He met Davis's force with force, his aggression with aggression. You punch me, I'll punch you.

Davis: "You see what's happened, I suggest to you, is that you have knee-dropped on him in an attempt to wind him. That's what you've done, isn't it?"

Hurley: "No, not at all."

Davis: "Try to subdue him?"

Hurley: "No."

Davis: "And in doing that, not knowing your own strength, you've killed him?"

Hurley: "No, I haven't."

Davis: "And then you've thought later on, Oh well, he's probably died of a heart attack or something. Why do I have to confess having dropped my knee into him? That's what's happened, isn't it?"

Hurley: "Not at all. You said yourself, sir, a hundred and fifteen kilograms—if I dropped a knee down onto a man and he was dead within an hour, the investigators come three hours later, they give me an opportunity in the first interview. On the second time they say, 'You didn't fall on him?' And so, 'Oh, yeah, yeah, I could've. Oh, that's right, yeah, I could've—'"

Davis: "Oh, is—?"

Hurley: "I could've fallen on him, you know?"

Davis: "Oh, that's the lie you'd tell, is that right?"

Hurley: "Well, that's what I could've told them."

Davis: "Is that the lie you'd tell?"

Hurley: "That's what I could've told if I'd done the knee drop . . . that you're saying I have."

Davis: "I see. So had you—?"

Hurley: "I could have easily written myself out of this."

Davis: "Oh, I see. I see. So your state of mind now is, the way you're thinking, the way you're telling this jury is that, had you done it, you would've lied your way out of it, is that right?"

Hurley: "No, I'm saying had I been the type of person that had done something like that, I may follow that up with a lie to get out of this, to cover your backside, or whatever the term is."

In effect, Hurley was saying: "If I had assaulted him, I could have—even might have—lied about it, and said I fell on him. But since I didn't lie, I didn't assault him." When he first told his story, however, he'd had no reason to tell such a lie—he did not yet know how Cameron had died, and had no reason to concoct the excuse of falling on him to explain his injuries. His friends had cleared him of misconduct before. If Hurley had been "the type of person that had done something like that," he could also be the type to know he'd get away with it—short of it killing Cameron.

Peter Davis asked: "Are you swearing on oath to this jury that there was not one skerrick of anger in you after you ended up on your own nose in the police station, falling into your own police station?"

Hurley now grew combative. "Depends on your definition of anger. I wasn't pleased. I wasn't pleased I was down, but I wasn't angry."

Davis: "He'd resisted, hadn't he?"

Hurley: "So what? That happens a lot out on the street."

Davis: "So that didn't anger you?"

Hurley: "No."

Davis: "What about a smack in the chops? Did that anger you?"

Hurley: "No, not at all."

Davis: "Not at all?"

Hurley: "It surprised me."

Davis: "Are you saying that an adult man bashing you in the face didn't raise any emotion of anger at all?"

Hurley: "Wasn't bashing. It was just a backhand from a fella that had drunk too much grog that day basically."

There was a brief recess and the jury left. Hurley, ashen-faced, walked from the witness box back to the dock. Eyes narrowed, he sat staring at his open hands. Penned there, he looked rotten, as if there were something poisonous inside him. I could almost see the bitter rage rocking through his head.

I thought of the cave painting I'd hiked to see in Laura, Cape York, showing the two-meter-tall police officer being bitten on the foot by a huge snake, perhaps the Rainbow Serpent—the totem of the Doomadgees' grandmother. Hurley had told his story as a man would suck venom from a bite. His life was at stake. And this was the only antidote.

Compared to his indignation, Hurley's remorse had a subtle note. Maybe the balance shifted from day to night, from public to private. Maybe it didn't. One of the Police Union men had told me Hurley felt betrayed by the Aboriginal community. For all these years he'd looked after the women and children, brought order where there was chaos—and they had all turned against him. I wondered how he felt now about Reconciliation.

I had sent Chris Hurley a number of letters through his solicitor, wanting to speak to him, but had received no reply. As he sat there, I wished I could ask him:

Do you ever dream you're falling?

Do you ever dream of Cameron Doomadgee?

What do you think of the places you once chose to live, where good and bad are blurred and where you thought you were good?

Do you still think you were?

And there was one other question: *How can I get you to talk to me?*

Then, for some reason, Hurley looked over at me. He was only meters away but his brow was so knitted, his glower so dark, I could not see his eyes. His glare had partially erased them, had sunk them even deeper into their sockets, so that it took a few seconds to realize I was its subject. I don't know if he knew who I was; I suspect he did. With a weak smile I turned away, feeling my blood surge. I did not have it in me to stare back. He was a man trying to save his life and he seemed to be saying, *How dare you judge me?*

THE COURT RESUMED and Peter Davis replayed the video reenactment. The jury held their transcripts as if they were scripts of a play. Hurley sat in front of the screen watching himself on Palm Island. He pulled his jacket tighter. Leaning forward, Davis took the accused man through the video frame by frame, asking him to account for the detail he'd been able to give investigators, seeing as his memory was impaired. But Davis got no traction. He seemed exasperated by the unlikely story that Hurley was telling. Yet Hurley seemed to grow more comfortable.

Davis: "We're in 'the gray area' now, aren't we?"

Hurley: "Yes."

Davis asked why, if it was so gray, Hurley had been able to "specifically direct the interviewers as to how you had Mr. Doomadgee, where he was standing, how he was crouching." Davis replayed the part where Hurley said, "No, lower, boss." He stopped it at the moment Hurley and "Doomadgee"—Inspector Webber—walked through the doorway. In the video, Hurley said he fell to the left and Doomadgee to the right.

Davis: "A hundred and something kilograms of you and seventy-something kilograms of Mr. Doomadgee, and you've come together on the floor of the police station heavily?"

Hurley: "Yes, obviously."

Davis: "And you've missed [falling on him]?"

Hurley: "Yes, I have, obviously."

Davis: "And that, that's your whole case?"

Hurley: "Yes, it is."

The senior sergeant's body had impacted with the force of a car smashing, with the force of a plane crashing. Peter Callaghan, the lawyer for the Doomadgees at the inquest, had always said, "Doomadgee didn't give himself a black eye," and this black eye was "unlikely to have been caused in the same action which damaged the liver." But Davis, focused on the fatal injury, did not choose to make much of the black eye, believing it a risky strategy without forensic proof. Some people watching the proceedings thought Davis's position was weak, they wished *they* had hired the mauling Steve Zillman.

Davis: "You can't assist us, can you, in explaining how or what part of your body impacted upon Mr. Doomadgee?"

Hurley: "No, I don't know what part. I can only say one hundred percent that I did not cause any deliberate force to Mr. Doomadgee."

It was Friday afternoon. Hurley had been examined and cross-examined for over two hours. But he was like one of the tall spirits not just in his size, but in his evasiveness. He seemed to find ways of hiding in the legal cracks. The law pretended it could pin him down, cut him to size. Each new proceeding claimed to be the place where the truth would be known, the shadows cast out, with the bright light of justice triumphing. And yet as Hurley returned from the witness box, his supporters stepped forward to congratulate him. He shook hands and was slapped on the back. He had done well.

Hurley was the only witness for the defense. All evidence had been taken, and on Monday the defense and the prosecution would deliver their summaries. I looked around for Cameron's family but couldn't see them. Tracy had found the forensic descriptions hard to bear and had not come back. Elizabeth had been keeping to herself, even sitting separately from her sisters. She too had not been well; her manner was frayed. I had seen her earlier in the day clutching a

face towel. These past three years had been too much. The top button of her collar was undone and she had a series of pink plastic
pads on her chest—her heart was being monitored.

The last time I'd visited Palm Island, three weeks earlier, Elizabeth's garden was a jungle of meter-high weeds. Some of the plant
cuttings had taken, most had not. She sat on her veranda with a
nursery catalog a neighbor had lent her, looking at pictures of lilies
and roses with full, perfect petals. She pointed out the bright red and
yellow lilies she liked, then turned the page. Inside, the house was
quiet. Ten days earlier all her foster children had been taken away
from her. They had been removed and put in foster care on the
mainland.

What had happened was unclear. Queensland's Child Protection
Services had come and taken them either before or after she'd
"tapped" a machete against some social workers' car windshield. The
machete, she told me, was blunt anyway. She had been on her way to
the island's workshop to have the blade sharpened for $5 so she
could slash the wild grass in her garden. Elizabeth said she'd apologized to the social workers and they had accepted her apology, but
still they took the children. When I asked for more details a fog rolled
in. I knew the story was more complicated than this, and also that
Elizabeth was too proud to ever tell me what had really happened.

I had the impression of her spinning. When we first met she had
a great stillness, a poise, which I knew was a front—but such a strong
front—for someone made of something quick, hot, of high voltage.
Now they had taken what she loved, the children—but why raise
them to die so young? I wondered if these were her thoughts too, not
just mine.

Amazing Grace

ACROSS THE WATER on Palm Island that weekend, a dormitory reunion was being held. I had thought about going but it was impossible to get a bed. Hundreds of people who had been taken from their families as children and sent to the island came from all over Australia to see the men and women with whom they'd grown up. Most of the old buildings, the physical history of the dormitories, had been razed. But on the Friday afternoon, the ferry to the island was full of Aunties and Uncles singing mission songs as the boat sailed through a storm.

I remembered a hot, clammy night in Doomadgee when I went to the hall where the women held a weekly prayer meeting. Elizabeth was there, sitting with women mostly in their fifties, sixties, or seventies. Toddlers wandered around—their grandchildren—exploring the plastic-pot plants, the old piano, rows of rust-colored chairs, and a locker full of Bibles that also held some children's books. A little girl of six came over to me. She had bright, watchful eyes and as she sucked a hot-pink lollypop that matched her hot-pink T-shirt, she silently produced two books she wanted me to read aloud to her. The first was *Shapes and Colours*. The other one, from the early 1970s, faded and creased, was *Let's Meet the Police*. She had picked the fundamentals.

The police recruits in the pictures were all white. They did star jumps in very tight shorts and T-shirts. As the old women sat looking through their Bibles, I started reading to the little girl:

Stephen and Jane were waiting for the parade to appear, then they saw some horses stepping proudly down the street. Father said, "Look, children, the parade is beginning. Here come the mounted police!"

Stephen looked at the horses and their uniformed riders and said, "I think it must be fun to lead a parade, I think I'll be a policeman when I grow up."

What had Chris Hurley dreamed of being? What had Cameron Doomadgee? The bitter joke of Reconciliation in Australia was to assume the lives of these two men could be weighed equally. When Hurley was doing rugby training at a Christian Brothers school, Doomadgee was in a youth detention center. By the time Hurley was setting up a sports club for the kids on Thursday Island, Cameron had a child and a broken relationship. By the time they were thirty-six, the odds were that Hurley had more than half his life in front of him; Cameron had about a decade. As Hurley picked his way along the police career path, the other man was like his shadow. The date of their meeting was gaining on him. Hurley had tumult in his name, Cameron had doom in his.

"How did you know it was a police officer, Jane?" asked Father.

"He was wearing a uniform," said Jane.

The women in the hall picked up their hymn books and began to sing: *Oh! What a wonder that Jesus loves me. I'm so glad that Jesus loves me . . . Yes, it was love made Him die on that tree . . . Jesus loves even me.* With no piano, their voices sounded thin and flat and raw: terrible and beautiful at the same time. Silence followed the last note. No one said a word, as if memories were warming them.

These women had grown up in the Doomadgee dormitory. Now they all wore the same simple cotton dresses—short-sleeved, with a few buttons down the bust, loose around the waist, balled from so much washing. I'd seen them hanging on clothes lines, their bright colors faded, all in a row like a kind of uniform. In the dormitory, they'd worn dresses made from burlap bags, and after the war, old woolen army uniforms that were donated to the mission. Elizabeth and Cameron's mother had been one of these women. Some in the hall that night were her cousins, some were her husband Arthur Doomadgee's cousins.

Running over, running over, my cup is full and running over. The women did hand gestures for "cup" and "running." *Since the Lord saved me, I'm as happy as can be, my cup is full and running over.*

While Hurley's mother was going to school and dreaming of becoming a nurse, Cameron's mother was in a place where, according to a government official, life was "indistinguishable from slavery," where girls had their mouths washed out with soap for speaking their tribal languages. If they fought with one another they were not fed. If one girl had a sweetheart they would all be punished: "Dong us all on the head with the Holy Bible, love, which is wrong," Aunty Betty had told me. They were hit, and some had their heads shaved.

Those who tried to run away were flogged. Doreen Cockatoo remembered the missionaries putting one young boy who tried to escape "in jailhouse with a chain on his leg." All the kids were taken to see him, as a deterrent.

In 1997 the "Report of the National Inquiry into the Separation of Aboriginal and Torres Strait Islander Children from Their Families" was delivered to the Australian Parliament. Known as "Bringing Them Home: The 'Stolen Children' Report," it disturbed the nation's conscience. Political leaders cried in public as they tried to recount the stories it told; stories of black parents who took their sick children to the hospital and then discovered they'd been adopted by white parents; stories of mothers and fathers who died of grief. The report found that many Indigenous children who were taken entered adulthood in "a cycle of damage from which it is difficult to escape." Often they had only the most basic education, an ingrained sense of inferiority, feelings of numbness, and trouble developing relationships and parenting their own children. They had worse health, were more likely to be imprisoned and to suffer from depression, violence, and substance abuse. They were more likely to die young.

At the Doomadgee prayer meeting, a voice said, "Number one seventy-two."

"Number one seventy-two," everyone repeated, and a moment later the singing started, so thinly I could barely distinguish the words. Then other voices melded and the song took off: *I've a wonderful savior. He will keep me forever. We'll be happy together, my savior and I!* The hymns all had a slightly romantic, swooning air, perhaps because in the old days, when boys over fifteen or sixteen were sent to work on cattle stations, all these maidens had been locked up and were not allowed to marry until they were twenty-one. With hymn singing the only sanctioned entertainment, they had sung then as they were singing now about the man who loved them: Jesus the savior, and the suitor and the Father—to girls who were stolen or surrendered. Now all of them, sisters and rivals, were together again, with all the men long gone.

THAT WEEKEND, while I was waiting for the trial to resume, wherever I went there were stacks of the *Townsville Bulletin* showing Hurley's face with its brooding, stoic expression. On the front page of the *Australian* he was featured walking into court flanked by two Police Union officials in matching suits and ties. His fists were clenched; he was blank-faced, hard, as if wearing armor. The headlining story, however, was not about Hurley; it read, *Nation's Child Abuse Shame.* A government-funded report titled *Little Children Are Sacred* had been handed down the day before, detailing widespread sexual abuse of Aboriginal children in the Northern Territory. The report's introduction put it like this:

HG was born in a remote Barkly community in 1960. In 1972, he was twice anally raped by an older Aboriginal man. He didn't report it because of the shame and embarrassment. He never told anyone about it until 2006 when he was seeking release from prison where he had been confined for many years as a dangerous sex offender. In 1980 and 1990, he had attempted to have sex with young girls. In 1993 he anally raped a 10-year-old girl, and in 1997, an eight-year-old boy (ZH). In 2004, ZH anally raped a five-year-old boy in the same community. That little boy complained: "ZH fucked me." Who will ensure that in years to come that little boy will not himself become an offender?

Reading of this horror as I waited in my hotel room for the trial to continue, I wondered what the point of justice for poor dead Cameron Doomadgee was. The war between police and Indigenous Australians is a false battleground. The spotlight on Hurley and Doomadgee locked in a death struggle ignored the great carnage taking place offstage. *Little Children Are Sacred* described Australia after the Fall. It seemed to me that concentrating on a white man killing a black man took the nation back to its original sin, as if expurgation of this would stem the rivers of grog and the tides of violence drowning life in these communities. If we could absolve ourselves of this first sin we might be able to pretend that the later ones—the ones now killing a generation—happened in a realm beyond our reach and responsibility.

In January 2007, in the Aboriginal community of Yarrabah, just south of Cairns, a fourteen-month-old baby had been raped and murdered: both the mother and the killer were from Palm Island. Who knew what had happened to them?

One Palm Island woman, Deniece Geia, told me that a lot of mothers don't even know how to say, "I love you," to their children, because they were never told themselves. There are reasons for complete social breakdown, and one of them must be people being forcibly taken from their parents, who had in turn been taken from their parents, who'd been taken from theirs.

· · ·

IN THE DOOMADGEE hall, it was the women's singing of "Amazing Grace" that left me winded. The Cherokee Indians sang their own version of this hymn when, forced from their homelands, they walked the Trail of Tears. *Through many dangers, toils, and snares.*

Across the road, an ambulance was parked outside the Yella Gundgimara Doomadgee hospital—named in honor of Lizzy Daylight. Was it delivering one of the riverbed people, one of these women's sons or grandsons? *The earth shall soon dissolve like snow, the sun forbear to shine.* Each wrong note sounded right. These women who'd worked on stations for no money, who'd lived without rights, who'd heard from their parents and grandparents about surviving Wild Time, now sang about grace. It was too much. Their own resigned grace was all that stood between them and chaos. And it was too much.

Outside the hall, the Gulf country's night sky was jammed with stars, the darkness vibrating. In 1850, up to a hundred Aboriginal languages were spoken across Queensland alone; now around the nation, less than twenty are in good health. It is one of Australia's great tragedies that most of the song cycles about these stars have also been lost since Europeans came. The songs contained knowledge about the Dreamtime, about the ancestral heroes' endeavors and epic travels—and therefore about Shooting Star Dreaming, Dingo Dreaming, Black Cockatoo Dreaming, Flying Fox Dreaming, Wind Dreaming, Hail Dreaming, Fog Dreaming, Sugarbag (wild honey) Dreaming, and Shark, Dugong, Louse, Moon, Water Lily, Barramundi, Wave, Mosquito, Kangaroo Dreaming—on and on. Song lines and ritual song cycles of phenomenal complication. There were songs to make people better, songs to make them sick, songs to sing to babies so as to "make him good fella, strong fella," songs for crows to come and eat all the camp's scraps, songs about unrequited love, love magic songs, songs of the obscene, songs about fighting, songs for country, songs for hunting, songs for the dead, songs for mourning, songs for widows so they might be set free, songs to change the weather, songs to make you move from one place to another "ever more quickly"—epic songs with hundreds of verses that took all night to sing.

Later I heard from one of the Palm Island women about the last moments of the dormitory reunion. When it was time to leave, the ferry started pulling out to sea and the women on board began singing old mission songs. The women on the jetty—their sisters and cousins and friends—sang them back. They hadn't seen one another for thirty, forty years. Most likely they would not meet again. They kept singing until the boat was out of sight, everyone weeping.

The Verdict

ON MONDAY MORNING, June 18, it was raining. A gang of reporters and cameramen were lined up at the back entrance to the Townsville courthouse. The union's media officer, Ross Musgrove, didn't want Hurley to walk up the slippery front steps. In his baggy, light-gray pinstriped suit, shiny shoes, and striped shirt, Musgrove looked like a Jazz Age flunky talking on a mobile phone: "Okay, mate." Ringing off, he held a finger in the air as would a director. "One minute!"

Soon a white car with tinted windows pulled up. Two union men stepped from the back, Hurley stepped from the front. The three marched toward the courthouse in single file, Hurley in the middle. As he approached the pack, Hurley took a millisecond to brace himself and turn stony. He looked straight ahead and tried not to flinch at the raindrops or the camera flashes. Their light on his ashen skin revealed the same heroic features and the same impassive stare. One blond reporter joked to another about throwing her knickers at him.

Inside the courtroom, the red-faced, mustached *Townsville Bulletin* reporter showed me the second page of his newspaper:

Racist Words Alarm Drivers

Police are investigating a sign which appeared outside a store in Abbott St., Oonoonba yesterday. The words "I hate niggers" were used on the moveable letter sign. They have since been removed. The disposal and camping shop where the sign was located was closed yesterday and the owners were unavailable for comment.

The reporter told me that the Police Union and Hurley's lawyers had rung the paper and asked for the piece to be dropped or reined in. At their behest, it was shortened and printed without a photograph of the sign. There was debate as to whether the disposal and camping shop was actually a gun store.

Tracy Twaddle had returned to court and sat in the back row with her head in her hands. Hurley's partner sat in the front row in an almost identical position, but she was pert, neat, tailored, made-up, bejeweled. Tracy looked broken and exhausted in an old faded shirt over a cotton dress and (despite the rain) thongs. She had spent the weekend at home, sick. She wasn't eating or sleeping. Tracy had never believed anything would happen to Hurley and she wasn't going to start believing it now.

Tracy sat with her hunched and frail white-haired mother, Mary. In her late seventies, Mary wore thick woolen hiking socks and slip-on sandals, their soles worn right down. When she was a child, she and her family had been removed from the Atherton Tablelands, inland from Cairns, and sent to Palm Island, where Mary grew up in the dormitory.

Elizabeth, Valmae, Jane, and Claudelle sat upstairs; Hurley's brothers sat downstairs. Both families knew what it was to live in sick limbo. They had that much in common, but it was about to end.

Hurley's mother sat with her shoulders slouched, as if conscious of being scrutinized. There were rings under her eyes, and her jaw had a sad, slackened cast. I'd noticed that she would glance down wincing as she heard in detail how her son, flesh of her flesh, had caused the death of a man the same age as himself, through accidental or deliberate force. She was said to believe completely in his innocence.

So did his older brother, Senior Sergeant Tony Hurley, who, five weeks after the trial, would publish an article in the *Police Union*

Journal describing the media as "poison-penned, fork-tongued, cloven-hooved satyrs," producing "caustic exhibitions" with their "lynch mob mentality." It seemed he shared Hurley's rage. "My elderly parents," he wrote, "have only kept their sanity through prayer and the constant support of family, friends, and well-wishers."

Robert Mulholland began his summing up. "What impression did he have on you?" he asked the jury.

Hurley shifted in his seat, looking vexed.

"In our submission, you would not have the slightest hesitation in accepting Mr. Hurley told you the truth. If you accept it, that's the end of the case." Taking off his glasses, Mulholland looked at the jury; then, replacing them, he leaned forward. The prosecution's case, he told them, was "nonsense," "superficial," "unfair," "ridiculous," "desperate," "absurd"; it assumed "a cynical view of police officers," and was full of "tawdry or cheap shots at Mr. Hurley and a determination to get him—*to get him*! Despite the evidence!" Mulholland's glasses, now in his hand, moved up and down in the air like a gavel. He stood before the jury, incensed for Hurley.

Hands on hips, he spun an example of why one should never rush to judgment:

> [T]he husband and wife on bad terms. Let us assume they go for a swim on a lonely beach together and imagine further that tragically one of them drowns. The one still living might be said to have had an opportunity to have caused the drowning . . . but that doesn't, of course, mean to say that he or she did it.

Mulholland's tone turned conversational as he pleaded with the jury to use their "common sense." At the police station, Hurley helped women and children. He dealt with a bunch of "drunken, disorderly residents . . . who made a nuisance of themselves and wanted to carry on about the police presence and used some bad language and so on." Mulholland reminded the jury that Cameron, on the other hand, had been drinking methylated spirits, that Patrick had been sniffing petrol—that all these people were drunk, swearing, and out of control.

Leaning right over the lectern now, with the casual manner of a man at a bar complaining about what coppers have to tolerate, he said:

> Members of the jury, isn't he precisely, precisely the sort of police officer you'd like to have as your local copper?
>
> When Senior Sergeant Hurley went out that morning . . . he was performing a service for all of us, no matter where we are and where we live in Queensland. Whether you're out in the back blocks somewhere, whether you're up in the Gulf or you're out in far western Queensland or you're down in the south, it doesn't matter. When Senior Sergeant Hurley went out that morning to respond to the request, he did it on our behalf.

In a promilitary town, a town where the street market sells 000-size ammo-print baby clothes, it made sense to play up the nobility of Hurley's service. Mulholland suggested that if this local copper hadn't locked up Cameron, there might have been "some further act of violence to the one that we know Roy Bramwell had mounted earlier in that day." Mulholland did not mention that the senior sergeant let Roy, having just bashed three women, back out into the community, nor that he did so after seeing their beaten faces at the hospital that morning, and with the knowledge that one of them was scared Roy would strike again.

An Aboriginal law student attending the trial with some Palm Island friends told me she had never been in a courtroom with a greater sense of "us" and "them." Tracy and her mother had moved to the gallery. Downstairs, everyone was now white. Upstairs, everyone was black: the seats were filled with the aggrieved, with people looking for one of "them" to be convicted.

There was the family of Errol Wyles, a boy killed four years earlier when a white driver repeatedly reversed into him while he was
riding a bicycle. The police did not tell his parents he was dead for
two days. Their son's killer was sentenced to fifteen months for dangerous driving.

There was Lex Wotton. Three months earlier, he had pleaded
guilty to rioting and was sent to jail while awaiting trial. Then, having decided he'd made a mistake, he successfully withdrew his plea
and was now out on bail. His trial was almost a year away. Seeing
Hurley in the dock was what he had been fighting for.

A lot of Palm Island families with only minor involvement in the
riot were still paying off debts from their legal troubles. Parents
who'd been sent to jail were just returning home, and their children
were often still affected by the police raids two and a half years earlier. Lex himself seemed partly broken. When I'd spoken with him
previously he was almost megalomaniacal about his calling. "I have
visions of myself at the United Nations, talking, traveling all over the
world, teaching my faith and giving people a sense of me . . ." Now
one of his front teeth was missing: in his cell he'd pulled it out to
stop the aching. Faced with the possibility of Hurley's acquittal and
his own potential jail time, he was subdued.

Also upstairs was David Bulsey, the father of Eric Doomadgee's
goddaughter with the irregular heartbeat. Staring down at the
jurors, Bulsey worried that they were too old, that they'd start for-
getting things. On Palm Island, sixty or seventy is close to geriatric.
Next to him, his wife, Yvette, thought one younger juror with honey-
streaked hair had Indigenous blood. Yvette could tell by her nose,
but the juror wouldn't look at them.

The lawyers spoke over the dull drumming of the rain. Through
the windows I could see the union men walking back and forth on
the concrete balcony. The room was cold. People were sniffing.
Members of the jury occasionally shivered. Elizabeth and Jane
Doomadgee were sharing an old ski parka. Valmae and Tracy had
bought a jacket each from Best & Less for $11. Townsville was in a

rain shadow; the skies here were stoic compared to the venting tropical storms in other parts of northern Queensland. Of course, in the
wet season you expected rain, but this was the dry season. And in a
town where you couldn't even buy a coat, airplanes were grounded
in the deluge. When we stopped for an afternoon break, rain still
bucketed down and the old Aboriginal women in flimsy sandals
stepped through the puddles.

The union men and Hurley's supporters had claimed one of
the court building's balconies and stood smoking, staring down on
the street. Edna Coolburra, who'd been chatting with Cameron the
morning he died, asked if she could share my umbrella. I could feel
the police watching intently as we crossed the wet road together:
She's one of those.

ROBERT MULHOLLAND had two modes, theatrical and legalistic.
Sometimes he talked with an arm of his glasses in his mouth, as if
pushing back his words—but to no avail. He did not favor brevity.
He began to read vast swathes of the trial transcript, recapping the
last few days verbatim, and as he did his skin turned waxy. Only
occasionally would he look up at the jury. Even Hurley was yawning. Mulholland had been speaking all day and gave no signs of
concluding. An earnest young constable outside the courtroom said,
"He's probably promised his wife a holiday, and he's budgeted so
much and has to keep going."

Conjuring a scene of whites doing it tough, Mulholland asked
the jury to imagine two family members on their drought-stricken
farm: "and this happens, as we know, would be happening today
throughout Queensland." Say one of them took a gun and committed suicide in front of the other, he went on. Say the survivor could
not remember the position of the gun. "That person, that member
of the family, would, according to the prosecution theory, be facing
a charge of manslaughter! Got the demonstration wrong, because in
the emotion and the dramatic circumstances, a recollection was
faulty! What's the difference?"

He spoke at length of Dr. Lampe and his opinion that a fall caused Cameron's death. "People involved in traumatic events," Mulholland told the jury, "indeed quite often do not remember things accurately." He described how hard it was to remember the events of a minor car accident. Or "incidents on the footy field where recollections differ." Or a pub brawl, where all the eyewitnesses remember seeing different things. He went through cases of mistaken identity. He described the sensation of slipping in the bathroom: "a moment of panic, terror even!"

"Is it my imagination or is there an air of desperation?" asked the *Townsville Bulletin* journalist, massaging his temples.

THE FOLLOWING MORNING, day six, Andrew Boe was sitting at the back of the courtroom in a navy suit and crisp white business shirt. He'd just flown in from the United States, where he was working on a case. He had no need to be in Townsville, but he couldn't stay away. The Doomadgee sisters were delighted. "My little Chinese kickboxing brother," Elizabeth called him.

I was relieved to see Boe too. I'd missed his courtroom energy and aggression. But I asked him whether, if he'd known how long the legal process would take, he would still have acted as he did on reading of Cameron's death.

"Would I do it again? I don't know the answer to that. It would be hard. To make sense of my life then I had to have a cause." This cause had preoccupied and even sustained Boe for two and a half years, but it had also exhausted him and taken him away from his family. And it was his greatest fear that the person to gain the most from the Palm Island case would be himself—the inquest had extended him as a lawyer and as a human being, but he was unsure if anything had fundamentally changed on Palm Island. And his efforts might yet leave nothing changed for the Doomadgees.

In the courtroom, bets were being placed on how much longer Mulholland could go on. Then, at 12:10 P.M., after a day and a half of summing up, his face locked in sudden outrage. He hooked his thumbs around the top of his robes and pulled them close, as if bolstering himself.

> The prosecution theory is absurd and offensive as well as unfair ... the prosecution doesn't have a case, never had a case against him. You would have to have eyes political to conclude that Senior Sergeant Hurley did what he is accused of.
>
> The death of Cameron Doomadgee on Palm Island on the 19th of November 2004 was and is a tragedy, as is any death in custody of a person black or white. The outstanding social, economic, and political issues of Palm Island and of other Aboriginal communities would make you weep. However, they are all complex issues and this trial is not concerned about whether those issues exist. It is concerned with the single question in each charge of whether the prosecution has proved beyond reasonable doubt the guilt of Senior Sergeant Hurley. And convicting a man who is not guilty of those offenses of manslaughter and assault will not bring Mr. Doomadgee back, nor will it do justice to his memory, indeed, quite the reverse. It will compound the tragedy of his death and will make for a double tragedy ...
>
> People who would discuss this case in racial terms have got the wrong attitude ... Mr. Hurley will never forget that he was the accidental instrument of another young man dying. That is a cross he will carry for the rest of his life, whatever happens here.

Now it was Peter Davis's turn. His concern for fairness seemed to deprive him of any sense of theater or showmanship. That was not his style. When he stood it took him awhile to straighten out. He stayed slightly hunched, hands in his pockets, serious, wry, cerebral. He rocked on his feet. Behind him sat Hurley with his fists clenched. The court was awake.

Hurley accepted that his body had in some way killed Cameron

Doomadgee, Davis said. There existed, therefore, two "factual possibilities." One: "a complicated fall whereby the injury occurs." Two:
manslaughter. Davis reminded the jurors of the two pathologists'
evidence: Cameron's body was immobilized on the floor while a
force was applied to his abdomen that pushed the organs back and
cleaved the liver around his spine. "In the history of recorded medical science an injury like this has never actually been caused and
recorded by blunt trauma. But it happened in the police station on
Palm Island."

Davis spoke in clear, straight lines. He spoke in a white heat
while keeping cool. He asked the jury to consider the defense's
theory:

> This is it: that Mulrunji is in front of the accused when the
> two of them trip into the police station. Mulrunji is facing
> into the police station, it seems, and the accused is behind
> him . . . and this is the bit that really defies belief. In the trip
> Mulrunji pirouettes in midair . . . so as to land on his back or
> nearly on his back while the accused, from a position some-
> where behind him . . . somehow falls over on top of him with
> such force as to take the contents of his abdomen and cleave
> them across his spine, thereby rupturing his portal vein and
> apparently creating medical history. And then four hours later
> when interviewed the accused person, Senior Sergeant Hur-
> ley, doesn't even realize he's fallen on him. And incidentally,
> not only does he not appreciate that he has fallen upon Mul-
> runji, but he gives a pretty detailed version of how he didn't
> fall on Mulrunji at all.

Hurley's girlfriend was escorted out of the courtroom by his brother
the police officer. The defendant now sat completely still, hands
clasped in his lap.

The jury, Davis noted, had been told repeatedly by Mulholland
to use their "common sense." Davis asked: "Can I offer one exam-

ple?" He cited Hurley's claim that he was not at all angered by Cameron Doomadgee's behavior. Cameron had hit him on the jaw, struggled with him, and made him trip hard through the doorway of his own police station.

> Now common sense might tell you [that] as soon as he starts admitting of anger, well, we can then start thinking what might have happened from the back of the police van to the door. Once he starts admitting of anger, could he have given him the jab Penny Sibley saw? Once he admits of anger, well we can start thinking then that there's a reason why he may have knee-dropped into Mulrunji when they've both fallen into the police station.
>
> So common sense might tell you that there's a little bit of a reason why in the context of this case, this accused may well want to play down the anger. But he doesn't play it down, does he? He disallows it completely. He says, "I was not angry at all."
>
> Well, what does common sense tell you about that? Does common sense tell you, well, perhaps he did get a bit upset? Perhaps he did get a bit angry? And if he is angry why is he saying he's not?
>
> And of course while we're on the topic of common sense, does it really strike you as according with your common sense, the notion that this accused could fall on Mulrunji with such force as to cleave his liver across his spine, and not remember falling on him at all? Does that accord with your common sense?

Peter Davis, donnish in his black court robes and with his long, thin white hands, made an unlikely boxer, but now he moved around lightly on his feet, as if led by his agile mind.

The senior sergeant sat scratching under his collar. All his copper mates were wired, sprung, ready to defend their own. Behind me, another two-meter-tall police officer leaned forward, breathing heavily. As Davis continued I could hear the cop cracking the knuckles of each finger.

Hurley's two brothers sat in close concentration, displaying no emotion. Did they believe you should ferry around a drunken woman who'd just been beaten and then have to listen to drunken men—the kind that had beaten her—call you a fucking cunt? Should you just take it? Did they believe that if a drunk slapped your face, you should turn the other cheek?

Hurley's mother, watching her son in the dock, looked so sad. She had not taken her eyes off him all the way through Davis's devastating summary.

Davis pointed out that Hurley and his lawyers had always said he could have lied to get out of this, lied and claimed he had fallen on Doomadgee. Davis said: "He just told the wrong lie." Hurley hadn't known how Doomadgee died, Davis reminded the jury, when he made his original statement; he didn't know the autopsy results and he assumed it was an aneurism or a heart condition. Why would he need to say he'd fallen on top of Doomadgee?

The conversation with Leafe is only a matter of an hour or so after the incident. The memory is clear in his mind because he says to Leafe, "Look, I fell next to him. I didn't fall on top of him." Then he has two interviews and he says the same thing and let's assume that's right. So let's assume he's right when he says I did not fall on top of him.

Well if he's right, he's guilty . . . What possible innocent explanation is there for the horrific injuries that the pathologists found on Mulrunji?

Davis crossed his arms and leaned toward the jury, affecting disbelief. "How could it be that the accused person could impact"—Davis made a fist and punched his hand—"with Mulrunji with the force that is usually only seen in motor vehicle accidents, cleave his liver in two almost across his spine (that must have been a smashing contact)"—he punched his hand again—"and he's missed it! He's missed it! That's the defense case: missed it!" Davis's hands were now in the air, in an *I know nothing* pose.

Hurley's mother gripped the side of her seat and stared straight down.

Peter Davis took his time. He kept up eye contact with the jury. They were all watching him. He'd built a relationship with them, speaking in soft, reasoning tones. "You may also harbor prejudice," he said frankly. "Can you please put that to one side? Prejudice is a normal human emotion and those of us who say we've never held it are probably not looking at ourselves closely enough."

The barrister had been on his feet for just over an hour. As he ended his address, he gathered his papers, picked them up, and banged them up and down on the lectern. "Don't dare convict this man! Don't you dare convict him unless you're satisfied beyond reasonable doubt. But gee, it really does look like he's done it, doesn't it?"

It was clunky. But there was a feeling that Davis had pulled it off. There was now among the blackfellas real hope, even quiet jubilation.

Chris Hurley looked numb, frozen in his own suit of fate, but for a moment the mask cracked. His bottom lip quivered. He wiped quickly at his eyes. Then he was still again, solemn.

Whatever the jurors thought, the defense lawyers looked badly rattled. All the bravado of the union men evaporated. Even the worst of the starers cast their eyes down. Tomorrow morning the judge would give his instructions and the jury would go out to deliberate. After listening to Davis, Andrew Boe thought Hurley's best hope was a hung jury.

Once the court had adjourned, Peter Davis met Andrew Boe and the Doomadgee family—Elizabeth, Valmae, Jane, Tracy Twaddle—and the black community on the floor below, where the walls brandished portraits of sallow-faced judges in their wigs. There were about thirty people, old and young, some coming forward to be near

Davis and Boe, others, such as Lex Wotton, hanging back. Davis had put his heart into this, and now, exhausted, he said, "A lot of people have had ideas on how the trial should have gone, but I have done the best I could. I don't know what the jury will come back and say."

Elizabeth was standing in the coat she was sharing with her sister Jane. Tracy sat next to her mother. Their grief over the deaths of Cameron and Doris and Eric had been subsumed by this bigger fight. They were not fighting just for Cameron. His death had led to better watch house conditions in all remote Queensland communities, to the installation of padded cells and round-the-clock surveillance cameras. And the women were proud of that, but now they were tired and anxious.

The Doomadgees had found the week's legal proceedings confusing. They didn't ask any questions of the lawyers, but when their supporters did, they nodded in agreement. A man asked Davis why Roy Bramwell had not been called. Or Lloyd Bengaroo. Davis and Boe explained that both men posed too great a risk. Roy would have been destroyed by the defense lawyers, due to his drinking and inconsistencies. Lloyd was considered "more copper than black-fella": the prosecution had not known what he would say, and neither had the defense, who also opted not to call him. Earlier in the year, Lloyd had been bashed in a Townsville park by a Palm Island man, one of Lex Wotton's relatives. Now he had finally been given a transfer off the island.

Peter Davis told the group that whatever happened, Hurley had admitted he was responsible for Cameron's death. He had been charged with manslaughter and the case had gone before a jury. These were major achievements. Neither had ever happened before. Davis said he knew that a blackfella just needed to half look at a copper and he'd get arrested, but regardless of the jury's decision, Hurley had admitted liability.

"How can we live our lives like that?" asked Lizzy Clay, the mother of Dougie, who'd given evidence at the inquest that Hurley had belted him across the Palm Island police station.

Wearily, Davis said he was sorry, but that was just too big an issue for him to solve.

For a moment there was a sense that some of them were angry with him. But the activist Gracelyn Smallwood turned it around.

"You did a fantastic job," she said. Gracelyn was sitting down, fielding calls on her phone, wearing her STOP BLACK DEATHS IN CUSTODY T-shirt, which she washed and dried each night. I'd heard Gracelyn talking furiously about the barristers, robed in their "Captain Cook outfits" while the Aboriginal witnesses sat shaking, but she could see how hard Davis had fought. "Whatever happens we have had a win," she said. "Every young copper on the street will now think differently. They won't want to go through this."

Then David Bulsey stepped forward, fixing Davis with his wonky, intense stare. This man who'd been arrested in the raids following the riot and sent to jail shook the lawyer's hand. It was so gracious. And then the family and their friends, people who had also been ground down by too much tragedy, all stepped forward to shake Davis's hand, for fighting on their behalf.

Seeing this, I went under. Tears seemed to come from nowhere and I had to leave. I walked down the hall to the women's toilets and looked at my red and swollen face. It was not the first time I had cried in the two and a half years I'd been following the story, but this time it felt pathetic to be standing there weeping, to fail to match the Doomadgees' composure—and what made it worse was Cameron's sisters following to offer comfort. Jane and Valmae came and took me in their arms, checking that *I* was all right.

Peter Davis told me later that after twenty years as a criminal barrister, dealing with rapists and baby killers, he had "developed an exterior where it all reflects." The legal details of this case would fade, but the handshakes at that meeting would remain one of the most touching moments of his life.

OF THE JOURNALISTS covering the trial, Tony Koch was the only one who had believed Hurley might be convicted. But Peter Davis's

summary created confusion among most of the others. I didn't have
a clue. I tried to think as a juror might. If Hurley had done violence
to Cameron Doomadgee, it wasn't the only violence done that day
on Palm Island. Going by the courts, perhaps it was manslaughter,
but might I not think, as a juror, that frontier justice had its own
laws?

A few weeks earlier, I'd met a young white man, John. He showed
me photos taken several years back: photos of his body covered in a
crisscross pattern of bruises that he said had been made with a police
baton. John and two friends had set out on a fishing and hunting trip
to a small Gulf region town. They bought a case of beer in Mount Isa
and drove in a beaten old ute along rough dirt roads.

Along the way they stopped at a pub, leaving their pit bull ter-
rier tied to the ute. Some contract workers were drinking in the pub
and the two groups took a dislike to each other. The pit bull somehow got loose and came into the hotel, where the workers had a blue
heeler. The two dogs started fighting. Then the men started fighting.
It turned into a full-scale brawl, with the publican crawling behind
the bar and the barmaid dodging a flying bar stool. John and his
friends decided it was time to go.

The publican put a radio call through to police, and soon John
came to a roadblock. The police van's headlights blazed through the
dark and the cops stood waiting, their shotguns drawn. John pulled
up beside them; one of the officers held a gun through the open window and screamed at him to switch off the engine. But John needed
a screwdriver to start the ute, and he had to stall to switch it off. A
second officer popped the hood and ripped a wire to kill the motor.

"By this stage [the officer holding the shotgun] is telling me to
get out of the car, and he's opened the door. And then he started
going off, saying, 'I'm going to shoot your dog, I'm going to shoot
your fucking dog.'"

John stepped out of the ute and "when I done that I had the
shotgun in my face. And that's when they all grabbed me and just,
whoosh, pinned me into the ground. And [the second officer's] got

on top with the baton. [He's] on top of me and he just starts cutting sick with the baton."

One of John's friends called out: "Oh, stop, man! That's enough! Stop!"

The officer looked up from beating John and answered, "You're next!" After locking John in the van, he went back for his friend. The man lay in the fetal position while the officer beat him with his baton.

Later, the town's nurse treated the men but refused to photograph their wounds. The policeman was her friend. And these types had got what they deserved. John asked someone else to take the photos.

"I had good welts all over me, man, he got me everywhere," John said. But this was the way of the world, the way of the frontier. He didn't report the incident. "You're not going to win against police," he told me—meaning, not even if you're white. The Tall Man comes in many guises, people say. He can change shape. But when he has got you down, black or white, the terror is the same.

THE NEXT DAY, Wednesday, the judge addressed the jury, stressing that this case was not about any previous deaths in custody, it was not about the police, it was not about Indigenous issues. These twelve men and women had to decide, beyond reasonable doubt, whether Christopher Hurley had killed Cameron Doomadgee.

The jury went out to deliberate. The sergeant overseeing security told me the verdict would "depend on the jury's values." A female court guard, who'd written a children's book titled *Do as You're Told,* said people from outside Townsville didn't know what it was like living alongside blacks. The jury took three hours, during which time they ate lunch. When the call came that they'd reached a decision, the players reassembled.

Andrew Boe sat at the back of the court once more. I turned to him as Hurley walked to the dock. "Not guilty," Boe mouthed. When the foreman made the news official, a howling cry of pain came from Cameron's sisters in the balcony, while Hurley's supporters erupted in jubilation. For the first time, we saw Hurley smile. Tough men wiped tears from their eyes. His friends, his mother, his girl-friend were crying. He leaned down, hugging them, while others patted him on the back.

Outside the courthouse, Gary Wilkinson of the Police Union stood next to Hurley and made a brief announcement. The senior sergeant would not be speaking. He wanted time alone with his family. Groups of riot squad police in plainclothes waited nearby, all of them wearing belt bags with guns inside. Up close, Hurley's face looked fleshier, as if it had suddenly come unsprung. I had a glimpse of what he would look like when older. He tried to maintain that straight-ahead stare, the focus on the middle distance that had kept him upright and unflinching throughout the trial. Rocking through his head, I imagined, were the words *I did not do it. I did not do it. It was not me.*

The next morning, it was raining so hard drivers turned their headlights on. Sirens rang out of the wet, long and angry. The Rainbow Serpent was whipping its tail, flashing its tongue. The whole city was shrouded, while the newspaper billboards bore the story:

**HURLEY
VERDICT:
"NOT
GUILTY"**

And:

**PALM ISLAND
OFFICER
CLEARED
OVER CELL
DEATH**

I met Elizabeth. She was standing in the rain wearing light clothes and flip-flops, but she seemed unperturbed. "I have my head held high," she told me, "because we got this far." She was not in the least surprised by the verdict. In fact, she seemed sorry I'd had to learn a harsh reality. "I knew it was coming my way. Every time I go to the courthouse nothing but whites there. Didn't feel right about it." It was as if her turning up all week were as much a charade, albeit one driven by a wary politesse, as the jury's brief deliberations. Everyone had been going through the motions. Elizabeth hadn't bothered to come and hear the verdict, instead she'd listened to hymns on the radio. She rang me afterward and told me she wasn't giving up. She had kept strong for three years. "I'll always be strong," she said. "I want justice." She called me her little white sister and held the phone up to the speakers so I could hear the hymn: *a wall of fire about me, I've nothing now to fear.*

Her sister Claudelle had also stayed away for the verdict. I had been walking with Andrew Boe that night when we ran into her in the empty mall as she was looking for dumpers—the detritus of old cigarette butts with which to make a smoke. She clung to Boe, howling, "He was my baby, he was my baby brother!" Boe, holding her in the dark, was also deeply upset, angry, unconsoled by the moment in court. "How come we not win?" Claudelle cried. "How come we not win?" Claudelle's seventeen-year-old son was named Cameron Francis, after her brother. She had breast-fed Eric when his mother left him. She was keening: "*My baby brother!* I loved him with all my heart. I loved him with all my heart."

But Elizabeth stood in the rain saying, "The Bible tell us, *Let not your heart be troubled.*"

That same day, less than twenty-four hours after Hurley's not-guilty verdict, Prime Minister John Howard announced his Northern Territory Intervention. The *Little Children Are Sacred* report had asked of government: "What will it take to make you, on behalf of the people of the Territory and Australia, realize the national shame and racial disorder existing in this lucky country and what will you do about it?"

Howard proposed a ban on all alcohol and pornography on

Aboriginal land, an increased police presence, enforced school attendance, and the quarantining of welfare payments. Ignoring most of the report's detailed recommendations urging community consultation, he also announced he would be sending in extra police and the army. Within days, news programs were showing footage of army officers in jungle fatigues boarding planes that looked bound for Iraq, which landed in the Northern Territory. "It's our Hurricane Katrina," the prime minister said, as though it were all down to nature. An election was looming and he trailed in the polls.

A few hours later, the Police Union held a press conference. I did not go. The union was launching a series of five radio advertisements: high-rotation gloating. One compared Queensland to Zimbabwe. Another quoted Martin Luther King: "*Injustice anywhere is a threat to justice everywhere.* Thankfully, justice has finally prevailed, but the damage for one Queenslander and his family has been done."

I didn't have a ticket and the airlines said all their flights were full, but I packed and took a taxi to the airport. Even if I had to fly somewhere else and wait for a connection, I didn't care, as long as I could leave. I had wanted to know more about my country and now I did—now I knew more than I wanted to. I waited for a ticket home and the guard who eventually scanned my bags saw Hurley's photo on my newspaper and said, "I've got a lot of sympathy for him. I've worked security in jails. A lot of them should be shot. The jail's just a motel between raping women."

Hurley had become a kind of folk hero. It was as if he'd been not so much acquitted as forgiven. And in forgiving him, people forgave themselves. Within an hour of the verdict, the senior sergeant had been reinstated in the Queensland Police Service, but before resuming duties he would first take an extended Southeast Asia vacation.

The last time I saw Chris Hurley was at the Queensland Police Union's inaugural Pride in Policing Day march, on Sunday, August 9, 2007, seven and a half weeks after the verdict. This was the march the union had threatened before Hurley's trial and they could now hold it with impunity. Police divisions were lined up under banners, preparing to walk through the streets of Brisbane to Parliament House. Officers had brought their children, some dressed in mini-police uniforms, as were their teddy bears. Bagpipes sounded—the Police Pipe and Drums. Onlookers waved Australian flags, white and blue pompoms, or handmade signs reading THANK YOU! It was the parade scene from the children's storybook about police.

I watched the police commissioner shake Hurley's hand. Then the senior sergeant joined his division. Other cops came over to congratulate him. Hurley, like his supporters, was wearing a blue band with his serial number, 6747, around his wrist. He shook more hands. Then he talked to a man holding a little blond girl. He leaned toward her, pretending to be a monster. "Grrrr!" he cried, holding his hands like clawed paws in front of his face. The girl laughed with delight. He tickled her. "Grrrr!" There he was, the Tall Man. But when I looked for him in the parade I couldn't find him. It was as if he'd dissolved into a long stream of blue.

Postscript

AT THE TIME of writing, Senior Sergeant Hurley is involved in legal action to have the Queensland deputy coroner's findings against him overturned. Andrew Boe's firm, Boe Lawyers, on behalf of the Doomadgee family and Tracy Twaddle, has launched civil action against the Queensland government and Senior Sergeant Hurley, claiming damages of nearly AU$1 million. Boe Lawyers has also instigated a personal injuries action for Barbara Pilot, the niece of Cameron Doomadgee who claims her foot was run over by Hurley.

The police officers in the Palm Island riot have received bravery awards.

Lex Wotton's case has not yet gone to trial.

Queensland's director of public prosecutions, Leanne Clare, who did not charge Hurley, has been appointed a District Court judge.

Hurley's friend and investigator Detective Senior Sergeant Kitching, has been promoted to inspector. The Crime and Misconduct Commission has recommended that Detective Sergeant Darren Robinson undertake "appropriate training in relation to cultural awareness and communicating with Indigenous witnesses." It's not known whether he has done so.

On February 13, 2008, Prime Minister Kevin Rudd formally apologized to the Aboriginal stolen generations for the pain and suffering caused by removals sanctioned by successive governments.

Acknowledgments

For their unfailing support and assistance with this book I thank
Andrew Boe, Elizabeth Doomadgee, Valmae Aplin, and other mem-
bers of the Doomadgee family. I also thank Tony Koch, Tracy Twad-
dle, Paula Morreau, Erykah Kyle, David Trigger, Betty O'Lockland,
the Yanner family, the Burketown Pub, Peter Callaghan, Tony
Moynihan, Nikola Lusk, Carly Nyst, Deniece Geia, Barry Moyle, the
Palm Island Aboriginal Council, the Doomadgee Council, April
Peter, Elaine Cairns, Mal Hansen, Col Dillon, Gracelyn Smallwood,
Stefan Armbruster, Matt Kennedy, Michael McKenna, Peter Davis,
Jonathan Horton, Steve Trezise, Michael Liddy, Barry Cundy, Father
Tony O'Brien, John Bulsey, Yvette Lenoy, Lex Wotton, Agnes Wot-
ton, Stewart Levitt, Frederick Cassis, Colin McDonald, the Clum-
point family, Edna Coolburra, Rosina Norman, Margaret Conway,
Elizabeth Clay, Bethel Smallwood, the Quinkan and Regional Cul-
tural Centre, and members of the Queensland Police Service, past
and present, who spoke to me.

For their encouragement and patience I thank Ben Ball, Mere-
dith Rose, Nan Graham, Dan Franklin, Andrew Wylie, Tracy Bohan,
Sean Wilsey, Morry Schwartz, Sally Warhaft, David Winter, *The
Monthly*.

Comments by witnesses in the text are quoted from the transcript of
Inquest No. COR2857-04 into the death of Mulrunji Doomadgee,
and from Indictment No. 4/2007, the Queen versus Christopher

James Hurley, courtesy of the Queensland Supreme Court. The author also gratefully acknowledges the following sources.

PREFACE Walter E. Roth, *Superstition, Magic and Medicine* (Government Printer, 1903), pp. 28–29. Henry Reynolds, *The Other Side of the Frontier: Aboriginal Responses to the Invasion of Australia* (Penguin, 1982), pp. 46–47. Reynolds writes, "The Aranda called bullets *mukataanna* or the fruits or kernels of muskets while the Kalkatunga coined an even more graphic term for rifle which meant literally hole maker."

THE ISLAND For historical information on Palm Island I am indebted to Joanne Watson, "Becoming Bwgcolman: Exile and Survival on Palm Island Reserve 1918 to the Present," Ph.D. thesis, Department of History, University of Queensland, 1993, pp. 10–21, 112; Henry Reynolds, *North of Capricorn* (Allen & Unwin, 2003), pp. 159–63; Rosalind Kidd, *The Way We Civilise* (University of Queensland Press, 2005), pp. 50–51, 104 (Kidd is the source of the quote on p. 11); Dr. Dawn May, "Race Relations in Queensland 1897–1971," Appendix 1(b) to "Regional Report of Inquiry in Queensland, Royal Commission into Aboriginal Deaths in Custody," 1991 (May is the source of the letter quoted on p. 12); J. P. M. Long, *Aboriginal Settlements: A Survey of Institutional Communities in Eastern Australia* (ANU Press, 1970), pp. 127–28 (Long is quoted on p. 12); Walter E. Roth, *North-West Central Queensland Aborigines* (Government Printer, 1887), pp. v, 71–90 (Roth is quoted on pp. 14–15).

THE DEATH For information about the Torres Strait Islands I have relied on Jeremy Beckett, *Torres Strait Islanders* (Cambridge, 1987), and Anna Shnukal, *Broken: An Introduction to the Creole Language of Torres Strait* (ANU, 1988). Mark Alexander's article "A Cop Who Cared" is quoted on p. 28, courtesy of *The Sunday Mail*, Brisbane (December 5, 2004).

• • •

THE INVESTIGATION   Information about Queensland police culture comes from G. E. "Tony" Fitzgerald, "Report of a Commission of Inquiry into Possible Illegal Activities and Associated Police Misconduct," 1989, pp. 200–203.

THE FAMILY   David Trigger discusses *Wanggala* Time and Wild Time in *Whitefella Comin': Aboriginal Responses to Colonialism in Northern Australia* (Cambridge University Press, 1992), pp. 17–21. Information about the traditional beliefs of the Waanyi people comes from the transcript of the "Nicholson River (Waanyi/Garawa) Land Claim" (Australian Government Publishing, 1985), and W. E. H. Stanner, "The Dreaming" (1953), in *White Man Got No Dreaming: Essays 1938–1973* (ANU Press, 1979), pp. 23–28. Lizzy Daylight is quoted on p. 48 from David Trigger's personal correspondence to the author. Chris Hurley is quoted on p. 49 from Michael Madigan, "Palm's Perilous Punch," *The Courier Mail,* February 26, 2005. R. D. Haynes's "Aboriginal Astrology," *Australian Journal of Astronomy,* April 1992, p. 129, is quoted on p. 51. W. E. Roth's *Superstition, Magic and Medicine* (Government Printer, 1903), p. 16, is quoted on pp. 51–52.

BELIEF   The quote on p. 70 is from Stanner, op. cit., p. 29. The quote on tribal sorcery (p. 78) is from Watson, "Becoming Bwgcolman," op. cit., pp. 109, 258; Watson also details the Curry incident, pp. 127–72, as does Renarta Prior in *Straight from the Yudaman's Mouth: The Life Story of Peter Prior* (James Cook University, 1993). For information about tall spirits I have consulted Percy Trezise, *Dream Road: A Journey of Discovery* (Allen & Unwin, 1993), p. 127; Jennifer Isaacs, *Australian Dreaming: 40,000 Years of Aboriginal History* (Landsdowne Press, 1980), p. 14; George Chaloupka, *Journey in Time: The World's Longest Continuing Art Tradition: The 50,000 Year Story of the Australian Aboriginal Rock Art of Arnhem Land* (Reed, 1993), p. 60 (Chaloupka is quoted on p. 76 with the permission of New Holland Publishers); Tommy George, "Our County, Our Art,

Our Quinkans" (Ang-Gnarra Aboriginal Corporation, 1995), quoted on p. 77 with permission.

THE INQUEST   Peter Sutton quotes the late Francis Yunka-porta's description of "tippin' elbow" in "The Politics of Suffering: Indigenous Policy in Australia Since the 1970s," *Anthropological Forum* 11, no. 2 (2001), p. 129. Tony Koch's article "Yanner's Bitter Dilemma" (pp. 96–97) is quoted with permission from the *Australian,* December 11, 2004.

DOOMADGEE   Robyn Davidson, "No Fixed Address: Nomads and the Fate of the Planet," *Quarterly Essay,* issue 24 (2006), p. 15 (p. 102); Peter Sutton quotes W. E. H. Stanner (pp. 102–3) in *Dreamings: The Art of Aboriginal Australia* (Penguin, 1989), p. 15. Details on Gulf seasons come from "Nicholson River (Waanyi/Garawa) Land Claim," prepared by David Trigger on behalf of Aboriginal people, 1982. I am also indebted to Dr. Trigger for translating the Ganggalida on pp. 115–16.

For information about the Doomadgee Mission I have referred to Trigger, *Whitefella Comin',* and to Vic Akehurst, *A Light in the Darkness: An Anecdotal History of the Doomadgee Mission* (Market Intelligence, 2007). The report quoted on p. 105 was written by the director of tuberculosis to the director general of Health and Medical Services, May 1950, Queensland State Archives, QS 505/1.

Trigger is quoted on p. 113 from *Whitefella Comin',* p. 20. Tony Roberts refers to the discovery of a cave of skeletons in *Frontier Justice: A History of the Gulf Country to 1900* (University of Queensland Press, 2005), pp. 50–51. Lizzy Daylight is quoted on p. 113 from "Nicholson River Land Claim: Report by the Aboriginal Land Commissioner, Mr. Justice Kearney, to the Minister for Aboriginal Affairs to the Administrator of the Northern Territory" (Australian Government Publishing, 1985), p. 4. Henry Reynolds quotes Caroline Creaghe (p. 114) on the practices of Lorne Hill Station in "The Aboriginals in Colonial Society, 1840–1897," Appendix 1(a), "Regional

Report of Inquiry in Queensland, Royal Commission into Aboriginal Deaths in Custody," p. 4.

BURKETOWN   W. E. Roth is quoted on p. 125 from *Notes on Government, Morals and Crime* (Government Printer, 1906), p. 6. The song "Hard, Hard Country" by David Kirkpatrick and Stanley Coaster is quoted on p. 128 with the permission of EMI Music Publishing Australia Pty Limited. Norman Mailer is quoted on p. 128 from *Armies of the Night* (Penguin, 1994), p. 148.

THE INQUEST RESUMES   Norman Mailer is quoted on p. 145 from *Armies of the Night,* p. 147–48. George Orwell on pp. 150–51 is quoted from "Shooting an Elephant," in *A Collection of Essays* (Harcourt Brace, 1981), pp. 148–53. Gillian Colinshaw is fascinating on the relationship between police and Aborigines in *Blackfellas, Whitefellas and the Hidden Injuries of Race* (Blackwell Publishing, 2004).

THE FUNERAL   Colin Tatz is quoted on p. 161 from *Aboriginal Suicide Is Different: A Portrait of Life and Self-Destruction* (Aboriginal Studies Press, 2001), pp. 75–78.

THE SUBMISSIONS   Peter Sutton is quoted on p. 170 from "The Politics of Suffering," p. 146. Sutton also quotes W. E. H. Stanner (p. 170) in *Dreamings,* pp. 14–16.

THE FINDINGS   Tony Koch's article "Bloody Disgrace: Saga Is State's Worst Injustice" is quoted on p. 176 with permission of the *Australian,* December 15, 2006. The quote on pp. 178–79 comes from Sir Laurence Street and Peter Davis's "Street Report."

THE TRIAL   The poll results quoted on pp. 197–98 (commissioned by Levitt Robinson Solicitors) are from "Community Consultation Report: Palm Island Riots," AEC Group, July 2006.

• • •

AMAZING GRACE   Doreen Cockatoo is quoted on p. 225 from "Broken Links: The Stolen Generation in Queensland," State Library of Queensland, 2007. The quote on pp. 226–27 is from *Ampe Akelyerneremane Meke Mekarle: "Little Children Are Sacred": Report of the Northern Territory Board of Inquiry into the Protection of Aboriginal Children from Sexual Abuse* (Northern Territory Government, 2007), p. 12. Information about song cycles in this chapter is from Walter E. Roth, *Games, Sports and Amusements* (Government Printer, 1902), p. 21; the "Nicholson River Land Claim" transcript; *Forget About Flinders: A Yanyuwa Families Atlas of the South West of the Gulf of Carpentaria,* by Yanyuwa families, John Bradley, and Nona Cameron, 2003.

THE VERDICT   The article "Racist Words Alarm Drivers" is quoted on pp. 230–31 from *Townsville Bulletin,* June 18, 2007. Tony Hurley is quoted on p. 232 from "943 Days," *Queensland Police Union Journal,* August 2007, p. 12.

IMAGES   P. vii: map of Queensland; credit: Alan Laver, used with permission. P. 5: Palm Island's clock tower; credit: Matt Kennedy, used with permission. P. 99: mothers with babies, circa 1940; credit: Doomadgee Mission Photograph Album, Queensland State Archives, item ID 337129, c.01/01/1940–31/12/1940. P. 135: Cameron Doomadgee's son, Eric, at his father's funeral holding his cross; credit: Andy Zakeli, courtesy of *The Sydney Morning Herald.* P. 191: Senior Sergeant Chris Hurley leaves the Townsville courthouse on June 15, 2007; credit: Darren Hilder, © Newspix/News Ltd/3rd Party Managed Reproduction & Supply Rights. Page 250: Cameron Doomadgee and his sister Valmae in 1986; credit: © Newspix/News Ltd/3rd Party Managed Reproduction & Supply Rights.

Printed in the United States
By Bookmasters